JINGLES
How To Write, Produce & Sell Commercial Music

ABOUT THE AUTHOR

Al Stone sold his first jingle for a chocolate-flavored soft drink in 1965. In 1977 he founded his own jingle production house, Stone Music Company. Since that time, he has written, produced, and sold hundreds of musical jingles for local, regional, and national advertising accounts. He continues to write and produce radio and TV commercials from his home studio in Noblesville, Indiana.

AL STONE, JR.

Cincinnati, Ohio

 Published by Writer's Digest Books, an imprint of F&W Publications, Inc., 1507 Dana Ave., Cincinnati, Ohio 45207. First edition.

94 93 92 91 90   5 4 3 2 1

Library of Congress Cataloging-in-Publication Data

Stone, Al
Jingles: how to write, produce & sell commercial music / Al Stone, Jr.
p. cm.
Includes index.
ISBN 0-89879-413-7
1. Jingles (Advertising songs) – Writing and publishing. 2. Singing commercials – Production and direction. I. Title.
MT67.S83 1990
781.5 – dc20   90-12663
CIP
MN

Design by Sandy Conopeotis.

Music engravings by William Holab, New York.

For my wife
Carol,
and my daughter,
MacKenna:
you are the
harmony of my life!

CONTENTS

ACKNOWLEDGMENTS

Although the perspective on writing, producing, and selling jingles you'll find in this book is my own, I have had enormous help in developing this approach. For any errors or omissions, I take full responsibility; however, for those successful methods and ideas which you find useful, I share credit with the dozens of musicians, singers, teachers, friends, family, and, most important, customers who contributed over the years to my personal success. To all of them, and those I've omitted, unintentionally, "thank you!"

Special Thanks

Mom and Dad Stone; my brother, Ed Stone, and my sister, Ellen Doukoullos, who both sold jingles for me; Richard "Doc" Lieber who gave me an appreciation for music and electronics; Carl Smith, who made my music come to life so many times; Don and Wanda Petty, Jim and Brenda Kornmann, Fan and Bill Spitz, Chris Slater, and good ol' Glenn Mitchell, customers who became friends along the way; my sister, Carol King, for her constant encouragement and her computer; Nancy Thomsen and Tony Stone, my other sister and brother who endured my early days as a musician; George Knott, my late uncle, for his piano; John Fish who taught me that music is more than just the notes; Bill Duke who bailed me out so often when I needed a keyboard player in the middle of the night; Ted Mau who played and sang with me through the good times and the bad; Mike Graham, the best engineer in the business; Jane Snyder and Sandy Butz for their knowledge about singing; Jerry Wilson, who wrote the book on selling; Jeff and Saly Fehn, who helped with "Mac;" Paul Legge and Kevin Meeks at IRC Audio; Brian Paulson at IRC Music; Hardin Cheatham; Julie Whaley and Mark Garvey, my editors at Writer's Digest Books, and all those other customers whose names are fading, but whose checks never bounced.

The Players

Steve and Margie Hanna, Chuck Nenneker, Larry Wiseman, Bob Wood, Jim Beckel, Ann and Larry Philpott, Greg and Corrine Imboden, Pam Miller, Wendy Paul, Karen Foster, Dianah Stauback, Flip Miller, Dick Dennis, Rex Thomas, Steve Dokken, Larry Sauer, Dana Hubbard, Mike Johnson, Jim Arnold, Jack Gilfoy, Bill and Lydia Earnhart, Kim Sullivan, Dave Meadows, Scott Ballentine, Mike and Pam Close, Bill Moring, Dave Smith, Mark Mayfield, Greg Anderson, Bill Warren, Doug Adams, Chris Browning, Steve Creech, Chris Lieber, and Ted Mau.

The Singers

Susan Herner, Sandy Gossling, Lori Smith, Sharon Fergusson, Mike Patty, Craig Patty, Sandy Patti, Cozette Byrd, Teresa Benge, Steve Moore, Steve Morse, Steve Green, Karl Hinkle, Rodney Jones, and Ted Mau.

INTRODUCTION

These are exciting times in the music business. Every year, the industry presents new opportunities to aspiring musicians and songwriters. Coupled with the astounding proliferation of affordable, high-quality recording equipment, novice composers can compete with established professionals for millions of dollars in music production budgets. One specific area of music production, jingles (music for radio and TV commercials), has gained more attention in recent years because musicians and composers have discovered how much more dependable and lucrative jingle writing can be than playing in saloons or submitting hundreds of songs to publishers.

Once the domain of a select few, the jingle business has opened its doors to new ideas, new trends, and new composers. No longer do advertising agencies that contract for jingles look only to traditional music meccas for their production materials. Writers in cities throughout the country compete with those in New York, Chicago, Los Angeles, and Nashville for jingle production assignments.

Nonetheless, people striving for success in the jingle business often fail because they don't understand that "doing" jingles is more than merely writing short songs. Although there is certainly a relationship between writing good songs and writing good jingles, writing music for radio and TV commercials requires a different set of skills and knowledge, not the least of which is the ability to function in the fast-paced world of advertising. Therefore, an aspiring jingle writer needs to learn as much about the advertising business as possible.

Because composing jingles is only part of the process, aspiring jingle writers need to familiarize themselves with the recording process with which they will produce their work. Modern recording practices often confound the beginner because of the myriad of choices available. Studio time and talent (musicians and singers) are expensive. Learning how to budget time and money, therefore, can be the best advantage the beginner develops.

Furthermore, success in the jingle business means knowing how to compete in business: how to set up and run a small company, how to advertise and promote your services, and how to get paid for your work. Whether you're a schooled musician or have never played an instrument, you will have to develop business skills if you want to be successful in this highly competitive industry. I often tell beginning jingle singers that singing jingles is more of an acting job than a singing assignment. Yes, you need a good voice and the ability to sing in tune, but you need to understand what you are singing and how to deliver the message for which the advertiser is paying. A similar analogy works for jingle writers. Jingle writing is as much a business writing assignment as it is a musical assignment.

Another important consideration for anyone trying to break in is the fact that the jingle business functions primarily during regular business hours. Though you may choose to write and produce jingles "after hours," your customers will expect to hear from you during the daytime, not in the evenings or on weekends. Getting started may present a problem if you are trying to hold down another daytime job, but it is certainly not impossible.

Finally, although a thorough knowledge of music theory and mastery of the piano are two extremely helpful skills, they are not essential for becoming a successful jingle writer/producer. You must, however, have a sense of music, a feel for rhythm, an ear for melody. You must be able to put words and notes together in an appealing manner, whether you can name the notes or not. At some point in the process, however, if you are not a musician, you will need to associate with someone who is musically competent who will transfer your musical ideas to paper for musicians and singers to read.

To compete successfully in the jingle business, you will need to understand the advertising business, the recording process, and the craft of jingle writing. The system I present in this book should help you in all three areas.

Al Stone, Jr.
Noblesville, Indiana

CHAPTER 1

Yes, You Can!

Welcome to the jingle business! Yes, even if you're not a musician, you can write, produce, and sell jingles, those sometimes annoying but always memorable little musical ditties that advertisers use to hammer home their messages thousands of times a day. Yes, you can write 'em, produce 'em, and make a lot of money selling 'em! And I'm going to show you how.

First, let me assure you, I am not a highly trained master musician. Yes, I read music, somewhat, and I play a few instruments, marginally. Yes, I've made a living as a performing musician, but no, I would not refer to myself as a schooled musician.

What I do possess is knowledge of and experience in the advertising business. What I will show you is how, with some measure of talent and creativity and a large amount of perseverance, you too can be successful writing, producing, and selling jingles, even if you're not a musician.

The second confession I must make is that although it's been nearly twenty-five years since I wrote and produced my first jingle, I'm still learning every day. I am impressed with the quality and diversity of talent that abounds in this business. I am at times overwhelmed with the outstanding creativity of those competitors, especially the younger ones, whose demonstration tapes I've had the privilege to hear. But I am not intimidated at all by the competition, and you shouldn't be either.

The commercial music field is as vast and complex as any other major business, yet there is always room for new ideas, new melodies, and new musical styles. So, if you have the desire and ability to write and produce commercial music, you should do it. It's the most exciting business I've ever been involved in and it is certainly the most competitive.

But be warned! The jingle business is frustrating. It is literally a jungle with a labyrinth of pitfalls and traps ready to snare the uneducated and inexperienced. Although the financial rewards are exceptional, the disappointments occur nearly every week. For every "spec" (speculative jingle) I've written and sold, I have at least five specs languishing in the closet, waiting for a new customer whose name and slogan might fit.

If you're going to get into this business, be prepared to toughen your skin, lose your ego, and get ready for war. The battle will rage with competitors, customers, agency reps, engineers, talent, and even overnight delivery services. My favorite maxim is, "The job isn't sold until the [customer's] check clears the bank!" And even then there may be a hitch.

One last comment before entering the fray. If you are a schooled musician, you have a definite advantage over those of us who are not. Nonetheless, though my musical terminology may offend your sensibility at times, if you have not competed in the jingle business, you have just as much to learn as the rest of us. So, please, ignore the elementary approach to music theory as I present it and look for the ideas that will help you succeed faster than you imagined. Now, let's jump in and get to work.

The Jingle Quiz

Directions: Fill in the blanks with the correct word or words from these famous jingles:

1. This is not ______ ______ Oldsmobile!
2. Can't beat the ______.
3. This Bud's ______ ______.
4. Give your breath long lasting freshness with ______ ______.
5. ______ ______, ______ ______ and touch someone.

(Score 5 points for each correct answer. A score of 25 means you're a likely candidate for the jingle business or else you've been chained to your television for the past ten years. A score of 0-5 means you're from the planet Oooom and don't know the difference between a Toyota and a tollbooth.)

The correct answers are:

1. your father's
2. feeling (Coca Cola)
3. for you (Budweiser beer)
4. Big Red (chewing gum)
5. Reach out, reach out (AT&T)

Taking this quiz should demonstrate that, like it or not, musical jingles affect us all. We hear them even when we aren't listening closely. Their messages sneak into our brains and cause us to act in certain ways. We buy products and services and may not even know why. We have been influenced by these creative messengers and we respond often in spite of our better judgment.

Jingles identify an advertiser and its message. Hearing the words alone, as in the quiz, can cause us to remember the melody. Conversely, hearing just the melody will often bring the words to mind. Commercial jingles do work extremely well. And someone, preferably you, has to write them.

Where the Jingle Writer Fits In

As jingle writers, we are members of the advertising community, and, as such, we offer an important service to our customers who are advertising agencies and direct accounts. The distinction here is simple. Ad agencies represent many different businesses for which they contract a variety of services. Ad agencies create total advertising campaigns with ads for print, electronic media, outdoor, and direct mail. A single agency may handle dozens of accounts, some of which may need music for their broadcast or non-broadcast advertising and promotion.

Direct accounts are simply businesses operating without advertising agencies. For several reasons, direct accounts prefer to handle their own advertising. Large companies, for example, often have in-house advertising departments that function in much the same way as an ad agency. These ad departments create the programs that their own companies will use to promote their products and services. Frequently, the media recognize these advertising departments as legitimate ad agencies and offer sales commissions (discounts) to the advertiser for placing ads in magazines and on radio or TV stations. By placing their own ads or spot announcements (commercials) themselves, these "house" agencies enjoy the same discounts on the cost of the advertisements, often as much as 15%, as the established ad agencies receive.

On the other hand, most small companies cannot afford to hire ad agencies full time, so they often try to do the work themselves. In most cases, they fail miserably because they are not advertising professionals and simply don't have the time and expertise required. Consequently, these small advertisers working without ad agencies are targets for your services, especially when you're just starting into the jingle business.

Advertising agencies and departments employ copywriters to create slogans, total advertising campaigns, filler copy, brochure notes, and a host of other writing assignments. But most agencies and departments, especially local ones, cannot afford to keep full-time jingle writers on staff. So, they job out the work to a jingle house, a company specializing in commercial music writing and production.

Occasionally, an ad agency will do some of the writing of the jingle before hiring a composer. Some agents enjoy writing lyrics, for example, and simply contract with a composer to set the words to music and produce the final recording. More often, however, the agency depends on the jingle writer to do nearly all of the work on both lyrics and music.

No matter how much or how little creative input you receive from your customer, as a jingle writer, your job is to come up with the "hottest-newest-most-unique-most-memorable" jingle ever written. At least, that's what your customer will expect. And with the competition raging today, you'd better come close on your first attempt for the customer or forget it.

As an aspiring jingle writer/producer, you should focus first on local advertisers, the flower shops, car dealers, drugstores, groceries, and other smaller retail accounts for whom you may write immediately. There will come a time when you'll be pitching those big national accounts. But there's a fortune to be made and a scoreful to learn writing for local accounts.

About now you might be asking yourself, "What do I care about advertising agencies, direct accounts, and house agencies? I want to learn how to write jingles!"

Stone's first rule of writing anything:
KNOW YOUR AUDIENCE!
Stone's second rule of writing:
KNOW WHAT YOU'RE WRITING AND WHY!

Knowing your audience means knowing who your advertising customer is, what it spends annually, why it needs a jingle, and how you can convince it to buy one from you. Knowing what you're writing and why includes not only knowing the basics of composing lyrics and music for a jingle, but also knowing why you're writing the words and music.

Over the years I've met dozens of exceptionally good songwriters and lyricists. Over that same period, I've met only a few outstanding jingle writers. The difference between the two groups should become more and more clear as you read on. But this fact remains consistent among all of the successful jingle writers I have known: every single one of them understands what the advertising business is all about and how they fit into that world.

A Typical Ad Agency

Let's look a little deeper into the advertising business, specifically, the way ad agencies or departments function. Suppose, for example, that an advertiser decides to hire an agency to handle its advertising. What kind of services should the advertiser expect from the agency?

Though no rules exist for the structure of an advertising agency, most formally structured agencies follow some fairly common practices. A typical ad agency divides along two or three primary lines: sales and account management, creative, and media buying. Often agencies operate in creative groups: committees made up of a member or two from each department who do all of the work—sales, creative, and media buying—for a particular client.

Depending on its size, focus of business, and market, a typical agency may have a creative director, an artist or art department, staff writers, account executives, media buyers, broadcast producers, and management and support teams.

The creative director is usually the person in charge of supervising all of the creative projects in the agency. The person who serves as creative director may or may not be an artist, a writer, a broadcast producer, or account executive; however, he or she should understand all of these positions and how they affect each other. Furthermore, by definition, the creative director should be a highly imaginative person, capable of motivating and managing other creative people.

When calling on advertising agencies, you will often be directed to the creative director. Beware! Some creative directors have absolutely no power whatsoever. They simply function as the mouthpiece of management, and their primary role is to collect samples from vendors and send finished ads to stations and newspapers. In other, more enlightened agencies, creative directors make the final decision on which products and services the agency will buy for its customers. Make sure you find out what kind of creative director you're pitching!

Let's take a look at why advertisers use music with or for their commercials. And by the way, these reasons will help you when you're selling your music.

Why Jingles?

There is one human characteristic we all share, in varying degrees: our love for and our attraction to music. Music is the great leveler. Music can enlighten and cause reflection. It can evoke emotional extremes, firing up a crowd at a ball game and motivating the masses to near-hysteria. Music can soothe the troubled soul or trigger fond childhood memories.

What I find most significant about the power of music is its uncanny way of forcing the mind to recall minute details. No matter what age, we all remember both positive and negative feelings when an old song comes on the radio. We remember where we were, what we were doing, and who we were with. We remember the cool autumn breeze, the glorious sunset, the view from the top of the mountain. Music does that to us. And for that reason, music can be the most powerful tool in an advertiser's arsenal.

A Typical Local Advertiser

To understand the important role music plays in advertising, let's examine some of the tools of the trade. We'll use the fictional ABC Flowers as an example of the typical local advertiser.

ABC has been in business for several years in a medium-size, Midwestern city. Over the years, ABC has expanded to five locations around town. For most of the past five years, ABC has experimented with many forms of advertising: direct mail, print, outdoor, telemarketing, and electronic media. ABC has been handling its own advertising; however, the company has recently decided to "shop" for an agency to handle the work. Let's review ABC's advertising history to identify the tools it has used.

Direct Mail. Direct mail advertising, simply defined, is sending out various pieces of advertising literature to a specific list of potential customers. In most major cities you'll find at least one company specializing in direct mail advertising for customers such as ABC. These direct mail shops may be ad agencies that offer full services, from concept to completion, including the actual mailing. Or they may be mailing houses that simply package and mail out the advertiser's preprinted materials to appropriate lists of potential customers.

Though some would call direct mail "junk mail," it is a viable method of advertising. Using direct mail, an advertiser, such as ABC Flowers, may choose its audience from a specific location, age group, or socioeconomic category. Direct mail, however, depends primarily on the effectiveness of one tool, the printed page. It also assumes that the target audience, those potential customers, will receive and read the material. Unfortunately, most direct mail winds up in the trash, unopened and unread.

ABC's direct mail campaign has consisted of a series of mailers announcing sales for special occasions, new locations, new gift-giving ideas, and so forth. A successful mailing returns roughly two to three percent to the advertiser, and ABC has experienced a less-than-average measurable return on its direct mail program.

Print. Print advertising refers to newspaper and magazine ads running locally, regionally, or nationally in general or trade publications. Print ads may simply service an account (giving the name, address, phone number, and a brief description of the business) or they may promote specific marketing programs such as seasonal sales, grand openings, new product/service lines, unique approaches to selling the product/service, and dozens more. Print advertising, more than any other media, covers the spectrum of products and services marketed throughout the world. There are thousands of products and services using print advertising exclusively to deliver their messages.

ABC has been doing print advertising since its inception. It runs weekly ads in the local newspapers. It has a regular, full-color ad in the monthly "city" magazine. It advertises in the weekly "shoppers" and neighborhood papers, and around various holidays, ABC places special print ads in the local high school and college papers. Print advertising has served ABC well over the years.

Outdoor. Throughout its brief history ABC has tried to use outdoor advertising (billboards) sparingly. In every instance, ABC has chosen to use outdoor primarily as location advertising, i.e., they put up boards announcing their new locations. Although it can be effective for some advertisers, outdoor depends heavily on the locations of the boards and how many people per day see the boards in those locations (gross impressions). Furthermore, a billboard offers only one message. The audience sees it several times, absorbs it, and either reacts to the message or doesn't. ABC, nonetheless, continues to buy at least one billboard space each month, year round.

Telemarketing. In recent years, ABC has experimented with both live and taped telemarketing, direct phone calls to individual customers. ABC's success ratio is difficult to measure because the messages delivered via telemarketing have been generic by design. "Hi! This is Jill and I just called to remind you that Mother's Day is just two weeks away, and we'd like you to stop by any one of ABC Flowers' five convenient locations and pick out your Mother's Day bouquet, before they're all gone!" Telemarketing appears to be a useful tool for some businesses, and ABC has just begun to tap the market with this form of advertising.

Direct mail, print, and outdoor advertising materials offer effective though limited use. Even though most advertisers reuse parts of their ads from week to week or year to year, most ads must be conceived, redrawn, and rewritten for every new campaign. Not so with jingles. Jingles have a lengthy shelf life, depending on the licensing arrangements, and jingles offer the greatest flexibility for the advertiser using electronic media.

Electronic Media. Radio, television, and nonbroadcast audiovisual presentations offer many advertisers the best buy for their advertising dollars and provide the jingle writer/producer unlimited opportunities for selling music. Though certainly not every advertiser can afford to buy thirty-second (:30) or sixty-second (:60) spot announcements during the Super Bowl or the top-rated network program, almost every small advertiser could afford to buy local radio or cable TV advertising time.

Furthermore, with more and more community-based low-power stations appearing each year, more local advertisers than ever before will have access to their potential customers who live and work near their stores or businesses. Low-power TV is similar to neighborhood weekly newspapers. It doesn't try to compete with the bigger network affiliates or long-established independent stations; consequently, the advertising fees on low-power TV are lower, obviously, because the size of the audience it delivers is smaller.

Cable TV is similar in some respects to low-power TV because the local insert avails (times reserved during each hour on cable channels for local cable operators to sell for ad revenues) offer smaller advertisers opportunities to reach a smaller though more well-defined audience. And no matter where the advertiser is running its spots (commercials), on network TV, local radio, or low-powered neighborhood TV, a jingle could be the most important part of its advertising campaign.

Because radio and TV advertising is within reach of the small advertiser, what ABC Flowers needs to do is analyze its advertising budget, carefully design a radio and TV campaign, and make room for a jingle! Let's see if and how ABC can accomplish this goal.

An Advertising Budget

First, let's define a budget for ABC Flowers that should help you understand the decisions a typical local advertiser must make. A realistic budget for all advertising materials, space, and time for a small chain of flower shops would be 15 to 18% of the company's annual gross sales. Now, you might ask, "Why do I care how much the flower shop spends on advertising?" The answer is not simply "because your paycheck is coming out of that budget." You need to understand how advertisers spend money so that you'll have a better way of analyzing your target customers. Also, you'll be able to price your work more realistically.

Let's assume that ABC Flowers has annual gross sales from all five stores of $1.2 million.

Gross sales	$1,200,000
15% of gross for advertising	180,000
Newspaper Advertising (60%)	108,000
Billboard Advertising (7%)	12,000
Amount remaining for all other advertising	$ 60,000

A $60,000 budget for all other advertising, after subtracting newspaper and billboard, sounds like a lot of money, especially for a small five-store chain of florists. But let's look closer.

In ABC's market (city), the average cost of radio spot advertising on the top five stations is $75 per minute. Prime-time TV shows cost between $500 to $3,500 per thirty-second spot. Local TV news commercial announcements cost between $300 to $700 per thirty-second spot. If we divide $60,000 by 12, ABC's gross expenditures are only $5,000 per month. How many prime-time TV spots or local drive time (the highest rated) radio spots on the number one station in town can ABC afford to buy each month? How effective can these purchases be; how many potential customers can ABC reach? It becomes a mathematical nightmare, unless you understand all the variables.

If, for example, ABC buys radio spots six days a week on the number one radio station in town at a discounted rate (because of the quantity ABC purchases) of $100 per spot, ABC would have only fifty spots to use during the month, or only two spots a day if it skipped Sundays! How effective would two radio spots a day be? Not very effective. And that's probably why ABC hasn't been doing any broadcast advertising. There's no room for it in the budget. And there's also no room for a jingle in the budget!

ABC will either have to restructure its advertising budget, reducing the amount of money designated for print, or it will have to allocate its broadcast budget to flights of air time, bunching up spots in groups of two or three days per week or two or three weeks per month.

ABC's New Ad Agency

Rather than hiring a jingle writer on its own, ABC Flowers has chosen an ad agency (XYZ Advertising) to create all of its advertising materials, including its jingle package. So what happens with the ABC account inside the agency? First, it is assigned an account executive, a sales rep whose function is to keep the client happy. In small- to medium-size agencies, account exec's handle several clients, often a dozen or more.

Next, depending on the agency's structure, ABC's owners will meet with the creative team consisting of writers, artists, producers, management, and, of course, the account executive. During this initial planning meeting, ABC's owners will tell the agency people their history in advertising, what they've been doing, what they'd like to be doing, and what they can afford to do. This first meeting with their new agency should be very open, very honest, and very productive in terms of setting the ground rules and deciding on a direction for the company. It often isn't!

Many ad agencies are so desperate for business that they become rubber stamps for their client's wishes. "Whatever ABC wants, they get!" bellows the creative director. It's the gutsy but successful agency that takes the position, "We're the advertising professionals; let us do our job!" Your job, as a freelance jingle writer, is to figure out what kind of agency you're dealing with.

So, ABC has a new agency, one with enough confidence to tell the owners, "Here's what we're going to do for ABC in the next twelve months." The creative director then outlines the various elements of the new advertising campaign for ABC Flowers. If the agency has made a presentation to ABC in order to win the account, some of the creative work may already be done.

In our example, XYZ Advertising has won the ABC Flowers' account because it did its homework. It analyzed ABC's previous five years of advertising. It discarded the folksy, late-sixties flower-child image and came up with a modern slogan, logo design, and storefront sign.

"Your new slogan," the creative director announces proudly, "is 'ABC Flowers with blooms for all rooms!' "

ABC's owners stare blankly at the artcard their new account executive is holding.

"Get it? Blooms for all rooms!" repeats the creative director. "We want people filling their homes, their offices, their factories, their RV's with flowers from ABC . . . blooms for all rooms. It's dynamite!"

ABC's owners blink in feeble agreement.

The account executive adds quickly, "Wait'll ya hear yer new song!"

And that's where you, the jingle writer, come in.

Getting Assignments

There are many ways a jingle writer gets assignments. The writer may be "pitching" with an agency to win an account. An agency may call in a writer for a new account it has already won without using a jingle in its presentation. An established account, with or without an agency, may call a writer in to do a new jingle or update an old one. Or, a writer may have contacted a direct account and convinced the advertiser to use music in its ad campaign.

Pitching with an agency is very common. Once a writer has established a relationship with an agency, the agency often calls with speculative projects that the writer may elect to do, usually for little or no money. Frequently, an agency will pay the cost of singers and musicians so that the jingle it is presenting to its client will sound as polished as possible.

If the agency wins the new account, the writer may, I emphasize may, get the assignment.

CHAPTER 2

Yours for a Song

Before you can compete effectively in the jingle business, you need to understand the basic components of a jingle. Though similar to songs in many respects, jingles are often more repetitious, certainly more compressed, and usually longer lasting than most songs. Local advertisers, for example, often use their jingles for many years; whereas, popular songs have a shelf life of only a few months.

We can talk about jingles using typical songwriting and poetic terminology: introduction, verse, chorus, bridge, tag, hook, and coda. We can analyze the jingle for melody, rhythm, rhyme, repetition, concatenation, and denouement. But first, let's examine the overall structure of a jingle beginning with length.

Length

As you compose your first jingle or musical ID (identification) package, you must understand that your song will be used as part of a total campaign, obviously for radio or TV advertising. Most advertisers buy time on radio or TV stations in lots of :10, :15, :30, or :60-second time units. Therefore, the commercial or "spot" (short for spot announcement), of which your jingle is a part, must be timed exactly to fit into the segment that the advertiser has purchased. The station's "traffic" department will reject a :31 or a :61-second spot, for example.

As a general rule, when you compose a jingle, you should strive to end the song at :29 or :59. In the case of a :10 or :15, you should cut a half-second off the length. Since most advertisers buy :10, :15, or :30-second length spots on television and since most TV stations require at least a half second of "roll time" to get their tape up to speed, cutting the length of your jingle by a full second will help the advertiser conform to industry standards and not have its commercial cut off abruptly before it's actually over.

So, one of your first investments as a jingle writer will be a good, dependable stopwatch, and then a good, dependable metronome. As you compose the jingle, your stopwatch and metronome will guide you to correct time length.

The Contents of a Typical Jingle Package

When you write a jingle for a customer you are composing a piece of music for radio and TV advertising that your customer may be running a year, two years, perhaps even five years down the road. No one can predict today precisely what your customer will need for his or her various spots in the future. Will he or she be running only :30 TV spots? Only :60 radio spots? Lots of cable TV two-minute spots? We can't predict, so, you will be selling your customer a jingle "package," i.e., a collection of "mixes" of the jingle you've composed.

Mixes. The recording term "mix" refers to the final recording or rerecording of instrumental and vocal performances of a song or jingle. For example, the final recording or mix of a hit song is usually just the singer singing and the instruments playing from start to finish for the entire arrangement of the song. The recording engineer raises or lowers the sound levels of the various instruments and vocalists until the producer decides the song sounds the way he or she wants it to sound. The engineer may also adjust the tone (equalization) of the various instruments and singers, and he or she may add special effects (see chapter 6).

Since most recording today occurs in "multi-track" studios, the engineer has total control over each separate instrument or instrumental section and each vocalist or vocal group. Therefore, the engineer can mix the sounds together in an unlimited number of ways, bringing instruments and singers in and out of the song whenever desired.

Once you have composed your jingle in whatever lengths you have predetermined in conference with your customer, you must plan the mixes in your package. You do this planning prior to recording the final tracks (instrumental and vocal recordings). In a typical jingle package for a local advertiser you may have the following mixes:

:60 Full sing (or full vox)
:60 Open-close (or donut)
:60 Tag (or stinger)
:60 Instrumental
:30 Full sing
:30 Open-close
:30 Tag
:30 Instrumental
:10 Full sing
:10 Instrumental

Let's define these mixes.

:60 Full Sing. Sometimes called the :60-second full vocal arrangement or "full vox" ("vox" is an abbreviation for "vocal"), the :60 full sing mix is the whole song from front to back with singers singing the lyrics you've written over an instrumental performed by any number of musicians. The full sing is the complete jingle in a :60-second format.

:60 Open-Close or Donut. The :60 open-close or "donut" gets its name from the hole in the middle of the jingle, i.e., the place where the singers are not singing. This hole allows time for an announcer to read specific commercial information (ad copy) that the advertiser may change as frequently as it wishes without changing or rerecording the entire jingle package. The term voice-over derives from this process of an announcer speaking over music. A typical :60 open-close mix begins with :05 to :10 seconds of singing, :30 to :40 seconds of instrumental "bed" (for the announcer to speak over), and :05 to :10 seconds of singing at the end.

:60 Tag. The :60 tag is simply the jingle mixed so that it begins with just the instruments playing—no singers—all the way through the jingle until the last :05 or :10 seconds. This final singing part is called the tag during which the singers usually sing the name of the company and/or the company's slogan.

The :60 tag allows the advertiser to use the bulk of the time announcing its particular message while maintaining the musical identification of the jingle underneath the announcer and singing the name or slogan at the end of the spot.

:60 Instrumental. When the advertiser needs all of the air time to promote its product or services, a special sale, a seasonal message, or other spoken information, he or she often chooses the :60 instrumental mix of the jingle. Since there is no singing whatsoever in this mix, the announcer has the full :60 (or :59) seconds to deliver the commercial announcement, but the advertiser still benefits from the jingle bed hammering home the musical identification underneath the announcer.

:30 Mixes. The :30-second mixes follow the same pattern as the :60s for the same reasons. The lengths of the beds will be shorter, of course, and the challenge to you, the writer, is to maintain the integrity of the song in the much shorter :30 mix.

:10 Mixes. The :10 mixes are usually just quick edits of the final tag of the jingle. We often plan our arrangements and recording sessions so that we may simply edit out the tag line easily and cleanly after the musicians and singers have finished. Occasionally, we will actually record a separate :10-second length jingle based on the :60.

Special Mixes. Frequently, you will take an assignment that requires special mixes of perhaps varying lengths, depending on the advertiser's needs. Examples of special mixes include: the weave, the bump or the spike, the stinger or button, and shorter or longer than standard-length mixes.

Weave. The weave mix is simply a variation on the open-close with the singing literally weaving in and out of the mix accenting specific lines of predetermined copy. For example, one of our advertisers requested that the name of his store "pop in about every five to ten seconds throughout" the jingle, even during the "mostly instrumental" mixes. So, what we produced is a jingle that begins with singing the advertiser's name, after a brief instrumental introduction, and continues with short instrumental segments, roughly ten seconds each, alternating with the singing of the name.

Bumps or Spikes. The bump or spike is similar to the weave in that a word or a line simply jumps up in the middle of a verse or chorus, almost out of context. For example, the original structure of a jingle might be V/B/C/T (verse, bridge, chorus, tag); however, with a bump or spike added, the modified structure appears as:

V(spike)V(spike)B(spike)B(spike)C(spike)C T

The bump or spike is used as an interruption of the flow of the jingle without destroying the overall effect of the track. The point is to accent or emphasize a key word or phrase the advertiser feels is critical to its campaign.

Here's an example:

Dented Rents (Auto Rental)

(Verse)
You need a car for a day or a week,
But you don't want to spend a lot
(Spike)
Rent a Dent!
(Verse)
You don't need to impress,
So there's no need to guess
(Spike)
Rent a Dent, Rent a Dent, Rent a Dent!
(Bridge)
Don't waste your money or time,
Shopping all over town
(Spike)
Rent a Dent, Rent a Dent
(Bridge)
Save yourself a lot of money
Save yourself a lot of time
Dented Rents the car you need
We've got cars of every kind!
(Chorus)
Rent a Dent from Dented Rents
It's so easy to do
(Spike)
Rent a Dent
(Chorus)
Rent a Dent from Dented Rents
We'll save money for you!
(Tag)
Dented Rents, the best car at the best price!

Stingers or Buttons. The stinger or button is simply a short jingle usually just singing the advertiser's name or slogan. We occasionally cut stingers for use in TV spots when the customer chooses not to order a complete jingle package. More often than not these stingers are simply the advertiser's name sung a cappella (without instrumental accompaniment).

Special Length Mixes. You may get requests for music shorter or longer than the standard lengths, :60, :30, and :10. In most cases these requests come from highly experienced advertisers who produce complex commercials using a host of audio and video tools. For example, an advertiser might commission you to compose and produce a melody in four different musical styles for use in a multitargeted advertising campaign. Each musical style might only last a few seconds or might be edited together to create a longer yet nonstandard-length piece of music.

Occasionally, you'll land an assignment that permits you to compose a theme song of three to four minutes' duration with edits for use as a jingle. These types of projects allow you to expand your imagination and increase your fees!

Working with your customer you will determine which mixes will be most useful for the advertising campaign. For example, your customer may request variations in the total package; I have produced jingle packages containing as many as thirty-five mixes. Your customer may tell you, "I only run :30s; I never run :60s, ever!" So, you may only cut a :30-second jingle for that customer, but you will cut a :60 instrumental for future sales. You deliver the :30s to your immediate customer, retaining the sales rights outside his or her market, and you keep the :60 instrumental mix "in the can" for that future time when you resell the jingle in another city (see chapter 8).

Jingle Structure

Now let's take a closer look at the specific elements of structure—the introduction, verse, chorus, bridge, tag, and hook.

The Instrumental Introduction. Even though the instrumental introduction in a typical popular song might be ten, fifteen, or even twenty seconds long, in a typical radio or TV jingle, the instrumental introduction is usually no longer than a beat or two, one or two seconds at the most. The reason should be obvious: if you're writing a :30-second jingle, three seconds equals 10% of the time allotted for the finished commercial, and 10% of a typical advertising broadcast budget could mean literally thousands of dollars a year spent "introducing" the commercial!

Quite often the jingle writer begins the jingle with a very simple introduction. It could be an a cappella vocal line or a quick drum beat "pick up." (Less than a full measure, a pick up, if used as an introduction, establishes the tempo and leads into the first full measure of music.) Below is an example of a two-beat pick up in 4/4 time (see chapter 4 for more on music notation):

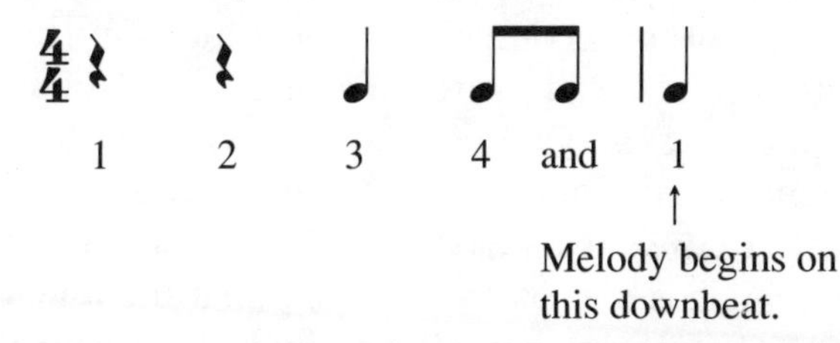

The possibilities for musical introductions are practically unlimited. A short horn (trumpet) punch, very staccato in fanfare fashion is effective. A sliding trombone ending with a cymbal crash or a quick crescendo of violins with harp serve well as introductions. Musical and nonmusical sound effects also add punch to the front of the song. Whatever choices you and your arranger make, you should be sure that the introduction is short, attention-getting, and consistent with the overall effect of the advertiser's campaign.

For example, several years ago I was commissioned to write a jingle for the Niagara County (New York) tourism department. The slogan at the time was "Niagara County is Rainbow Country." The ad agency creative director requested that the introduction of the song include "something that indicates Niagara Falls and rainbows." Interesting request.

In the final production we used cascading violins and a harp to suggest the waterfalls. The melody line of the slogan that opened the jingle was very soft, smooth-flowing, and transparent, like a rainbow. The musical effect was to suggest the bubbling rush of water and the clearing skies revealing a rainbow. It worked.

For a chain of quick-stop convenience stores and gas stations throughout New York and New England we created a calliope sound effect for the opening of the jingle. The stores' theme was built around a circus atmosphere.

A newspaper in northern Indiana requested a soft, middle-of-the-road sound for their new advertising campaign. We used violins, flutes, and oboe following a single thump on a bass drum as the introduction.

Over the years I've used every imaginable sound effect and musical instrument to introduce jingles, each chosen for the specific purpose of getting the listener's attention. In broadcasting today, the audience hears thousands of commercials; therefore the challenge is to make your jingle stand out from the crowd. Creating a short but strong, identifiable introduction will help you accomplish this goal.

Verses, Choruses, Bridges, and Tags. Your placement of verses, choruses, bridges, and tags defines the overall structure of the jingle. If we assign the letters V, C, B, and T to represent verse, chorus, bridge, and tag, respectively, your choices for the overall structure of a jingle might include these and other "song patterns":

VCVCBCT
TVCVCT
VVCTCT
VCBVCT
CTVBCT
VCBCT

The song patterns vary according to your design of lyrics. If you think in terms of the advertiser's name and slogan being the most important part of the jingle, you will find that building either from or to the tag (T) is very logical. A good rule of thumb is to try to include the advertiser's name at least five times in a :60 and at least three times in a :30.

For example, the pattern VCVCBCT (verse, chorus, verse, chorus, bridge, chorus, tag) might look something like this:

(First verse)
line 1
line 2
line 3
line 4

(First chorus)
line 1
line 2 (contains advertiser's name)

(Second verse)
line 1
line 2
line 3
line 4

(Second chorus)
line 1
line 2 (contains advertiser's name)

(Bridge)
line 1 (contains name)

(Bridge)
line 2 (contains name)

(Third chorus)
line 1
line 2 (contains name)

(Tag)
line 1 (contains name and slogan)

In this example of structure, the advertiser's name appears at least six times and the slogan once. In the following chapter we will examine various sets of lyrics based on several of these song patterns.

The Verse or Stanza. Before moving further into writing lyrics (chapter 3), let's take a look at the specific components beginning with the verse more accurately defined as the stanza. Throughout this text I will use the two terms interchangeably.

In songs and poetry, verses or stanzas serve as the primary source for expository information, simply stated, the facts. When the songwriter "tells the story," the details of love gone wrong, for example, the verse carries these facts as the writer interprets them. Moving from one verse to the next, the writer may offer details that further develop the theme or clarify the important ideas.

As the song unfolds, the listener is drawn into the story and tries to understand the writer's point of view, attitude, and feeling about the subject. The effectiveness of this communication depends upon the writer's ability to paint word pictures, to capture abstractions in concrete language in a manner that the listener not only understands but also enjoys.

In a jingle, the writer's goal is similar to a songwriter's. The jingle writer wants to explain, motivate, and entertain the listener. However, because the goal of advertising is to bring customers into an advertiser's place of business, the jingle writer's job is a little more difficult than the songwriter's or poet's.

The jingle writer has far less time than either the songwriter or the poet to establish The Idea and to motivate the listener to act. In only thirty or sixty seconds of lyrics, the jingle writer must introduce the product or service; explain the features and benefits; repeat the advertiser's name, slogan, and perhaps address and phone number; and motivate the listener to rush out and buy the product or service.

The Chorus and the Hook. The chorus and the hook of a jingle is that part of the song that the listener most often remembers. If you think about your favorite popular songs and try to recall the words, you usually will recall the choruses and the hooks. The same is true for jingles.

The chorus actually contains the "hook," the short musical and lyrical expression that capsulizes The Idea the advertiser wants the listener to remember. Through repetition, the chorus causes the listener to lock into the theme better than any other part of the jingle. Whereas choruses in songs may be four to eight lines, choruses in jingles are usually two to four lines. Compression once again: trying to pack as much information into as small a time frame as possible.

The purpose, then, of the jingle chorus is to hammer home the advertiser's name and slogan, usually placed in the hook. It's the best shot and perhaps the last shot the advertiser has to affix The Idea firmly in the listener's mind.

"Give your breath long-lasting freshness with Big Red!"

"You deserve a break today . . . at McDonald's"
"Coke is it!"
"Double your pleasure, double your fun,
With Double good, Double good,
Doublemint Gum"

Each of these hooks or slogans has been burned into the consciousness of Americans over the past ten or twenty years; yet few of us remember much more than these few words of each jingle.

The Bridge. If the verse or stanza communicates the details of the jingle, and the chorus contains the hook, what then is the bridge? Simply, the bridge is a short section of a jingle that permits the writer to create a resting place for the ear. The bridge contains a different melody and a different set of lyrics than the verses or chorus. The bridge allows for a change of direction, a break in what could have become the monotony of the verse-chorus-verse-chorus pattern of the song.

But bridges can serve another function in a jingle, namely a place to put lyrics that the advertiser will not need beyond the initial airing of the jingle, if at all.

For example, some of your customers may only need room to sing lyrics at the beginning and ending of the jingle. They need only an open-close mix with plenty of room in the middle (donut) to put announcer copy. Car dealers come to mind immediately. Most car dealers stress the same concepts in their advertising—"service, selection, and low prices." Although they often buy fully produced jingle packages, car dealers usually wind up using only the open-close, the tag, or instrumental mixes in their ongoing campaigns and promotions. They usually run the full sing mixes only for a short time, a few weeks, to introduce the new theme song. The lyrics you write for the bridge, therefore, should be disposable, easily dropped without harming the overall effect of the jingle.

The reason I choose to write these disposable lyrics in the bridge structure rather than a verse or chorus is to maintain the musical and lyrical integrity of the jingle that the listener will hear most often. Once the advertiser drops the bridge lyrics in favor of announcer voice-over, the focus shifts more toward the announcer away from the jingle. The music however, remains beneath the announcer, carrying the musical theme and reinforcing the advertiser's message.

Since they usually want their name sung at the beginning and end of the track, car dealers may not even ask for bridge lyrics. "We wanna sell cars!" they tell you. "We wanna push prices," they bellow. "So sing the name and get outa the way! Let the announcer sell!"

I'm not exaggerating.

For this type of customer you might design a jingle with this pattern: VBCT—a verse, a bridge, a chorus, and a tag.

The verse might only be two lines and the chorus might only be four lines building toward the single-line tag. Most of the jingle would be the bridge, an instrumental section of forty to forty-five seconds, echoing the musical theme of the chorus at times, yet standing apart from both verse and chorus in structure and melody.

Here's an example:

(Tag)
Powers Swain Chevrolet Geo
(Verse)
Our minipayments will scare the competition away and put a smile on your face
So just smile and say "boo!"
(Verse)
Our miniprices will beat the other dealers around and put a smile on your face
So just smile and say "boo!"
(Chorus)
Powers Swain saves you more
Shop the minipayment store
Find out why we scare the competition
(Bridge)
Powers Swain
Just say "boo" and start a new tradition
Powers Swain, the minipayment store
(Inst bridge)
(Chorus)
Powers Swain saves you more
Shop the minipayment store
Find out why we scare the competition
(Tag)
Powers Swain Chevrolet Geo
The minipayment store
Powers Swain Chevrolet Geo

The minipayment store
Powers Swain!

In this example, we actually mixed the final jingle without any singing during the short (:11 seconds) instrumental bridge. We then created mixes using just the opening tag line and the closing tag as written above. The result was a :60-second open-close jingle with a long, :48-second instrument bed. The lyrics we wrote for the bridge were disposable.

Here's another example:

(Verse)
When you feel like dining out
But you don't know where to go,
Follow the signs to Chesterfield
For dinner and a show!
(Chorus)
Chesterfield is theatre, fine dining, and much more!
Chesterfield has everything you've been looking for.
(Bridge)
Seven days a week, we're here for you
With special group rates and special shows for you.
Chesterfield is an experience for one and all,
Great food, great fun, great theatre, c'mon
Come along!
(Chorus)
Chesterfield is theatre, fine dining, and much more!
Chesterfield, yes Chesterfield
(Tag)
We're what you're looking for!

In this example, we can easily drop the bridge lyrics without destroying continuity. Since this jingle is a rather slow tempo piece, the bridge runs approximately :25 seconds, a sufficient amount of time for an open-close mix.

The Melody

The goal for every hit songwriter and every jingle writer is finding that "hummable" tune. It is the melody that stays with us long after the words have faded. The more memorable the tune, the more effective the song. If I had to rule out all elements of a good jingle except one, I would choose melody.

Creating good melodies, however, can be frustrating. Every time you come up with a good one, someone reminds you of the hit song from ten years ago that used the same set of notes! As a writer or composer of melodies, I find that working with the lyrics first helps me arrive at more original tunes than if I simply start with the music. Even if you're not a musician, you can "write" excellent melodies. Just use a small cassette recorder so that you don't lose your composition before you get with a musician!

A second approach I use is to find a rhythm for the jingle—a beat—before trying to find the melody. Up-tempo jingles often require fewer words. If I can establish the rhythm and tempo of the piece first, I can narrow my choices for lyrics and melody considerably. In chapter 4 you will find some exercises to help you find those tunes bouncing around in your head.

How you decide to put the jingle together depends on how the jingle will be used and for whom you are writing. Some jingle writers claim they "always write thirty seconds of verse/chorus, twenty seconds of bridge, and ten seconds of tag." Others admit that they have no design in mind, but merely sit down and begin writing . . . "it just sorta comes out . . ." Still others work closely with their arrangers, carefully plotting each and every note, each and every measure, each and every word, finally achieving a miniature symphonic piece worthy of any major orchestra.

The point is there is no one process you must follow when writing jingles, but there are some common-sense approaches you will begin to learn in the following chapters.

Musical Styles for Jingles

Throughout the brief history of the jingle business, writers have used every imaginable style of music. Popular songs have beome jingles and some jingles have become popular songs. Whatever the latest style of music, you'll find a jingle writer out there trying to incorporate it into a new track.

Often the advertiser or agency will request a specific style(s) of music for the new jingle package. Sometimes they will leave the decision to the writer with little or no guidance whatsoever. In either case, you should be ready for anything, and I mean *anything*.

I have had some of the most unbelievable requests for mixing musical styles. We've mixed a classical string quartet with a gutbucket country style in the same :30 jingle. I've had customers ask me to produce the BBC (British Broadcasting Corporation) theme song with lyrics for a local British-theme restaurant. Another inventive agency rep (advertising account executive) ordered a track with nothing but flutes; he just loved flutes!

To prepare yourself for this onslaught of sometimes inane but often quite reasonable requests, you should familiarize yourself with as many musical styles as possible. Even though your forte may be contemporary synthesized rock, you should become quite adept at writing old forties swing music. Although the number one-rated rock act may be your favorite group to listen to, you should dig back in the files and pull out some early fifties vocal groups such as The Four Lads, The McGuire Sisters, The Four Freshmen, even The Weavers so that you'll be able to capture those styles or blend them into your jingles as needed.

You probably will receive requests for jingle packages in multiple styles—one melody developed in several different styles of music. We have written and arranged jingles in as many as seven different styles, from a full :60 a cappella version to a forties swing piece to a contemporary rock version. With some minor adjustments in melody and lyric, multiple styles present no serious problem, and they can increase the size of your fee dramatically.

So, dig out those old 78s and start studying!

Production Steps

I see a jingle going through at least two of the four steps in production: the rough idea (perhaps just a melody and a sketchy lyric), the spec (a complete melodic and lyric idea presented with minimal production), the demo (a more polished presentation of the jingle), and the final production (a fully arranged jingle ready for broadcast). Frequently, I have sold jingles from simply a rough idea—me banging on a box guitar singing my brains out into a portable cassette recorder. Occasionally, I've sold a track singing and playing the jingle "live" over the phone or in person. Any time you can skip a step from the rough idea to final, do it. The better you are as a writer and salesperson, the easier it is to sell from rough ideas.

The Rough Idea. Think of the rough idea step as an artist's sketch pad. While working on a jingle assignment you will stumble upon melodies, lyrics, even single words that you try to fit into a comprehensive whole that will become the jingle. At the rough idea stage you are literally an artist at work. The jingle is just becoming a reality. You may have written only a chorus, a hook line, a line or two for a verse, or just a hot new slogan.

Rather than plunging ahead with these rough ideas, you can save time by contacting the agency or the customer and giving the ideas a first hearing. If you can, sing the melody or just read the lyrics or slogan. You'll get a reaction, often a positive one. More importantly, if you're on the wrong track, the customer will usually tell you. A word of caution: Some people have absolutely no imagination. Before presenting fragmented rough ideas, you should analyze your customer carefully. If you doubt his or her ability to make the leap from rough idea to final production, save yourself a headache and continue working toward the spec.

The Spec. The spec or speculative jingle demonstrates three properties: the proposed lyrics, the melody, and the overall structure of the jingle. Jingle companies have various names for specs; however, most companies do these rough tracks at no charge or for very little financial compensation. On the other hand, some of the more famous, sought-after composers can command a high fee, in the thousands, for a spec.

When you produce a spec, you spend just as much creative time writing the music and lyrics as you would if you were getting paid for the assignment but you spend much less time producing the jingle on tape. You should not be investing your own money in studio time, talent, and tape on specs. A spec simply puts you in the game and validates your ability to write for the particular assignment in question. Your customer should understand before hearing the spec precisely what a spec is and is not.

Whenever I work with someone who is not familiar with jingles, I give them a copy of a tape I call, "From Spec to Final." This tape has been invaluable in defining the steps in the evolution of a jingle so the customer unfamiliar with the process will understand how I work and what a spec is. The tape is very simple. The first cut on the tape is a very rough spec, just a singer with piano accompaniment. The next cut is a demo, a professional jingle singer and a three- or four-piece rhythm section. The final cut on the tape is the finished jingle with full orchestration and a group of professional jingle singers. Once you're ready to start selling jingles, you should work up your own version of a "spec to final" tape. It will save you time and headaches explaining the process to the inexperienced customer.

Years ago one of my competitors told me that "it's all in the spec." If the spec doesn't sound good, you're out of the game. I agree, especially today with literally hundreds of people writing and selling jingles all over the country. Therefore, without contradicting myself, you should spend the time necessary to produce a good-sounding spec—not a finished, polished commercial, but a demo that can compete with what other jingle writers are pitching. If that means working out a deal with a professional jingle singer and an experienced studio musician, do it. Strike a deal that helps all parties win. Agree to pay the singer and the musician full rate if the spec sells.

The Demo. The demonstration tape or demo is a more polished version of the spec. In producing a demo you use more professional musicians and singers and try to closely approximate the sound of the final jingle. In the early days, I produced demos free—a classic mistake. Since even at the demo stage a jingle is still speculative, it just doesn't make sense to gamble your own money. Consequently, you should try to get all or part of the production costs paid for a demo.

Most demos are cut (recorded) as if they were actually final productions. The difference is in the number of musicians and singers used on the track. Usually, a three- or four-piece rhythm section and one good singer is sufficient for demos. The costs are reasonable, and if the customer is serious about hearing the track in near-finished form, he or she will pay these costs.

The purpose of the demo is to show how the jingle will sound when professionally recorded, using excellent studio musicians and singers. On specs I often sing the jingle myself or hire a beginning singer who will work gratis, being paid only if the track sells. On demos I hire experienced singers and musicians and pay them a spec rate, usually half the cost of the final production rates. You may record demos for agencies or customers who can't imagine how the spec will sound when fully produced. Furthermore, an agency may pay for a demo so that it has a stronger chance of winning a new account for which it's competing.

The Final. The final is, obviously, the finished product. Once you have ironed out all of the lyric, melodic, arranging, and editing problems, you schedule studio time, book your musicians and singers, and prepare for the big show.

Final recording sessions are usually exciting and rewarding experiences. It's the time when you get to hear your music played and sung by the best talent you can find. It's frequently the time when you get to do a little dog and pony show for your customer who may never have been in a recording studio.

Your goal in the final recording session is to complete the jingle on time and on budget. Your chances for succeeding are dependent upon your ability to coordinate all the activities of a number of individuals: musicians, singers, arrangers, conductors, engineers, assistant engineers, and customers. Yes, customers can be quite difficult at final recording sessions.

Keeping in mind that we will discuss in detail the recording process (chapter 6), your job as the writer/producer of jingles is to please all of the people all of the time. The problems that develop during recording sessions range from equipment failures to tardy musicians to temperamental customers. Unless you are prepared for any contingency, you could lose precious time that, in the jingle business, means terrifying sums of money for studio and musician fees.

During the final recording session you will record all of the instrumental parts and vocal parts for the jingle in the various time lengths and styles you've predetermined with your customer. After recording all the parts, you will mix down the parts to a master tape, making copies for your customer to use on the air. Don't forget to pick up your check before handing over the tapes!

For the Nonmusician

As I've suggested earlier, if you're not a musician, or if you're a lousy one, you can still compete in the jingle business. Obviously, at some point you'll have to engage the services of a schooled musician to help you produce your tracks in both spec (speculative) and final form. However, you can do a lot of the groundwork before collaborating with a musician.

Though the purists will argue that the person who writes the notes on paper is the composer, it has been my experience over the past twenty-five years that although a solid background in music theory is certainly helpful, it is not essential for writing good music or good jingles. If you're not musically adept, you do need a crutch, a way of operating that will enable you to perform as a musician though lacking those skills.

Happily today you have several advantages.

Since I've already urged you to start spending money on things such as stopwatches and metronomes, you won't be surprised when I suggest that your next purchase be an inexpensive but dependable cassette recorder. The hand-held type that uses standard cassettes is fine.

With this small recorder you will be able to "compose" the music for your jingles simply by singing into the microphone. Once you've worked out the lyrics, the melody, the structure, and the timing, you may present your "very rough spec" to your musician friend who can then translate your vocal work to paper in the form of a lead sheet or "chart." A lead sheet or chart is simply the melody and chords of the jingle written out in musical notation with the lyrics printed below the notes.

With your lead sheet in hand, you can work with any schooled musician to produce a polished spec, a demo, or even a final production of your jingle. And no one will ever know—unless you tell them—that you didn't "write" the music. It's my opinion that you did, in fact, write it. No apologies necessary.

What you must do, however, *before* contracting the services of a musician to help you, is work out an agreement on who owns the music. You may decide to pay the musician for his or her services on a buy-out basis and own all the rights to the music yourself. Or, you may wish to work out some kind of "payment upon sale" of the work.

You may even want to form a partnership or small company with a musician and share both the profits and risks of being in business together. And finally, you might deal with several musicians at the same time so that you always have a variety of talent available when the work load increases.

As with any matter that could become grounds for a lawsuit, legal agreements, contracts, partnerships, and corporations are the purview of attorneys. You should contact an attorney knowledgeable in matters of contracts, performance agreements, copyrights, and publishing. Your attorney should draft all agreements you plan to use in your business and should review all forms and agreements included in this text prior to your use of them.

Collaboration can be the most exciting part of being in the jingle business. Certainly from a performance standpoint, collaboration can be extremely rewarding. Back in the early eighties we had the privilege to work with a young lady who was to become one of the most outstanding gospel singers of this generation, Sandi Patti. Today, she is world renowned for her gospel albums and concerts. She was then and is today a remarkable talent, a soprano with the ability to make a song soar. I've often pointed to the first jingle Sandi sang for us back in 1979 as the turning point for our company—the day we became "legit" in the business—because with Sandi singing our songs, we sounded legitimate! So, by all means, collaborate. But choose your partners carefully.

What should you look for in a musician on whom you may have to rely to communicate your musical ideas? First, choose a keyboardist (we no longer call them pianists). The keyboard offers the widest range of possibilities for composing of any of the instruments. It is the most versatile, especially if the player owns or has access to a powerful electronic synthesizer.

A keyboardist can recreate the parts of your composition better than any other instrumentalist. The keyboard "covers" the range of all instruments; consequently, you can hear those sweet violins up top and that hard-driving bass line on the bottom.

If the keyboard you're using contains stored samples of real instruments, you can actually hear digital reproductions of all the instruments and sound effects. In fact, you can produce a fully orchestrated finished jingle package using only one instrument. It's incredible!

So, what's the process of collaboration between you, the nonmusician writer, and your keyboardist-extraordinaire? Assuming you've struck a deal so that the legal ramifications are covered, you will supply the keyboardist with your ideas for a spec (speculative) jingle.

The conversation might go something like this:

You: I've got a shot at this new account, Julie (your keyboardist). It's ABC Flowers, and I've got an idea for a slogan and a melody.

Julie: Great. Let's hear what you've got.

You: As you can see, the lyrics are a little rough right now, but I think the tune could go (humming) . . .

Julie: That's nice. How about this harmony part for the last chorus (hums harmony) . . .

You: Good idea. Now, for the spec, all we'll need is a basic piano/vocal track that you can probably cover yourself, right?

Julie: No problem.

You: So, here's the lyric sheet, and here's a cassette of my singing . . . and I use the term "singing" loosely. See what you can come up with as far as a chord progression. And you might try to smooth out that bridge melody for me, OK?

Julie: Sure, just leave it to me.

Now, as this brief conversation demonstrates, the nonmusician/jingle writer may know very little about instruments, notes, intervals, chords, charts, and arrangements. What he or she should know is that they exist. Although you may not be able to talk intelligently about quarter notes and rests, you should develop an appreciation for those people who do speak the language. You should work hard at understanding the basics of music theory, not so you will be able to read music and play instruments, though that would be an ideal goal toward which to work; no, the reason you should begin to learn a little bit about music theory is because you will be hearing the jargon in the studio and you'll be expected to know what the musicians are talking about.

For example, suppose the musicians suggest, "Let's put an eighth rest here at the end of measure 26, so the singers can get a breath before that long, fast-paced section, 27 through 31, OK?" If you don't know that a rest is literally a pause in the music, you won't know how to respond to the question. You may not know how long an eighth note rest is, but at least you'll know what the musician is talking about.

Auditing a few music theory classes, studying an introduction to music theory textbook, or following musical scores while listening to recordings can help you develop a conversational ability in music theory. Beyond this simple familiarization, you should consider enrolling in music theory courses. Again, the goal is not so that you can become a great performer, composer, or arranger, but so that you can communicate with musicians using their language. More ideas and information for the nonmusician can be found in chapter 7.

After you've given your rough idea cassette and lyric sheet to Julie and she's had time to work with the melody and chord progression, you'll be ready to produce either a spec or a demo of the new jingle.

CHAPTER 3

In Your Ear

The great debate in the jingle business is over which element listeners remember most: a wonderfully turned phrase or a captivating melody. Who knows? As a seller of jingles, I constantly emphasize the musical side of the argument. "Music sells!" I proclaim. "Without music, your ad campaign is flat; with it, you'll increase your sales ten thousand per cent!" Well, maybe not ten thousand, but music sure helps.

Yet every advertiser has a message to send to the public, a message most often communicated in words and images. Very few local and regional advertisers have the financial luxury of developing a musical theme that sells by itself. Only after years of market penetration through repetition and thousands of dollars in air time can advertisers such as McDonald's, State Farm Insurance, Allstate Insurance, The U.S. Army, Miller Beer, Alka Seltzer, and others rely simply on the melodies of their jingles to say it all. Even with these memorable tunes, the big guys still sing the songs, often changing lyrics from campaign to campaign. But they still sing the words. Who could forget these lines:

"You deserve a break today"; "And like a good neighbor, State Farm is there"; "You're in good hands with Allstate"; "Be all that you can be"; "If you've got the time, we've got the beer"; and the classic, "Plop, plop, fizz, fizz, oh what a relief it is."

Writing lyrics will be as challenging and as important as any other part of your job as a jingle writer, especially for local advertisers who plan to use their tracks for years and years.

So, where do you start when writing jingle lyrics? First, you must have some input from your customer. Over the years we've developed a very simple contact sheet that we fill out for every assignment. The contact sheet reminds us to ask specific questions of the advertiser to get creative input for the jingle. Here's a copy of our contact sheet.

In addition to completing a contact sheet for each assignment, we request copies of the advertiser's print and radio/TV ads. We try to collect as much information as possible before beginning to write. Now, let's analyze the contact sheet for clarification.

Exact Name of the Business as Advertised. Many of the customers for whom you are writing may be located in cities you've never visited. The customer may call and say, "I need a jingle for ABC Florists." If you don't ask, "what's the name *as advertised*" you may write the jingle with the wrong name. By asking the question you may cause a careless account exec to check his or her facts. "Oh, yeah, the name is ABC Flowers, not florists!"

Specific Locations to Be Used in Jingle. Rarely will any advertiser want you to sing its address (though it has happened), but asking for specific locations will reveal information that might be useful as part of the lyrics. If, for example, the advertiser's "fifteen convenient locations" is a competitive advantage, you may write a line expressing this advantage. Also, knowing the number of locations gives you an idea of the size of the account. As you will soon discover, the contact sheet gives you more information than simply the creative input you need for writing lyrics. It will reveal budgetary considerations.

So, if the answer to the locations question is, "Well, they've got about fifty stores nationwide,"

CONTACT SHEET

Exact name of the business *as advertised:* ____________________

Specific locations (if any) to be used in jingle: ____________________

Specific products or services: ____________________

Estimated budget for production: ____________________

Advertiser's target audience (age range, economic background, ethnic considerations): __________

____

Musical style preferred or that best fits the advertiser's image: ____________________

Examples of songs or other jingles in the musical style requested: ____________________

Formats of radio stations advertiser uses most often: ____________________

Does the advertiser use TV: ____________________

Advertiser's current slogan or positioning statement: ____________________

Will the advertiser be using this music package locally, regionally, or nationally: __________

Creative input (any specific information relative to lyric content—product names, services, locations, points to stress, e.g., prices, hours, selection, competitive advantages):

____

____

____

____

____

____

____

____

____

____

____

____

you've got yourself a regional or national account.

Specific Products or Services. Asking the advertiser to list specific products or services may seem silly when you're doing a jingle for a car dealer or a restaurant, but simply by asking the question you force the advertiser to determine those characteristics of his or her business he or she feels are most important to sing about. Rather than answering "food," a restaurant owner may consider the fifty thousand dollars she just poured into new furnishings and wallpaper. Her answer may come back as "great food served in beautiful surroundings!" And you're halfway to a new slogan.

In other cases, the name of the business may not tell you all there is to know about the advertiser's products or services. For example, years ago I wrote a jingle for Smith Restaurant Supply in Syracuse, New York. Now, on the surface, what do you think of when you hear the name Smith Restaurant Supply? Big pots and pans used in restaurants, right? Institutional flatware and china? Massive stoves and refrigerators? Probably. But the store was expanding into the retail market and selling unique items from all over the world for individuals, not businesses.

So, we sang about "traveling all around the world" to find "exciting and unique" things for the kitchen. We designed the simple slogan, "your kitchen is our world," to capture the international flavor with a twist.

Estimated Budget for Production. We put this question early on the list because we hope the advertiser might answer it without thinking much beyond its apparent simplicity. Trying to get budget figures from some advertisers or their agents is difficult. Frequently, the response to such a question is, "whatever it takes," or "as little as possible," or some other vague answer. Getting a specific answer to the budget question helps you qualify the customer (verify that the project is legitimate).

If, for example, the advertiser gives you a ridiculously low figure, you'll know that the production will have to be minimal, probably an instrument or two and one singer. On the other hand, if the budget is bountiful, you can plan to pull out the stops and write some heavy arrangements, perhaps even some multiple versions of the jingle.

Secondly, knowing the budget helps you decide if you even want to pitch the job. Over the years we have taken on small budget projects that have cost us as much time as most large budget productions. In fact, I would take the bold position that the smaller the budget, the more headaches you'll develop trying to please an unrealistic or simply cheap customer.

So I try to get the budget question answered early in the development of the project.

Advertiser's Target Audience. As a writer, knowing your audience is your first responsibility. We ask the advertiser to define its demographics, its target customer, by age, socioeconomic position, geographic location, and any other useful profile material identifying the potential customers. In most instances, the target audience will be obvious; nonetheless, you should ask the question just in case the advertiser is planning to shift to a secondary target.

For example, a retail store selling only denim wear for young adults and children may be planning to expand into a line of western wear for all ages. If you don't ask about the target audience and write a strong rock piece appealing to younger people, you may miss the advertiser's new market completely.

Musical Style Preferred. The question of what musical style the advertiser prefers is tricky. Many advertisers and even their agents try to create campaigns that are effective in reaching the target audience and that please themselves as well. The conflict should be obvious. Many advertisers don't know what their audience likes or dislikes in music. And many believe that what they like, personally, is what you should write.

In explaining this very important question to the advertiser, I usually ask for examples of musical artists the advertiser thinks his or her customers listen to. If he or she doesn't know, then I know we must do more research, ask more questions, and nail down precisely the musical style that best fits the campaign.

Radio Station Formats. Tied closely to the musical styles question is the question about radio station formats. Knowing the formats (type of programming) of the stations on which the advertiser usually runs its commercials helps define the musical direction the jingle should take. If the advertiser buys only country-western formats, you'll probably drag out that banjo for the jingle. If the stations run the gamut from adult contemporary to gospel, you're probably going to write an MOR (middle-of-the-road) track, something that won't offend anyone.

Also, knowing how many stations the advertiser uses gives you more information about the size of the account. In most cases, the more stations the advertiser uses, the higher the advertising budget. . . the higher your production budget!

Does the Advertiser Use TV? You should ask about TV for two reasons. First, you'll find out if you need to write a :29-, a :15-, or a :10-second arrangement of the jingle. Second, once again, you'll know a little more about the budget.

But a more important consideration for asking the TV question is to determine if you will be writing a jingle that goes along with specific visuals, perhaps a jingle that needs to sync with (synchronize or match) a video track. Writing for TV requires a little more attention to timing than writing for radio. For example, you often have to write lyrics that hit exactly at predetermined moments in the commercial, often within tenths of a second. You may have to match precisely a piece of animation. You might even write a jingle that actors lip-sync on camera during the commercial. Introducing TV into the formula can make your job more complex.

Advertiser's Slogan or Positioning Statement. If the advertiser has a slogan or positioning statement that it wants to continue to use, fine. Frequently, however, the advertiser will ask you to create a slogan. Although the ideal would be for the advertiser to pay you separately for this creative effort, more often you will create a slogan as part of the jingle package price.

Slogans or positioning statements can be the most powerful lyric lines you write; consequently, most of your research into the account should reveal information that will help you design a powerful, memorable slogan that capsulizes the advertiser's message for years to come. In most cases, you will create a slogan that functions as the hook in the jingle.

Local, Regional, or National Use of the Jingle. You need to know from the outset where the advertiser will use your jingle so that you can price your package accordingly. Prices for jingles used locally—in one city or ADI (area of dominant influence)—usually include a local buy-out license. But when the advertiser is regional or national, the price of the package should increase dramatically since you are leasing the package for use in a much larger geographic area. I'll have more to say on licensing in chapter 8.

Creative Input. This section of the contact sheet should be the most revealing. Frequently, advertisers will simply discuss this section with me on the phone or in person. I have found using a small cassette recorder most helpful in capturing the ideas the advertiser wants to use in the jingle.

No matter how you retrieve the creative input, your goal is to coax the advertiser to be specific and to use as much concrete information as possible. Although the majority of the lyrics you'll create will be a mixture of abstract and concrete words, you want the advertiser to give you as much down-to-earth language as possible so you can formulate the strongest selling lines for the jingle.

Typical of the vague responses we've received from customers over the years in this section of the contact sheet are:

"we do it all; we have everything covered"
"we're full service; we can take care of any problem"
"our goal is to be number one in customer service"
"our name says it all"
"we have the best products and the lowest prices"
"our (store) is the most convenient"
"we offer the best price, the best quality, the best . . ."

As you can see, these types of responses are helpful only to a point. To make a jingle stand out from the crowd, you need to get the listener involved with specifics. You're painting word pictures carried along with melody and rhythm, so you try to avoid the cliché, and you try to limit the use of abstractions.

In the examples of lyrics we've written (that appear in the appendix), you will find many clichés. The problem is that advertisers frequently think in clichés and won't let us use our imaginations to help them improve their images. A striking contradiction to this attitude are the lyrics we wrote for a trendy leather goods store.

The owner allowed us the freedom to be creative while still demanding that the jingle reflect both the high-quality leather products and sophisticated atmosphere of his stores.

The name of the store is simply "Leathers" and it started as a boutique in the late sixties when handmade products were in high demand. The store had grown from a very small, craft-oriented sole proprietorship into a glitzy, fashion-mall location with tasty decoration and knowledgeable sales people. Yet the owner wanted to maintain the charm and uniqueness reflecting his earlier business while adding the pizzazz of the (1982) present. He even wanted the name of his Great DAne ("Moondog") included in the jingle because the dog lived at the store. Here's what we came up with:

Leathers Magic

(Verse)
We started small; we've done it all, and
We made it right.
Now it's fashion footwear for that fashion look both day and night.
And the magic that we do is better than before.
(Chorus)
It's Leathers magic, fashion magic,
Leathers makes magic for you!
Leathers magic, midnight magic
Leathers makes magic!
(Verse)
We search the world for the finest styles
And bring them home to you.
For belts, bags, and coats
Leathers is the place for you
And the magic we perform
Will turn you into now!
(Chorus)
It's Leathers magic, casual magic
Leathers makes magic for you.
Leathers magic, Moondog magic
Leathers makes magic!
(repeat and fade)

Looking at the creative input section of the contact sheet for Leathers, you find simple words and phrases:

"magic"
"started small"
"worked hard to create quality products"
"buy styles from all over the world"
"fashion, fashion, fashion!"
"shoes, purses, belts, coats; men's, women's, children's"
"night-on-the-town look"
"Moondog lives at the store!"

These words and phrases, though not thoroughtly concrete, were most helpful in finding the right lines for the song. The lyrics worked well and the repetition of the "magic" idea hammered home the unique marketing approach.

So, once you have your contact sheet in hand, you can begin to sketch out the first draft of your lyrics.

The First Attempt at Lyrics

Whether you write the words and the music simultaneously or independently, you should try to establish a process of writing that will allow the most freedom to explore ideas both in word and song. The process you design will evolve with each assignment you complete. There is no absolute method; however, there are several helpful approaches to keep in mind.

Let's begin developing a process by returning to the mythical ABC Flowers and examining its completed contact sheet.

As you look over this sample contact sheet, what strikes you as the key ingredient? The demographics? The locations? The variety of services? Perhaps all of these ideas are important. But the one comment the advertiser makes in the creative input section that speaks loudest to me is "we'd like to develop a list of regular weekly or monthly customers who fill their rooms with blooms all the time." What any business needs is repeat business, regular customers. And what a florist needs is more customers coming in more frequently. If I were writing a jingle for ABC Flowers, I'd start there: focusing on changing the occasional customer into a regular, weekly customer.

Analyze the Data. The first step in developing your jingle-writing method or process is, then, to analyze the raw data you've collected. Going over the contact sheet carefully and asking yourself questions will cause the significant ideas to blossom (sorry). Look for information the customer has repeated. Look for a logical progression of ideas from the beginning of the information to the end. People often tell you what they feel most strongly about last,

CONTACT SHEET

Exact name of the business *as advertised:* ABC Flowers

Specific locations (if any) to be used in jingle: Five stores all around town

Specific products or services: Flowers, gifts, cards, free delivery; tele-florist

Estimated budget for production: $3000 to $4,000

Advertiser's target audience (age range, economic background, ethnic considerations): Everyone!

Musical style preferred or that best fits the advertiser's image: soft but not sleepy, new age

Examples of songs or other jingles in the musical style requested: Al Jarreau, Kenny G.

Formats of radio stations advertiser uses most often: Adult contemp., C/W, some Rock

Does the advertiser use TV: Possibly in the future

Advertiser's current slogan or positioning statement: Blooms for all rooms

Will the advertiser be using this music package locally, regionally, or nationally: Local

Creative input (any specific information relative to lyric content—product names, services, locations, points to stress, e.g., prices, hours, selection, competitive advantages):

In business 5 years. Name is known but we've grown and added services ("speedy delivery & full service"). Amazing variety of arrangements and gifts. Want people to use florist for more than just special occasions—want to develop regular customers ("people who fill their rooms with blooms all the time"). Call one phone—555-9999—we'll route call to the nearest store.

so read all the way through the creative input section, searching for the strongest idea.

Experiment with a Verse. Once you've done your analysis and found what you believe is the most important idea, The Idea, write it down at the top of a blank sheet of notebook paper:

"We'd like to develop a list of regular weekly or monthly customers who fill their rooms with blooms all the time."

Next, start reducing The Idea to phrases:
"regular customers . . . fill rooms with blooms all the time"

Chop a little more, bend it, reshape it:
"you . . . fill your rooms with blooms every week"

A little more modification:
"Filling your rooms with blooms for fun!"

Modify a little more and experiment with a verse:
"Every week, every day, every minute, every hour
nothing says it better, better than flowers,
Filling your rooms with beautiful blooms
That's what you can do at ABC Flowers!"

See how it works?

You take the idea, chop it down to size, then expand it using rhythm, rhyme, repetition, and imagery to create, as in this example, a verse. Try it yourself, right now.

Here's a second attempt at the same process;
First, The Idea:

"We'd like to develop a list of regular weekly or monthly customers who fill their rooms with blooms all the time."

Next, start reducing The Idea to phrases:
"Regular customers . . . weekly . . . blooms—rooms"

Chop a little more:
"Weekly blooms for all rooms—special"

Experiment:
Make every week so special with blooms for every room,
At ABC we'll help you find the perfect floral tune"

Well, maybe not so good. But you're experimenting with images, concrete expressions, sounds, rhythms. As you execute this initial attempt to find lyrical sensibility, you are expanding the possibilities for your customer. In fact, since writing is discovering what you know about your subject, you are expanding your own possibilities for not only this account but also every account in the future.

The process will work for you. The beauty and the curse of writing jingles is that you have a given amount of time to fill. You know going in that you're limited to :60 or :30 seconds.

Set the Hook. The second step in the process is to look for the strongest place for the hook. Once you've focused on The Idea of the song, and perhaps penned a few potential lyric lines, you should begin working on structure deciding where specific lines, including the hook, should go. The choices are many.

Opening with the Hook. You may decide that because the advertiser will not be running the :60 or :30 full sing very often, you will open and close the jingle with the hook line. When the advertiser uses the :60 open-close or :60 tag mixes, the hook will still be there.

Using the first experimental lyrics as a point of departure for attacking structure, let's develop a hook line for our ABC Flowers example and place it at the beginning of the song.

"Every week, every day, every minute, every hour
nothing says it better, better than flowers,
Filling your rooms with beautiful blooms
That's what you can do at ABC Flowers!"

Here's a possible hook:
"Fill your rooms with blooms from ABC Flowers!"

Let's open the jingle with that line.

Recalling the song patterns from chapter 2, we'll assign the letter T to the hook line. Now, let's create a verse that we'll label V.

"Every week, every day, every minute, every hour,
Make your life so special with beautiful flowers,
In the hallway, in the kitchen, in the bedroom, by the stairs,
Use your imagination, put flowers everywhere!"

OK. Remember the idea: "We want our customers to buy flowers more often—every week . . ." Remember their slogan, "Blooms for all rooms." We now have a hook and a verse. We're not passing judgment on them at this time; we're merely identifying them. So far, our song pattern is T V, and depending on tempo, we may have filled only about fifteen seconds.

Putting the Hook at the End of a Verse Line. Let's experiment with putting the hook at the end of the first verse, but let's cut that first verse in half so that the hook still comes early in the jingle in case we need more time for the instrumental bed:

> *"Every week, every day, every minute, every hour,*
> *Make your life so special with beautiful flowers,*
> *Fill your rooms with blooms from ABC Flowers!"*
> *"In the hallway, in the kitchen, in the bedroom, by the stairs,*
> *Use your imagination, put flowers everywhere!*
> *Fill your rooms with blooms from ABC Flowers!"*

In this arrangement we have some repetition of the slogan and we've forced a break in what could be a monotonous rhythm in the four verse lines. It might work.

Putting the Hook at the End of a Chorus Line. Now, assuming a different song pattern, V C T, with C serving as a chorus, we could tack the hook onto the chorus or let it serve as the last line of a chorus. Let's first create a chorus:

> *"Why not live it up a little bit and brighten your day*
> *It's so easy, you can do it, we're a phone call away!"*

and now, the hook:

> *"Fill your rooms with blooms from ABC Flowers!"*

Now, our jingle lyrics read:

(Verse)
Every week, every day, every minute, every hour,
Make your life so special with beautiful flowers,
In the hallway, in the kitchen, in the bedroom, by the stairs,
Using your imagination, put flowers everywhere.
(Chorus)
Why not live it up a little bit and brighten your day
It's so easy, you can do it, we're a phone call away!
(Tag)
Fill your rooms with blooms from ABC Flowers!

Our song pattern is V C T. With a short instrumental introduction, a repetition of the hook line at the end, and a short instrumental tag for the announcer to give the phone number, we've got a :30.

The Bridge. The third step in the process is developing a set of lyrics for the bridge. Remembering that the bridge should be both musically and lyrically different from the verse and the chorus, our bridge lyrics might evolve from other areas of the contact sheet information, ideas comparatively less important than the hook, verse, and chorus.

Reviewing the contact sheet we find that ABC offers one phone number to reach any of the five locations around the tri-county area. Perhaps the bridge would be a good place to mention the phone number and the concept of "one call reaches all" five stores. Let's go back to our process and grab a specific line from the contact sheet:

"We have one local phone number that anyone can call from any part of town and we'll route the call to the nearest store. That number is 555-9999."

Let's chop it up:

> *"one local phone number . . . any part of town . . . nearest store . . . 555-9999."*

Modify a little:

> *"call five, fifty-five, ninety-nine, ninety nine . . . wherever you are . . . you're on the line"*

Now, experiment and create a four-line bridge:

> *"No matter where you live, get on the line,*
> *call five, fifty-five, ninety-nine, ninety-nine,*
> *ABC Flowers makes it easy for you*
> *to get flowers today, just a phone call away!"*

Again, don't pass judgment on these lyrics; we're just experimenting, trying out ideas, words, and phrases. But we have a bridge, structurally speaking that is. Let's look at the song up to this point:

(Verse)
Every week, every day, every minute, every hour,
Make your life so special with beautiful flowers,
In the hallway, in the kitchen, in the bedroom, by the stairs,
Using your imagination, put flowers everywhere.
(Chorus)
Why not live it up a little bit and brighten your day
It's so easy, you can do it, we're a phone call away!
(Tag)
Fill your rooms with blooms from ABC Flowers!
(Bridge)
No matter where you live, get on the line,
call five, fifty-five, ninety-nine, ninety-nine,

ABC Flowers makes it easy for you
to get flowers today, just a phone call away!

Coming out of the bridge, perhaps, the hook line again?

(Tag)
Fill your rooms with blooms from ABC Flowers!

Add the chorus-hook sequence again and you're done!

(Chorus)
Why not live it up a little bit and brighten your day
It's so easy, you can do it, we're a phone call away!
(Tag)
Fill your rooms with blooms from ABC Flowers!

What I want you to see is the simplicity of the process. You gather information on the contact sheet. You discuss the information with your client, taking notes, recording the conversation if possible, and then you adjourn to write. You analyze the contact sheet, searching for The Idea that best fits the advertiser's purpose—the theme, the focus, the controlling idea. Then through experimentation using the advertiser's own words, you develop a lyric line or two or more. With an eye on structure you begin to play around with phrases, images, words. You move the hook around until you're satisfied with its placement. You create a verse-chorus-bridge structure. You may decide at some point down the road to discard nearly everything you've written, but for the moment, you have a rough idea of the jingle. And that's the goal of the initial process: a rough idea of the jingle. Nothing more.

Analyzing the Lyric

We haven't discussed melody, rhythm patterns, chord progressions, voices, instruments, nothing musical at all. Just lyrics! And yet, we have a rough jingle on paper. Before we leave this example, let's analyze each line of the rough jingle lyrics for strategies that sell, both jingles and products.

"Every week, every day, every minute, every hour." Since the primary goal of this jingle for ABC is to convert the occasional customer into a regular weekly or monthly customer, I've chosen to use units of time as an introductory concept. Starting with "week" and "day" and then moving to "minute" and "hour," I'm attempting to cause the listener to think about time and the timelessness of flowers. The repetition of the word "every" creates a pleasant rhythmical pattern that establishes the feel of the jingle from the beginning. It also subtly reinforces The Idea, buying flowers "every" week or at least regularly.

"Make your life so special with beautiful flowers." Using the rhyme "hour/flowers" may seem forced, but it works. More important, we're completing the thought that flowers can make every week, every day, every minute, every hour special, better, beautiful, exciting.

"In the hallway, in the kitchen, in the bedroom, by the stairs." This line moves the jingle from the abstract, making life special, to the concrete, places in which people display flowers. I've used the repetitious "in the" to mirror the rhythm of "every" in line 1, maintaining rhythmic integrity of the lyric.

"Using your imagination, put flowers everywhere." An appeal to the ridiculous, more precisely, hyperbole: "Why, Mr. Jones, you could put flowers in every possible place in your house! Even in the shower stall!" The attempt here is to involve the listener, to trigger his or her imagination. "Where would flowers look interesting in my house?" is the question we want the listener to consider. And then the chorus:

"Why not live it up a little bit and brighten your day." We ask the listener for a commitment, a small contract to do something special for himself or herself. Since traditionally people give flowers to everyone else on special occasions, with this line we are asking the listener to break from tradition, live it up a little, go ahead, buy some flowers for yourself.

"It's so easy, you can do it, we're a phone call away." Yes, once we've hooked them, we begin to reel them in. "Aw, c'mon, just pick up the phone . . . it's easy . . . even a child can do it . . ." Encouragement, removal of fear, ease of operation, simplicity: all of the pluses are here to motivate the customer to action.

"Fill your rooms with blooms from ABC Flowers." This is the mythical ad agency's line, so technically, I shouldn't have to analyze it; however, if you choose to use someone else's exact words in your jingle, you'd better be able to justify it. The client will insist on it!

My answer would be that "filling your rooms with

blooms" is a catchy, clever, and memorable way to describe a rather ordinary process, buying flowers. I like the idea of "filling" rather than merely "getting" or "buying" flowers. The internal rhyming of rooms and blooms is different and memorable, and using the coinage "blooms" for flowers in general is original. The line itself serves well as a hook because it's short, rhythmically appealing, and dynamic.

Now, let's look closely at some of the other ingredients to use in crafting lyrics that sell.

Repetition. Because jingles compete with thousands of other commercials every day, your job as a writer is to repeat important words and ideas in the song so that the listener can't miss them. The listener may only hear part of your jingle. He or she may tune in, literally, in the middle of the jingle. He or she may be distracted before the jingle is over. Repeating the important words and phrases helps the advertiser get its message across even if it has the listener's attention only for a few seconds.

I've mentioned repeating the customer's name several times in the jingle, but what other kinds of repetition should you use? Let's look at several other real-life jingles for repetition of words, phrases, ideas, and sounds.

Our contact sheet for a newspaper in northern Indiana reveals two pieces of information critical to its jingle: the newspaper wants to tell the public that "whatever you need to know, you'll find in the *Tribune*." The assumption is that "when it's important to know something, anything, pick up the newspaper."

South Bend (Indiana) Tribune Newspaper (first half of the :60)

When it's important that you know all about
who's in the news, and what's in the news;
And where and when and why it's happening
you'll find it in the Tribune, *seven days a week;*
For nobody in Michiana delivers news the way we do,
South Bend Tribune *sheds more light on you!*

For the last half of the :60, we simply change the musical key (modulate up a half-step) and sing exactly the same lyrics. Talk about repetition! By the way, "Michiana" is a coinage used to describe an area in northern Indiana and southern Michigan. The locals understand it.

For a chain of car washes that have never been on radio or TV and that are trying to establish a new name in the market, we use repetition of the name of the business. Also, the customer wants to establish the idea that "keeping your car clean helps increase its resale value."

Autobath Car Wash (:60 Full Sing)

Take good care of your car; it'll take care of you;
Anytime, make it shine, (make it shine)
Autobath is open 24 hours;
Automatic or self-service (Autobath)
A classy place to wash your car;
Autobath your car today!
Your car will be worth more
if you keep it clean, shiny and new;
So Autobath at least once a week,
Your car will love you too;
you might hear it say:
"Wash me at Autobath" (come see us today)
"Wash me at Autobath" (wash your car today)
"Wash me at Autobath" (the Autobath way)

The words in parentheses are sung as "echoes" by the background singers (see chapter 4).

Writing for a bank is a challenge because banks are rather staid organizations, conservative and somewhat resistant to change. The National Bank of South Bend wants to let their customers know that "we're working hard to serve you, and we'll work harder than any other bank." Here's how we handled the assignment. Notice the repetition of words, sounds, and images.

The National Bank of South Bend (:60 Full Sing)

Here's to you, Michiana,
At National Bank, we're workin' hard for you,
Here's to you, because of you,
We're working harder at the things we do for you.
You're the reason why we keep our standards high,
The National Bank of South Bend
Here's to you, Michiana
At National Bank, we're workin' hard for you,
Here's to you, yes, here's to you;
You, you're the reason that we do the things we do;
Our business is banking, so our business is you;
The National Bank of South Bend!

How many times did you read the word "you" or "you're" in the National Bank jingle?

In the following jingle for a sporting goods store, pay particular attention to the repetition of the positioning statement, "Your total sporting goods store." This company wants to establish itself as "the one place in town to find anything and everything you need for sports."

Em-Roe Sporting Goods

We make your play time, Em-Roe Sporting Goods Store
Your total sporting goods store!
Put your hard day behind you and break away for some fun;
Em-Roe's got all you need to make you look great
and feel number one;
Come in and get more out of life at Em-Roe
(Em-Roe, Em-Roe)
Your total sporting goods store!
At Em-Roe we take the time for what's important to you;
The best in value and more, we know you've got a lot of livin' to do;
Come in and get more out of life at Em-Roe!
We make your play time, Em-Roe Sporting Goods Store
Your total sporting goods store!

A chain of convenience stores in New York has changed its name and needs to tell the public about that change. Also, it wants to let everyone know that "Country Pride stores have the widest selection of products" found in convenience stores anywhere in the area.

Country Pride (Convenience Stores) (:60 Open-Close)

Step inside Country Pride, we'll take care of you!
When you're really in a hurry; when you need to take a break;
On you way to work or headin' home, we've got what it takes.
When you need to pick up something quick and don't know what to do;
Step inside Country Pride, 'cos we'll take care of you.
Country Pride, Country Pride,
The little store with so much more.
Country Pride, Country Pride,
Convenience and more,
Country Pride's my favorite store!
(instrumental bed)
Country Pride, Country Pride,
The little store with so much more.
Country Pride, Country Pride,
Convenience and more,
Country Pride's my favorite store!

In each of these jingles we use repetition to stress the name of the business, the slogan, and any special ideas or concepts the customer wants to stress. If you read the lyrics closely, however, you'll notice our use of rhyme (repetition of vowel sounds) and alliteration (repetition of consonant sounds).

Rhyme. Rhyming can be the strongest weapon you have in attacking the problem of communicating ideas in song that don't necessarily lend themselves to song. Rhyme captivates the listener's attention; it's appealing. It urges us to complete a thought and link ideas together. It helps to answer the questions, "How do you sing about a bank? A car wash? A leather goods store? A flower shop?"

Well, singing about a flower shop is easy: flowers are romantic and poetic. But how do we make a convenience store appealing in song? Rhyme can help. Let's go back to the Country Pride jingle and look at the rhyme:

Step inside Country Pride, we'll take care of you!

There's no mystery to the rhyme in the first line of the verse. I was trying to find something that rhymed with "pride," so I grabbed my rhyming dictionary and began listing words that might be in the ballpark: wide, side, dried, cried, bide, lied, hide. Nothing seemed to jump off the page. I looked for close or near rhymes: size, wise, wine, line. Still couldn't find it. I was stumped. I sat there thinking about the words "country pride." I said them over and over again, out loud. I heard and felt the rhythm of the words: coun-try pride . . . da da dum.

As I tapped out the rhythm of the words and spoke "da da–ide," it just came to me. "Da da–ide"; "step in-side" Country Pride. That's it. "Step inside Country Pride." I had used rhythm to find the rhyme. And what did the customer want? What was his goal: To get more people inside his stores . . . stepping inside his Country Pride stores. So, the rhyme helps define the line. Step inside Country Pride becomes the tag and the slogan.

When you're really in a hurry; when you need to take a break;
On your way to work or headin' home, we've got what it takes.
When you need to pick up something quick and don't

know what to do;
Step inside Country Pride, 'cos we'll take care of you.

The rhyme scheme for the verse is simple: break/takes, do/you. But notice that the rhyming words cause the listener to move along. The first line of the verse presents a problem: when you're in a hurry or need to take a break. You don't have much time; you're rushed—the problem. The second line is more concrete in defining the problem: you're going to work or rushing home. Ah, now the solution: we've (Country Pride's) got what it takes. The end rhyme on these two lines functions, as you would imagine, to pull the problem and solution together; but there's more.

The third line is very concrete, very specific: when you need to pick up something quick and don't know what to do. The solution: just drop on by our store and we'll take care of you. Simple but effective repetition of vowel sounds to keep the ideas flowing smoothly in the song.

In the chorus we rhyme "store" and "more" twice to emphasize the variety of items the customer can find in the stores. It's not only convenient, but it's loaded with goodies . . . "so much more!" We could call it, "the more store."

Country Pride, Country Pride,
The little store with so much more.
Country Pride, Country Pride,
Convenience and more,
Country Pride's my favorite store!

Rhyme accomplishes several goals. It emphasizes ideas, pulls thought together, adds a natural musicality to the song, and carries the listener along. It also causes listeners to remember the words to the jingle.

Alliteration. Rhyme is only one of many poetic devices you may choose as a jingle writer. Alliteration is another effective way to accomplish the same goals.

In the *South Bend Tribune* jingle, notice the repetition of the word "news" and the alliterative use of the "w" sound in "what's," "where," "when," and "why." Using the five W's of journalism (who, what, where, when, and why) in a jingle about a newspaper seems not only appropriate, but also poetically effective. The alliteration is fun to hear and easy to recall.

In the Autobath lyrics, notice the alliterative use of "c" and in the National Bank and the Country Pride lyrics, the repetition of "w" sounds. Both rhyme and alliteration link lines to lines, verses to verses, and images to images creating continuity and a tight overall effect.

Art for Art's Sake? In the advertising business, many writers forget the purpose of advertising: to bring customers into a store. Too often jingle writers fail to create lyrics that achieve this goal because they get bogged down in the creative process. Although the jingle writer, as any other artist, strives to produce the best possible work, the writer must maintain a balance between creativity and solid advertising sense.

It's one thing to compose lyrics that create strong visual imagery, delightful-sounding phrases, and colorful metaphors. It's quite another thing to compose artistic lyrics that communicate the advertiser's message forcefully, without losing The Idea in a barrage of vague impressions and ineffective statements. Borrowing a phrase, jingle writing is not brain surgery, but the skill required to produce an effective jingle does require an understanding of what sells and what doesn't.

Here are some examples of lyrics that masquerade as art, but fail as advertising. These lines are from specs that, not surprisingly, did not sell.

(for a fast food chain, selling gourmet potatoes)
"We've got the potato, the Pompous Potato.
It's all nutritious and so delicious.
It's a culinary delight (that's right);
I said potato, the Pompous Potato;
It's the taste you'll really like!"

(for an audio store)
"Oasis Audio would like to talk to you
We have the perfect system,
So give a listen to Oasis Audio
We've got the sound for you
Oasis Audio . . ."

(for a beauty shop and school)
"Professional Hair Care, our interest is you.
You want to look right;
Your star's shining bright;

Your hair's a reflection of you.
The Professionals always use Redken Hair Products,
so you know your hair's treated right!"

(for a florist)

"Jarrel's is here for the special moments of your life;
for flowers mean love, and you've got so much to share.
For the love of your life, it's Jarrels.
You're number one because we know you care.

In each of these examples the failed phrases jump off the page. Is it strong positioning to use the phrase, "It's a culinary delight" when describing a potato? It's clever; it's different. But does the average person understand what "culinary delight" means in reference to a fast-food potato store?

"The perfect system" and "the sound for you" are vague statements when they are all that we are singing other than the name of the audio store. And what does "your star's shining bright" mean? None of these phrases communicates directly to the masses. And, with the exception of the Pompous Potato spec, the music for each of these examples was exceedingly bland and unimaginative.

So, how do you create lyrics that sell and still reveal your creativity? The answer is with balance, common sense, and an understanding of the different types of jingles. Customers want you to be creative. They want you to come up with a clever phrase, a wonderful new slogan, an exciting metaphor. But they also want the lyrics to make sense to their audience. There is little if any room on a local level for "artsy" lyrics that only hint at the advertiser's message. You must balance your poetic instincts with your newfound understanding of sensible advertising theory.

Different Types of Jingles

First, let's define types of jingles and then tackle the problem of shaping a good lyric from a bad lyric.

Image Jingles. An image jingle, simply defined, creates a general effect in a listener's mind. Image commercials give impressions rather than facts. For example, a restaurant may use abstract words and phrases to create the impression that it is the most popular eatery in town. A health club might use symbols and images to suggest that not only can people get in shape but also they can meet other like-minded singles at the club. Rather than selling specific products or services, the image track creates an overall impression of the customer's business.

Here are some image lyrics for a mythical restaurant, Imagination, catering to the very chic.

"Imagine rubbing shoulders with Garbo or MacLaine,
enjoying conversation over delicate champagne.
Imagine, if you will, the kind of dining that's just right;
Imagination requests the pleasure of your company tonight."

Straight-Sell Jingles. A straight-sell jingle, on the other hand, is concerned with getting very concrete information across to the listener. The statements about products or services are clearly defined, not generalized. "We keep over four thousand pairs of boots in stock at all times." "Our fast delivery service is guaranteed. If we're late, you don't pay."

Here are straight-sell lyrics for Imagination, now defined as a family restaurant.

"Use your imagination at Imagination,
Bring your hungry friends and family today.
You'll find Imagination has a menu you will love,
No matter what your taste, we know you're gonna say,
Imagination has everything, Imagination is real,
Imagination is the perfect place for a family meal."

Hard-Sell Jingles. The hard-sell jingle breaks down barriers and often attacks the competition. Lyrics such as, "Don't do it! Don't pay more at the other stores," and "Why settle for less than the best, when you can have it all, right here, right now," or "Nobody, but nobody sells for less" hit the listener in the face. The advertiser wants to jolt the customer primarily to get his or her attention. The announcers scream the copy, and the music is fast-paced and exciting.

Try to imagine these lyrics set to a strong rock beat with a powerful male tenor growling that "Imagination is *the* place to be!"

"If ya wanna go to town, if ya wanna party down,
Imagination! Imagination!
Ya won't believe how much you'll eat,
and the music and the beat's
Imagination! Imagination!
So, get yer tail in gear and
We will see ya right here,
Imagination is the place to be! The only place!
Imagination!"

Multiple-Use Jingles. If you're fortunate, one day you'll encounter a syndicator, an agency or production company that specializes in syndicating promotions and advertising campaigns around the country. A syndicator produces a theme for a campaign and simply customizes the various tools: newspaper and magazine ads, radio and TV commercials, jingles, for a specific customer in an exclusive market.

These customers commission you to write multiple-use jingles, tracks that you can easily customize with different store names. For example, we work with an animation house that has produced a complete advertising campaign for car dealers around the country. To date, this production company has sold the program in at least fifty markets. Every time he sells the campaign, we have to sing the name of a new car dealer in the original jingle.

Although the multiple-use jingle is not a style but rather an application of styles, you should be aware that such tracks exist and require a slightly different approach to writing. Primarily, when you are writing for syndication, you have to create a space in the jingle that will accept varying-length names (name drops). You may sing, for example, Butler Toyota, as the original name in the jingle. However, a month later, you may have to fit Bob Smith Pontiac and GMC into the same space.

Comic Jingles. The general rule in writing local jingles is to avoid comedy. Comedy is funny the first time the listener hears it. The second time it's not quite as funny. The third time it's deadly. And beyond the third time, the listener is ready to attack the advertiser. We have written comic tracks, jingles that employ comic devices such as sound effects, puns, unusual instruments, and strange voices. But we have tried to balance the comic effect with a strong melody and instrumental production that permits the advertiser to discard the comic lyrics and still retain the music for its campaign.

On a regional or national level, your audience is much larger; consequently, comic jingles are more effective. Also, regional and national advertisers change jingles more frequently than local advertisers, so the initial impact of the comic jingle is primarily what the advertiser wants. Most of the comedy advertising you hear on radio or TV today promotes regional or national accounts with the voice-over copy rather than with a jingle.

Making a Bad Jingle Better

Now, let's return to the Professional Hair Care spec lyrics (see page 30) and demonstrate how to reshape these bad lyrics into more salable lyrics. We want to eliminate vagueness without sacrificing creativity.

The owners of Professional Hair Care requested a contemporary piece of music appealing to recent female high school graduates up to age thirty. The wrinkle in the assignment, however, was that the customer wanted to use the name Redken Hair Products in the jingle to qualify for advertising co-op money (a percentage of the customer's total advertising bill paid by a supplier). So, the assignment is both image and straight sell.

Professional Hair Care

"You're on the move; you're exciting,
You won't accept less than the best.
For your hair that means Redken,
You can forget about the rest.
Professional Hair Care is ready to take good care of you.
You're a nineties kind of woman; you've got better things to do.
Professional Hair Care, Professional Hair Care
because you are important to you!"

How does this first attempt at revision work for you? Is it better than the first set of lyrics? Worse? About the same? I think it's improved, but it's not quite strong enough. The lyric still contains too much fluff, not enough straight sell. Let's revise this revision.

First, let's throw out all the vague statements:

"You're on the move," goes. "Forget about the rest," same. "Take good care of you," likewise. Now, what do we put back in that can communicate the ideas these three lines failed to say? Instead of "you're on the move," which is a cliché, how about "your career's important to you?" No. "You love your job, you love your friends, you love life, but do you love your hair?" That could work.

Let's create a new slogan to open the jingle and then add the new lines we've just written.

"Professional Hair Care for the woman who cares!"

Now, add the new lines:

"You love your job, you love your friends,
You love your life, but it depends
on looking good, every day,
and there's so little time."

See where I'm going? Here's the rest of the verse.

"Take some time out for yourself,
Let us help you look your best,
Professional Hair Care and Redken,
For the woman who cares."

Our structure is T V T. We have about twenty seconds, a good open for an open-close mix. Now compare these lyrics with the original spec lyrics. Rather than singing, "you're on the move," we have defined the listener in positive, concrete terms. We sing about loving "your job, your friends, your life," but then we submit the problem, "you love your life but it depends on looking good every day, and there's so little time" to take care of your hair. The solution? Professional Hair Care and Redken products. The appeal to the ego, "take some time out for yourself," is a variation on the cliché, "do yourself a favor."

All we need to do is write a thirty-second bridge mentioning convenient locations, special evening and Saturday hours, and Redken products again. We then bring in the "take some time out for yourself, let us help you look your best" line, add the tag, and we're finished.

When tackling an assignment that requires a mixture of image and straight sell, your challenge is to avoid clichés and vagueness and establish a balance between the images and the factual information you want to communicate.

Customer-Supplied Lyrics. Another assignment you may encounter is working with lyrics your customer gives you. First, you must determine if you will be allowed to change any or all of the lyrics. No matter what the answer, if the lyrics are bad, plan to revise them. Presenting your excellent lyrics along with the bad lyrics will help your customer see the difference. However, you may still have to produce the jingle with the bad lyrics. Some customers simply won't give in.

Also, when working with supplied lyrics, ask the customer what specific words and phrases you should emphasize. If you are allowed to revise the lyrics, you may need this guidance.

Here are the supplied lyrics I received from a customer recently. He designed the jingle to work with a TV spot featuring an animated mouse that jumps and yells, "boo," scaring away the competition. Many of the lines are merely ideas, rather than lyrics.

Powers Swain Chevrolet Geo!

Our minipayments scare the competition,
But they'll put a smile on your face.
Our miniprices scare the competition,
But they'll put a smile on your face.
Our bigger trade-ins will make you smile,
We make the deals others only talk about!
The good peoples' minipayment store saves you more!
If you've shopped the other stores,
Our minipayments will put a smile on your face.
Our minipayments leave more money in your pockets!
When you shop the other stores, just smile, say "boo" and disappear.

The customer gave me complete latitude on changing words and phrases, but he had chosen to use the music from a jingle that we recorded for another one of his customers a few years earlier. So, I had to make his new "lyrics" fit an old piece of music. Here are the revised lyrics.

Powers Swain Chevrolet Geo!

Our minipayments will scare
The competition away and
Put a smile on your face
So just smile and say "boo!"
Our miniprices will beat
The other dealers around and
Put a smile on your face
So just smile and say "boo!"
Powers Swain saves you more
Shop the minipayment store,
Find out why we scare the competition!
Powers Swain!
Just say "boo" and start a new tradition!
Powers Swain!
The minipayment store.

With some cutting and pasting I managed to make most of his ideas fit into the existing jingle. Compare the two sets of lyrics and you'll see how I accomplished this task. The lines I've chosen to emphasize fit The Idea my customer wants to communicate.

Relyrics. One of the most lucrative aspects of the jingle business is selling the same music over and over again. Since you should retain the copyrights to your jingles (excluding those jingles you sell out completely for an astronomical fee), you may reap the benefits of reselling the music in markets not protected by a license you've granted to another customer. The relyric business gives you the opportunity to realize more profit on an existing piece of music simply by writing new lyrics to fit an existing melody, just as I did for Powers Swain Chevrolet Geo.

Writing new words to fit an existing jingle may mean modifying the melody to accommodate the new customer's lyric ideas. Suppose we are going to relyric the ABC Flowers jingle for another customer, a restaurant named "Flappers." Let's compare our first line from the ABC Flowers lyrics with a line for Flappers.

Every week, every day, every minute, every hour
When you want to make your lunch something special, something fun

Try saying our new relyric line, at the same tempo (speed) as the original ABC Flowers line, counting the beats in each measure as I described earlier. Notice that the words "when you" function as a pick-up to the first beat (downbeat) of measure number one. The word "want" hits on the downbeat, count 1 of measure number one.

Here's our second relyric line:
Lunch at Flappers in the mall out on Highway 401

Remember, I'm creating a mythical restaurant in an imaginary mall on Highway 401. Let's skip to the chorus of our relyric:
Why not live it up a little bit and brighten your day

Yep. It's the same line from the ABC Flowers jingle. Here's the second line of the chorus:
C'mon and book yourself at Flappers; we're a phone call away

And the tag:
Fine food is only where we start, at Flappers!

With this tag line, we will have to modify the melody of the ABC Flowers jingle (see chapter 4) because the rhythm of the words in the new tag line is significantly different from the rhythm of the ABC Flowers tag line. But that's OK. As long as you can make the words fit comfortably with the original instrumental track and overlay a melody that still sells, you've got a relyric.

Before you move to chapter 4 and work on writing music for the ABC Flowers jingle, go ahead and experiment with the lyrics for Flappers using the ideas I've suggested thus far. Just imagine a restaurant built around the old "Roaring Twenties" theme. Assume that the advertiser wants to build its lunchtime business and is shooting for young professionals working in office buildings surrounding the mall in which Flappers is located.

The menu is loaded with healthy salads, quick meals, daily specials, and a host of cleverly named sandwiches. The waiters and waitresses dress in "Roaring Twenties" attire, and customers enter through a secret passageway in the lobby after giving a password. Have fun with this one!

A Checklist for Writing Lyrics. As you begin to write lyrics for jingles, try to keep these ten concepts in mind.

1. Collect as much information from your customers as possible, using the Contact Sheet. You can't have too much data.

2. Sort the information into groups to reveal similarities of thought and focus and to find The Idea.

3. Develop a short, catchy phrase or sentence containing The Idea and use it as the lyrical and musical hook of the jingle.

4. Review every line you write for visual and aural imagery. Let the listener see and hear the images your customer wants to communicate.

5. Eliminate clichés.

6. Use concrete rather than abstract words whenever possible.

7. Try to focus on "you" throughout the jingle. Get the listener (the "you") involved in the song.

8. Organize the lyrics into a logical structure that permits the most flexibility. Remember that the advertiser will stop using some of the lyrics, so place the most important lines either at the beginning (the open) or the ending (the close or tag) of the jingle.

9. Experiment with patterns, moving sections

around. Try starting with the tag or starting with a chorus, for example.

10. Draw upon current events for lyric ideas. Use trends, fads, and historical achievements (moon landings, centennials, championships, etc.) to help define The Idea.

Once you've written your specs, compare them with our finished versions published in appendix B. See how different yours and ours are. See if you can find areas for improving what you've written or areas that you consider better than ours. Play the two jingles back-to-back and have some friends tell you what they think. If you want an honest appraisal, don't let them know which jingles you wrote. Good luck.

CHAPTER 4

Practice Makes . . . Music!

Now that you've had a chance to work on your lyric writing, you need to add the music that will bring your jingles to life. Even if you're not a schooled musician, you can "write" the music for your jingles. You will need to capture your melodies and harmonies on tape, so once again, you should invest in some type of easy-to-use cassette recorder, preferably a hand-held, standard cassette model. I suggest the standard cassette-size type because you may be sending your rough cassettes to musicians or arrangers, and not everyone has the micro or minicassette type of machines.

A Little Music Theory

Before describing a method for finding and writing melodies for jingles, let's wade through some elementary music theory. If you're already conversant in theory, you may skip ahead to the section "Finding the Music in Your Head." Understanding these fundamentals of music theory will help you follow the development of the melody for the ABC Flowers jingle that I will compose in this chapter. Let's begin with the fundamentals of notation, which means, simply, writing the music on paper.

Pitch. In order to write music, we use a system that shows rhythm and pitch simultaneously. Composers use a device called the "staff" made up of five horizontal lines and four spaces. Each line and space represents a musical sound we call "pitch."

Staff

How high or low a pitch sounds is represented by its position on the staff, higher pitches at the top and lower pitches at the bottom. Furthermore, not all pitches fit on a single staff; consequently, we have different symbols, called "clef signs" or simply "clefs," to indicate where a pitch sounds in the spectrum of music notes. For our purposes, we use the treble clef sign to represent higher pitches and the bass clef to represent lower pitches. The composer places the clef signs on the left side of each staff:

Treble Clef Bass Clef

The Grand Staff. The easiest way to represent the entire spectrum of notes we may sing or play is the Grand Staff. If you've ever looked at piano sheet music, you've seen a Grand Staff that is simply two staffs, a treble clef drawn above a bass clef with the words of the song in between.

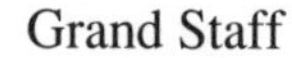

Grand Staff

The treble clef sign curls around the line of the staff used to represent G.

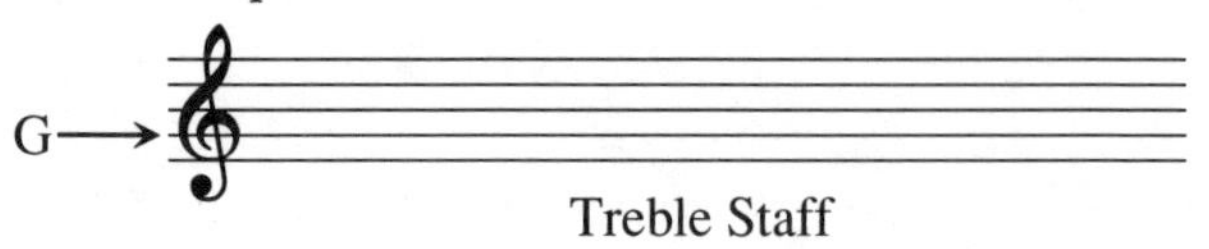

Treble Staff

Likewise, the bass clef sign shows the exact position of the pitch we identify as F on the staff.

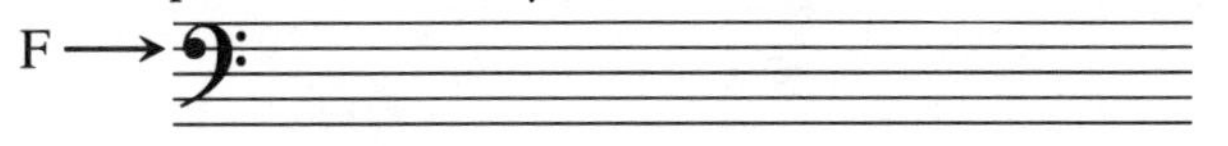

Bass Staff

These two staffs combine to create the Grand Staff with the treble on top and the bass on the bottom. Both ends of the staffs are connected with a vertical line from the top of the treble to the bottom of the bass.

Grand Staff
with End Bars

Since we've started to discuss pitches by name (F and G), we should mention that in music we use an alphabet of seven notes from A to G to name the pitches on the Grand Staff. The letters on the Grand Staff indicate the names of the pitches. Since we know that G is the second line of the treble clef and that F is the fourth line of the bass clef, using the musical alphabet, we can name the lines and spaces in between.

In order to complete the alphabet, ascending from F in the bass clef to G in the treble clef, we need to add a short horizontal line called a "ledger line" for the pitch C in the middle between the two staffs. This is that famous note known as "Middle C!" The space immediately below middle C is B; the space immediately above middle C is D. Look at the Grand Staff below and notice the addition of these three pitches in between the two staffs.

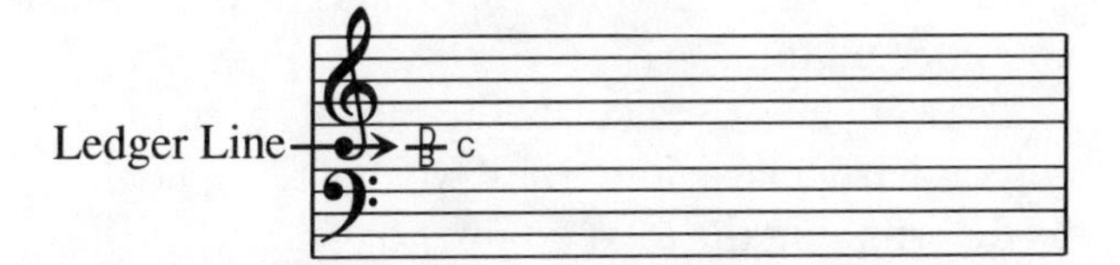

We may now fill in the remaining letter names for the pitches on the two staffs. Since the musical alphabet only uses the first seven letters, A, B, C, D, E, F, G, we fill in the remaining notes on the treble and bass staffs using these letter names, in order.

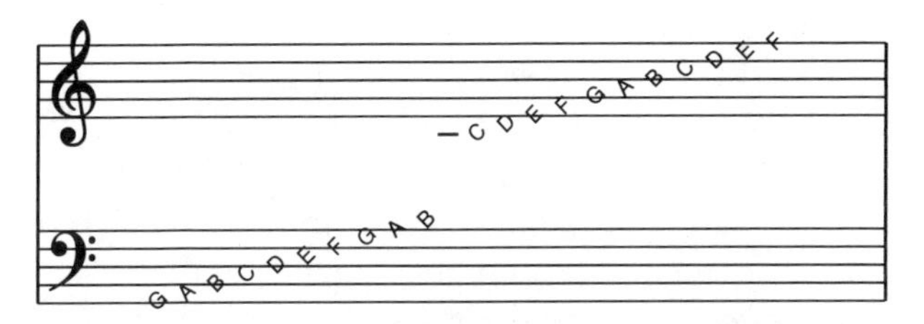

Simply by adding ledger lines and continuing the labeling, using the seven-letter musical alphabet, we can add notes above and below each staff to represent all the pitches we can play or sing.

However, there is one exception: there are pitches *between* these "natural notes" on the staff. These pitches are represented by altering the natural notes using "accidentals" called "sharps" (♯) and "flats" (♭). A sharp raises a natural pitch a half step; a flat lowers a natural pitch a half step. The half step is the smallest distance between pitches used in popular music; a whole step is made up of two half steps. Using all these different pitches in certain predetermined combinations, we create "scales."

A scale is a series of notes in step-order on the staff, starting on a predetermined note, in an organized pattern of whole steps and half steps. Scales determine the "key" of a song. Key is a term we use to describe a combination of notes organized around a central note (the tonic) according to the rules of harmony. The tonic note names the key. Since I'm going to write the melody for the ABC Flowers jingle in the key of C Major, here is a C Major scale. Notice the key of C Major has no sharps or flats.

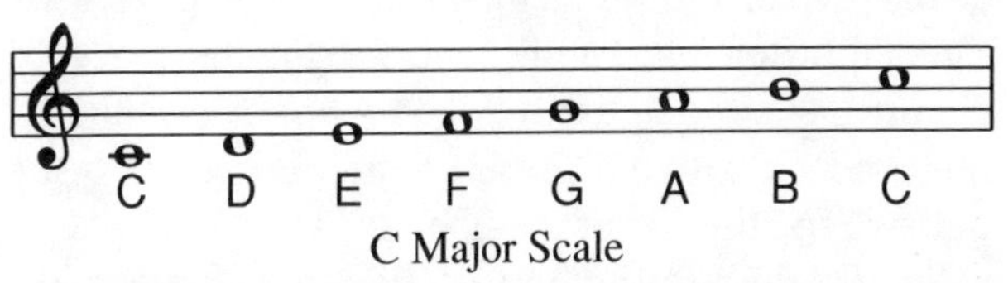

C Major Scale

Rhythm. Rhythm is the most fundamental aspect of music. You can have music without pitch but rarely without rhythm. Rhythm is a musical expression superimposed over a pulse. We call this pulse "the beat." When discussing rhythm, we use the term "value" to describe the length of time a note sounds. In modern music notation, the note value assigned to the beat is commonly a quarter note; therefore, the quarter note is the written representation of the pulse of the song. The pulse may be represented by other values, but for our purposes, we use the quarter note. When a quarter note gets one beat, the whole note equals four beats. The actual length of time a whole note plays depends upon the speed of the beat. The whole note can be divided into two half notes, four quarter notes, eight eighth notes, sixteen sixteenth notes, thirty-two thirty-second notes, and sixty-four sixty-fourth notes. The thirty-second and sixty-fourth note values are rarely used in pop music.

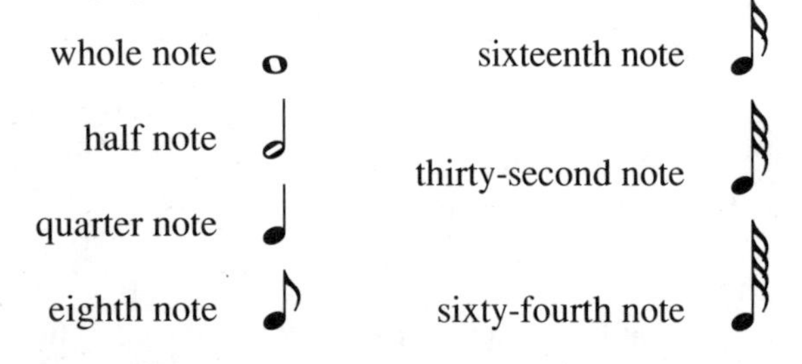

Some rhythms follow the beat exactly; every note plays on the beat as in simple nursery rhyme songs (think of "Mary Had a Little Lamb"). Sometimes the notes fall between beats or are added together to cover more than one single beat, creating rhythmic interest. But no matter where the notes fall, on the beat, between the beats, or added together, the effect on the listener is physical and emotional rather than intellectual. We speak of "feeling" the beat, the musicians translate this feeling into music using notes.

The beat is organized into strong and weak pulses that give us "meter," a term describing the number of pulses in a group. "Downbeat" is a term that identifies the strong pulses in a group. Meter comes in duple, triple, and quadruple pulse groups. If we assign a quarter note to the beat, we can create 2/4, 3/4, and 4/4 "time signatures." The upper number in the time signature represents the number of beats per group; the lower number represents the note value assigned to the beat, in this case, the quarter note. What I'm describing here is called "simple" meter, the kind most often employed in commercial music.

When we put music on paper, we create "measures," the written expressions of pulse groupings. For example, in 4/4 time, each measure has four beats with rhythmic notations adding up to the equivalent of a whole note: four quarter notes, two half notes, eight eighth notes, and various combinations thereof. The symbol for indicating the length of a measure is a vertical line called a "bar line." Musicians often refer to measures as "bars."

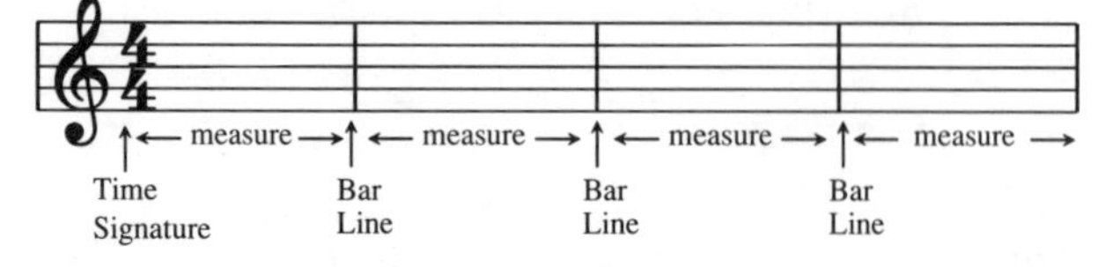

Because note values can be divided or added together, you can create whatever you want to happen rhythmically in the music. For example, instead of having four quarter notes in every measure, you may choose other note values, either longer or shorter than quarter notes, in order to express your musical ideas and avoid monotony.

Rests. When the writer wants intentional silence in music, he or she uses "rests," symbols corresponding to note values: the whole rest, the half rest, the quarter rest, the eighth rest, the sixteenth rest, and so forth.

whole rest 𝄻 quarter rest 𝄽

half rest 𝄼 eighth rest 𝄾

sixteenth rest 𝄿

Speed. Note values and rests are all relative to one another. When one value speeds up or slows down, all others speed up or slow down depending on the tempo (rate of speed) you choose to play the notes. If you set your metronome at 120 beats per minute (bpm), you are defining the tempo of your song as 120 quarter notes per minute. And the note values throughout the song occur relative to the value of the quarter note at the speed of 120 beats per minute. In other words, in a sixty-second piece of music (jingle), played at 120 beats per minute, you could have two quarter notes per second, one half note per second, a whole note every two seconds, or any combination of note values that equals 120 quarter notes per minute.

Knowing how to calculate the rate of speed of the notes is particularly important when writing jingles. By determining the total number of beats in the jingle and knowing the amount of time into which the jingle must fit (:10, :15, :30, :60), you can easily determine how fast the beats must go (beats per minute). Set your metronome at that rate and you should come out on time.

Intervals. The distance between pitches is made

up of combinations of half steps, and these distances are called "intervals." As you write melodies for jingles, the intervals will determine the shape of the melody, its movement up and down in pitch. Intervals have names according to their size, such as "seconds," "thirds," "fifths," and quality, such as "major," "minor," and "perfect." For example, we speak of "major thirds," "minor thirds," and "perfect fifths." These definitions, again, describe what is happening in a melody. Even if you're not a musician, you can write melodies without knowing the names of the intervals.

Finding the Music in Your Head

The first time you try to come up with an original melody for a jingle you may become frustrated. Furthermore, you may find a melody but discover that it's boring and trite or that someone else, probably Irving Berlin, has already used it. Don't give up.

All of us have melodies floating around in our minds. We have hummed songs since childhood, repeating the melodies of simple nursery rhyme songs such as "Twinkle, Twinkle Little Star," "The Farmer in the Dell," and "Pop Goes the Weasel." If you stop and analyze these fundamental melodies you'll discover the basis for all good melody writing: simplicity, ease of recall, repetition of motif, sensible progression, and completion of thought.

Though simplicity may seem counterproductive when considering the art of jingle-writing—no one wants his or her jingle to sound like "Twinkle, Twinkle Little Star," for example—as you begin composing melodies for jingles you should think simplicity. Keep the melody simple though not simplistic. Let's look at the melody of "Twinkle" for a moment. (If possible, study this section while sitting at a piano so you or a musician friend can pick out the notes.)

Illustrated below is the melody of the first line in the key of C.

Simple, right? Now what's going on in this line?

First of all, the melody goes up, starting on C, and comes all the way down, ending on C. All of the notes are within the same octave (eight notes), so the voice range is small. Nearly anyone can sing the song.

Second, the note values (length of time each note plays or sounds) are consistent. All the notes in the line, except for "star" and "are," are the same value. Sing or play the melody now so you can hear what I'm talking about. It has a very even, steady rhythm.

Third, because of the simple pattern, the melody is easy to recall. You hear it once or twice and you've got it, note for note. Fourth, the notes follow a logical or sensible progression, ascending and descending without giant leaps or odd half steps. If the melody moved from /C C/ (Twink- le) to /G-flat G/ (Twinkle), the half step from G-flat to G, though pleasing, would make the melody sound quite different and not as easy to recall. Play those four notes and listen to the difference. Or suppose the notes were /C C/ (Twink- le) to /C an octave above middle C G/ (Twink- le). There's nothing wrong with either of these variations, of course, but the intervals I'm describing are not "simple" or easy to sing on first or second hearing.

Fifth, the original melody offers a sense of completion. The line starting on C moves up and then down ending on C. It doesn't leave you hanging or expecting more movement. Again, I'm describing simplicity.

Now, let's consider these five elements and see how to apply them to melody-writing for jingles. Remember, this approach is a process that unfolds, step by step. The first line in our spec ABC Flowers jingle is:

Every week, every day, every minute, every hour.

First, let's consider the rhythm of this line. I'll use this symbol (ˇ) to indicate unstressed notes and this symbol (´) for stressed notes. For example, if we assigned two notes to the word "football" our notation would look like this:

fóot -băll

The words "every week," "every day," and "every

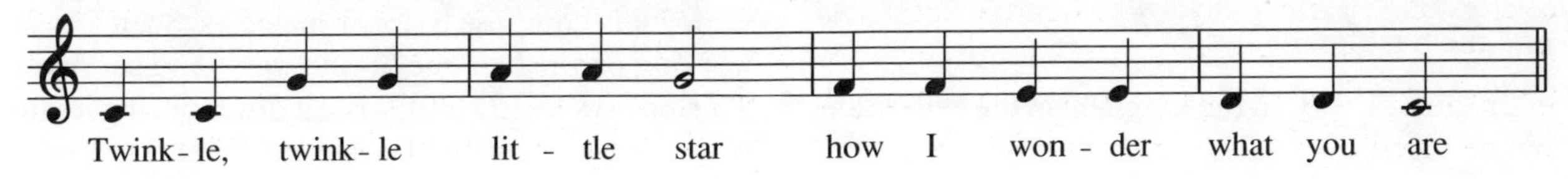

hour" have the same rhythm pattern: (ˇ ˇ ´). But in the middle are the words "every minute," which have a slightly different rhythm (ˇ ˇ ´ ˇ). The rhythm pattern for the line is:

Ěv- eřy wéek, ěv- eřy dáy, ěv- eřy mín-ŭte, ěv- eřy hóur

Tap out a 4/4 count on your desk and set your metronome at 120 bpm (beats per minute). Now, simply speak the words accenting the appropriate syllables so that you can say the whole line within four beats.

What you'll notice is that the first syllable "ev-" actually starts on the pickup (beat 4), and "week" falls on the downbeat. Here's how it looks. The numberals are beats per measure; we have two measures of four beats each for a total of eight beats plus the pickup beat.

4 1 2 3 4 1 2 3 4

4/4

Eve-ry week, eve-ry day, eve-ry min-ute, eve-ry hour

Now that you have established a rhythm pattern for the line, you begin to develop a melody simply by experimenting with intervals (distances between notes).

For simplicity of experimentation, let's write the melody in the key of C (no sharps and flats). Start on the E above middle C on the piano and play or sing these notes:

Notice the simplicity, the ease of recall, and the repetition. Now, add the second line of lyric. Sketch out the rhythm pattern.

Măke yŏur lífe šo śpec- ĭal wĭth béau- tĭ- fŭl flów- ěrs

Experiment with some notes:

and the next line:

Ĭn ťhe háll- w̆ay, ĭn ťhe kít- chěn, ĭn ťhe béd- rŏom, bў ťhe stáirs

Add some notes:

And the next line:

Ŭs- ĭng yóur ĭ- m̆a- ğĭ- ńa- tĭon, p̆ut flów- ěrs ěv- eřy whére

Some notes:

and, voila, we have a melody for our first verse!

Let's pause and consider what's missing. Using this reductive method of pulling melodies from your head and putting them on paper or tape, I am ignoring for the moment the business of harmony, i.e., putting chords with the melody, but I am assuming that we are staying in the key of C. I'm also ignoring the subtle and not so subtle rhythmic variations that make the value of notes and rests (absence of notes) in a line more interesting (see appendix B for a finished arrangement of the ABC Flowers jingle). Using my simple stressed and unstressed notation, I am also oversimplifying the process of determining the subtle musical shaping that composers use to create excitement, variation, anticipation, and dynamics in their work. But this process has produced a first draft, a beginning melody, not a finished product.

Hang in there. You will begin to develop your own method for pulling those melodies out of your head by beginning with my simple process. Write the lyrics, determine the patterns of stressed and unstressed syllables, experiment with some notes and intervals, and record your musical idea on a cassette.

Now, you may find, as I have over the years, that the words and the music come out at roughly the same time. And that's fine. You should have some idea of what style of music you're writing before you sit down to compose lyrics or melodies. So, if you're working on the first line of your verse and suddenly a melody comes in mind, write it down or sing it into your cassette recorder. Do it immediately because, I guarantee, you'll lose it if you don't.

Back to ABC Flowers.

We've got a rough melody for our spec jingle's first (and in this case, only) verse. We've built the melody so that it starts low in the scale of notes on an E and moves upward, ending, without resolution, on a high D. At the end of the verse, the listener knows there's more coming. We have left the listener hanging on purpose. What we're doing is pointing up (leading the listener's ear toward) the chorus. We want to pull the listener along, coaxing with notes that rise up the scale, drop back a few, rise up a little further, and reach a turning point that sails into the chorus. The chorus carries the hook, The Idea, which the advertiser wants the listener to remember most.

Our two-line chorus for ABC mirrors the rhythms we've established in the verse; however, what I hear in my head as we approach the chorus is a distinct pause before and a slowing down (ritard) of the melody on the first two words of the chorus, "why not." As we end the last line of the verse ". . . put flowers everywhere," we might have a one-and-a-half-beat pause (rest) before starting the chorus. Borrowing from the theater, call it the dramatic pause.

The first two notes of the chorus, for the words "why" and "not," will sound for two full beats each. Then the remaining notes will revert to the quick rhythmic pattern of the verse. Here's how I hear it (see below). And the tag could go like this:

fill your rooms with blooms_ from "A B C Flowers"_

Now, let's tackle the bridge. The bridge functions musically as a digression or relief from the patterns you establish in the verse and chorus. For advertising purposes, the bridge is the section that communicates some of the details that may change over the life of the jingle or some information that may be less important to drill into the listener's mind.

I try to find a countermelody for the bridge that reflects both the rhythm and melody of the verse without simply repeating the lines note for note. For our ABC Flowers bridge, the lyrics focus on the phone number the advertiser wants the listener to call. In a sense, this bridge functions in perhaps a more important way than most others. Since part of ABC's goal is to get the phone to ring in their central office, plugging the phone number in the bridge means that ABC may be planning to run the :60 full-sing version more often than most other advertisers.

Although the choices for rhythm and melody in the bridge are practically unlimited, I'm going to maintain the same basic rhythm pattern as I've used in the verse and chorus for consistency of feel. The melody of the bridge falls in a similar voice range as the verse and chorus and builds to a climax at the end leading back into the tag. Here's how the melody for the bridge looks (see second illustration at the bottom of the page).

OK. We have a verse, a chorus, a tag, and a bridge. At this point, I usually check the timing of the sections I have written to see how much time I have left to complete the jingle. After experimenting with several different speeds, I've set my metronome at 140 bpm and, using a stopwatch, I determine that through the end of the bridge I've used approximately :40 seconds. By timing each section at 140

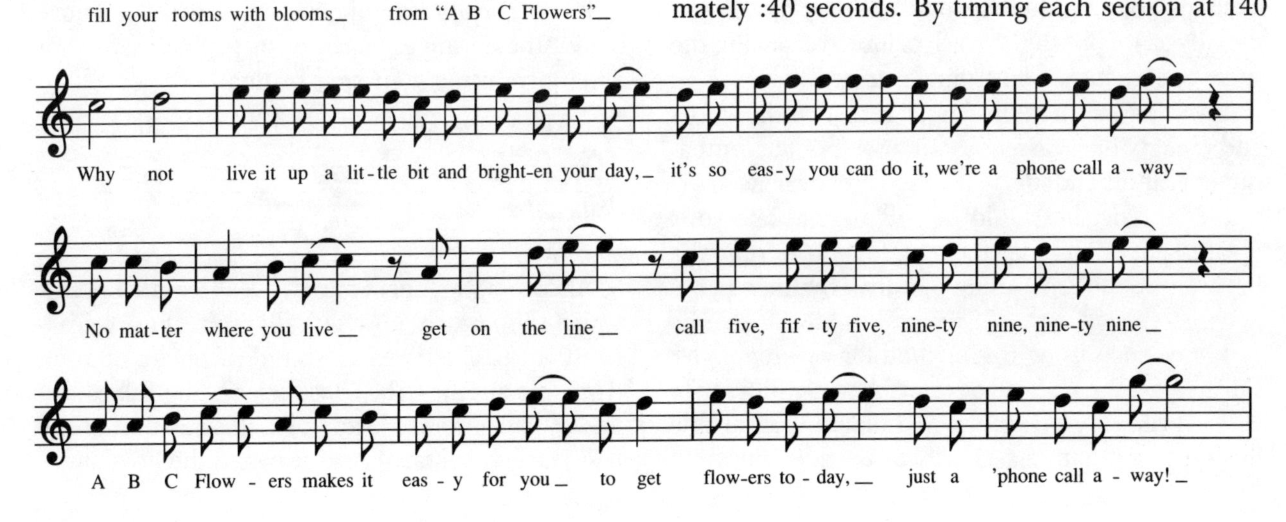

bpm, I find that into the remainder of the :60, I can fit the tag, the chorus, and the tag again.

I use a couple of approaches to make sure the timing of the jinge is accurate, whether I need a :10, :15, :30, or :60. I may establish a tempo (in beats per minute or bpm) with a metronome as I begin writing. Then I can calculate the number of measures simply by dividing the beats per minute by the number of beats per measure—or I simply write the jingle, guessing at a speed and the timing. When I'm finished I go back and time the jingle, using my metronome, adding or subtracting measures as needed to fit into the time frame required. It's trial and error.

If, for example, I am writing a jingle with my metronome set at 140 bpm, and I remain in 4/4 time (4 beats per measure), then I know at the outset that I will have no more and no less than 35 measures to fill to reach :60 seconds. If, on the other hand, I simply start writing until I think I have completed a jingle and then go back, choose a comfortable speed with my metronome setting (bpm) and find that I'm too long or short, I know that I have to eliminate or add a specific number of beats to make the jingle fit or change the tempo.

As you write your jingles, you'll find that simple experimentation, speeding up or slowing down, adding or subtracting measures, will eliminate any timing problems. After you've written a few dozen jingles, the process will become nearly automatic: you'll develop the ability to write a :60- or a :30-second jingle at practically any speed, without looking at your stopwatch.

We have a rough idea for the ABC jingle, though perhaps not a finished melody. We may modify the melody as we polish the track prior to recording the spec; but we have a basic jingle written.

If you had written this jingle, recorded the words and melody on a cassette, with or without accompaniment, and handed the tape to an experienced arranger, he or she would be able to translate your ideas to paper and play the song for you, adding the harmonies and smoothing out any rhythmic problems.

I have been using this method for writing jingles for the past ten or twelve years. The only difference is that I play (by ear) guitar and piano, so I am able to add accompanying chords to the melodies. My chords, however, are very basic, and I rely heavily on arrangers to breathe more life into my harmonies. If you don't play an instrument, you should find someone who does to help you get started. A music teacher, a church organist, a high school or college student, anyone who plays piano, can help you understand the fundamentals of pitch and value, rhythm and harmony, key and tempo as I've discussed at the beginning of this chapter. But I guarantee, you can pull those melodies out of your head and shape them into a complete, identifiable song.

Some Tips on Melody Writing

Before moving to the next step, polishing your jingle and preparing to record, here are a few tips for working on melodies. One of the problems I've encountered over the years is that I often write melodies very few humans could possibly sing. Many of my less-than-memorable tunes have vocal ranges approaching three octaves. The voice is a musical instrument and most singers have a limited range of notes they can sing well. Suppose, for instance, you're writing a melody for a female vocalist, an alto, and you start down low on a scale and then you soar up the scale to a few high notes above her range. You may be writing yourself into a corner.

Good altos have a singing range from approximately G below middle C to D an octave above middle C. Sopranos usually sing between middle C to an A above the next C. Tenors can usually handle a B, one octave plus one note below middle C, to a G or an A above middle C. Basses feel comfortable with parts ranging from an E, one octave and five notes below middle C, up to middle C. Writing a melody that swings from several notes below to several notes above these ranges may cause problems for you when producing your spec or final.

Also, female singers have a break point, a note at which they switch automatically from chest voice to head voice. These voices sound distinctly different from one another, the chest voice being full-sounding and strong, the head voice thinner though not necessarily weaker. Writing around the break point for a female vocalist will help eliminate strange shifts in sound during the performance. You should contact the singers you plan to use and simply ask them where their break point is—what note. They sould know.

Similarly, male singers shift to a falsetto voice at their break. The falsetto sounds dramatically different from the male's straight voice. The best examples I can think of in recent history are the high background vocals The Beach Boys used, Frankie Valli's lead vocal on the early Four Seasons recordings, and Smokey Robinson's lead vocal sound. Writing parts for which a male singer must use his falsetto results in a highly stylized song, one that will definitely grab the listener's attention.

Next, when you're working both on the melody and the lyrics, you should experiment with the speed at which you're asking the singers to sing your words. Stringing a dozen words together in a single line may be an unusual and clever approach to an assignment, but if the singers can't sing the words clearly enough to be understood, you've accomplished nothing. Though fast-moving jingles catch the listener's attention and create excitement, they present significant problems for the singers if the writer has ignored common sense when developing the lyrics. Now that's an important statement . . . ignoring common sense occurs daily in the advertising business!

If you must write fast-moving, hard-driving jingles with lyrics that would choke a mule, give the singers a break, literally. Write in a rest (pause) at strategic places during the difficult lines so the singers can breathe. If you get agency-supplied lyrics that are just impossible, have the courage to say so and negotiate some revisions.

Also, pay attention to trends in both popular music and jingles you hear on radio and TV. For the past dozen years and for the foreseeable future, the trend has been to use tenors or altos on lead vocals. Before you try writing a jingle, find out what vocal range you sing in, soprano, alto, tenor, bass, and if necessary instruct your arranger to transpose (change key) to fit the singer you have in mind.

You may discover that the tenor voice is preferable over bass or baritone voices because the tenor stands out better on radio or TV. Of course, you and I have heard dozens of marvelous basses and baritones singing national commercials, so my statement is not a rule, merely a suggestion. Although I have used both altos and sopranos for lead vocals for years, I prefer to use alto voices for lead simply because I like the lush, warm sound of an alto voice. Also, good altos are easier to find than good sopranos. Your choice of singers may be limited to who is available in your market.

Polishing Your Melody. Our rough melody for ABC Flowers might be strong enough to stand on its own as a spec; nonetheless, before we commit to producing the tape, let's experiment with the melody to see if it's the best it can be.

Let's go after the melody in the first two lines and see if we can modify it somewhat to make it more interesting. Here are the two lines as we wrote them previously (see bottom of the page).

Suppose we change the first line to this:

Notice that instead of returning to the E on "every minute," I move up (a half step) to F. Play or sing this melody and notice the difference. It may not seem to be an important shift and it may not work out, but this change forces the melody upward, faster. Where do we go from here? Let's see what happens next.

So that I don't force the melody up too much, I return to A on "make you" and the remainder of the line is the same as before. Play or sing it this way.

Now, why did I make these changes? First of all, I'm thinking about the mixes that we'll probably cre-

ate for the customer. By forcing the melody up faster in the first line, I am creating the possibility of having a more exciting one-line opening for a long-bed open-close mix. Suppose we simply use the first line as the open. By forcing the melody up faster in the first line, we accomplish our goal of creating a more exciting experience on this one single line.

But why don't I continue on up on the second line? If you follow through the lines in the verse, increasing by one note the starting note for each line, we will wind up the last line of the verse ". . . put flowers everywhere" on an E. What's more important is that if we make the change in the first line (up one note) and continue on up throughout the verse, we are pushing the melody of the chorus into the ozone, creating a difficult singing assignment.

The range of notes from the lowest (E) to the highest in the chorus on the word "a- way" (F) is an octave plus one note. This range may not be a problem for the good jingle singer, but what's happening to the melody? If we continue moving up a note, something sounds wrong. Let's look for the problem between the end of line one and the beginning of line two. Here's the revised first line:

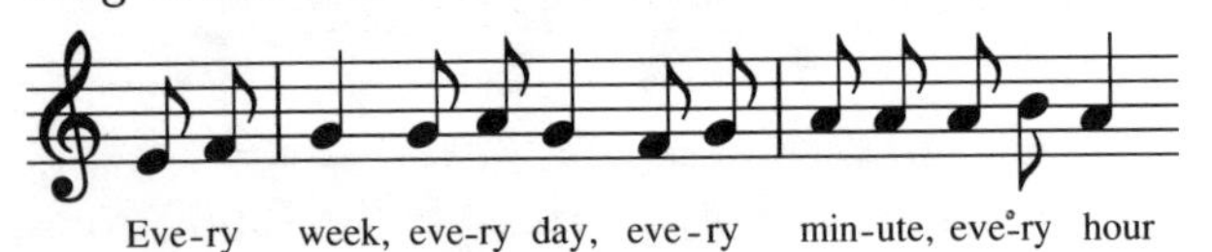

We end on A ("hour"). Now, here's what the second line looks like if we continue on up.

Play or sing these notes and stop when you have played or sung "make your life." Hear it? The interval between "hour" and "make" (A to G) sounds awkward. Compare this interval with the original one moving from G ("hour") down to F ("make"). Hear the difference? The notes in the revised melody, at this point in the song, simply don't work as well as in the original. Don't worry about why this phenomenon exists (unless you're a music major), simply understand that sometimes even a seemingly subtle shift in melody can create enormous problems.

Let's move on and play around with the chorus and add a tag line. We have ended the verse in our slightly revised verse on a D, precisely where we ended in the original. So, we start the chorus with the C–D interval ("why not") just as before. But now, let's try a variation on where the melody might go (see bottom of the page).

I don't like it. If I were to start on C ("why not") and move up, the voice range becomes practically unsingable, too wide. But if I drop down an octave to a G below middle C on "live," the interval sounds silly and, again, is very difficult to sing. So, at this point in the development of the jingle, I'll stick with the original melody. Or, if I have time, I continue the process of experimentation with alternate melodies for the chorus, the bridge, and the tag until I am satisfied that I have found the best tune in my head.

Repeating Words and Notes. Now, let's turn our attention to another part of melody-writing that helps drive home the musical and lyrical message in a jingle: repetition.

Overlapping, Echoes, and Answers. Suppose we took the first line of the chorus and as the lead singer completes the phrase "live it up a little bit," the background singers repeat (echo) the words "live it up a little bit" starting when the lead singer sings "bit." It's overlapping and looks like this (see first illustration on the next page).

The background singers don't sing the lead mel-

ody but rather a harmony melody based on whatever chord supports the lead melody.

See how it works? If not overdone it can be quite effective. And what if we have the background singers sing "ABC" at the end of both lines of the chorus. This "answer" device looks like this (see second example at bottom of the page).

You can substitute any words that fit the space and make a point of answering or expanding on the lyrical ideas given in the verse.

If you're not a musician, you'll need to associate with an arranger who can help you find basic chords to harmonize the melody. It's important to choose an arranger familiar with the musical style of your jingle because each musical style has its own harmonic language: the types of chords and progressions you write.

Your arranger will begin by identifying the key of the jingle, and will build a simple chord progression starting with the first note. Our sample jingle for ABC Flowers is in the key of C. The first note is E. We will first build a very simple chord progression for a light rock piece, starting with a C chord. Because of the simplicity of the melody, we discover that we need only four basic chords for harmony. The four chords, C, F, G, and D minor, contain all of the notes in the melody. A simple lead sheet illustrating the melody with basic harmony and the lyrics is on page 46.

We're nearly ready to produce a spec of the ABC Flowers jingle. We've polished the melody, we've added some background vocal echoes and answers, and we've added some rudimentary chords. All that's necessary is to contact a professional jingle singer, rent a studio for a couple of hours, and record the track.

Depending on your own musical background, your contacts in the industry, your access to a MIDI studio, and the time you can devote to recording the spec, you may produce a synthesized rhythm section with one or more singers. This kind of production at the spec level will certainly help your prospective customer understand what you have in mind for the final production. It is still my firm belief, however, that a well-crafted melody, sung clearly and in tune, and accompanied by a single, well-played instrument (piano or guitar) will sell without any studio embellishment. However, if you feel more comfortable showing more of the musical arrangement to your customer at the spec level, by all means do so. Just don't bet the farm on a spec—don't put much money into it!

Some Real-Life Projects

Now, it's time to try out your skills on some real-life projects. The following assignments come from my files of actual jingle jobs that I either won or lost. The fact sheets contained in this chapter are real;

ABC FLOWERS
Key of C
:60 Full Sing
A.S., arr. CES
Fast
Ev - e - ry week, eve - ry day, eve - ry min - ute, eve - ry hour, make your
life so spec - ial with beau - ti - ful flowers. In the hall - way, in the kitch - en, in the
bed - room, by the stairs, us - ing your im - ag - in - a - tion put flow - ers eve - ry - where.
Why not live it up a lit - tle bit and
bright - en your day? It's so eas - y you can do it, we're a 'phone call a - way.
Fill your rooms with blooms from A - B - C Flowers! No mat - ter
where you live get on the line call five fif - ty five, nine - ty
nine, nine - ty nine. A - B - C Flowers makes it eas - y for you to get
flow - ers to - day just a 'phone call a - way. Fill your rooms with blooms
from A - B - C Flowers. Why not
live it up a lit - tle bit and bright - en your day? It's so eas - y you can do it we're a
'phone call a - way. Fill your rooms with blooms from A - B - C Flowers!
© 1990 Al Stone

the customer requests are real; the assignments are real.

Your task is to write a jingle for each of these assignments. When you've finished, when you've written the best jingle you can possibly write, compare your finished product with mine published in appendix C. Every bit of information the customers gave me for each assignment, you will find on the fact sheets. Good luck!

Assignment #1

Name of customer: Jim Dandy Restaurants

Slogan: "We're lookin' better all the time!"

Target market: Families, retirees, young couples

Projected media buy: Four radio stations, no TV

Style of music preferred by customer: No comment

Lyric input: In addition to the slogan, Jim Dandy Restaurants are trying to change their image from a fast-food place to a family dining restaurant. Full menu; good locations; clean, bright surroundings. They want a patriotic theme, if possible, and play on the idea or word "changing," i.e., for the better.

(Note: This assignment came in during the hostage crisis and shortly after the energy crisis—patriotism was on the rise in America, and the restaurant wanted to play on that theme.)

Hints: In conversations with the advertising agency I discovered that the owners did not want anything that sounded remotely contemporary. Their restaurants were located in small, rural towns, and they wanted to cater to more family-oriented people who resisted change and appreciated old-fashioned values. Also, the agency suggested that the final jingle sound "all-American," like a "brass band" though *not* like a marching band.

Budget: Medium

Assignment: Write a :60 and a :30 full sing that uses the line, "We're Jim Dandy Restaurants; we're lookin' better all the time!"

Assignment #2

Name of customer: In Bank

Slogan: Needs new one—name change

Target market: 18-34, new customers, young working couples

Projected media buy: Radio and TV, large market

Style of music preferred by customer: Don't know

Lyric input: Stress the word "In" in the new name. Think about all the services you need in a bank; we're the oldest, and one of the top 100 banks in the country.

Hints: I actually missed on this one. The agency ordered the job, then canceled at the last moment with almost no explanation. They paid for the spec as I recall. I tried to come up with as many words as possible using "in" at the beginning of each word. The jingle I wrote is an upbeat, light rock piece. Very little creative input from agency.

Budget: Large

Assignment: Write one (1) :60 full sing using the phrase "in banking" somewhere in the jingle.

Assignment #3

Name of customer: Henselmeier's

Slogan: There's Only One Henselmeier's, The Big Real Western Store

Target market: Boots and jeans buyers

Projected media buy: Radio and TV, large market

Style of music preferred by customer: Country-western, female lead vocalist, and country harmonies in background vocals

Lyric input: Store carries a complete line of jeans, western wear, boots, hats, other leather accessories. Agency rep reports that store owner likes strong, exciting music with a "strong beat." Boots are the specialty of the store. Largest store in the area (only one location). Typical full-service western-wear store.

Hints: Classic country, with strong horn section; good old foot stompin' music but with a classy "Nashville horn" sound.

Budget: Medium

Assignment: Write a :60 only using the slogan as written above with an emphasis on "western" wear, "big," and "real." Also, stress the idea that store has everything for both guys and gals. Also, leave about three seconds of instrumental bed at end of jingle for a permanent announcer voice-over giving store location and hours.

Assignment #4

Name of customer: Niagara County (New York)

Slogan: Niagara County is Rainbow Country

Target market: Tourists/campers/ vacationers

Projected media buy: Radio only

Style of music preferred: Up-tempo, but not rock; light, lots of strings

Lyric input: The slogan should open and close the jingle. Cheap vacation; don't need to spend a lot of money on gasoline; put some color in your life (Rainbow Country). Twenty parks, fishing, camping, "Seventh wonder of the world," lit up with colored lights at night. Come to Niagara and see; year 'round fun; not just the Falls. Family fun!

(Note: This project came in just before Christmas and the agency needed the finished product, not the spec, the finished product before the end of the year! Fast turnaround necessary.)

Hint: We used the slogan to open and close the jingle as well as a spike in the middle.

Budget: Medium

Assignment: Write a :60 full sing.

Assignment #5

Name of customer: B & W Plumbing

Slogan: "The name that you can trust"

Target market: Homeowners

Projected media buy: Multiple radio station buy, large market

Style of music preferred: MOR, easy rock, but soft, group vocals

Lyric input: Use the slogan and company name in the same sentence.

Hints: The plumbing company has been in business for many years but needs to increase its retail sales. Will use only a :60 open-close on radio, so concentrate on writing a strong verse for the open, ending with a chorus/tag, then come back in with the chorus/tag combination for the end of the jingle. Try to identify typical plumbing problems and stress the fact that B & W guarantees to do the job right, the first time.

Budget: Medium

Assignment: Write only a :60 open-close

Assignment #6

Name of customer: River Bend (large suburban apartment complex)

Slogan: "The best part of living is just around the bend"

Target market: Young professionals

Projected media buy: Radio and TV, various stations

Style of music preferred by customer: Very soft, classy, not a ballad, but very light.

Lyric input: This is a brand new apartment center located just west of the fastest-growing section of a major Midwestern city. The style of architecture is described (by the developer) as "Southern California" or the "southern coast of Spain"; very light-colored brick with red tile roofs; the center sits on the bend of a river, nestled among beautiful trees, overlooking a small, manmade lake. Developer wants to describe the atmosphere of the place with the jingle.

Hints: We produced an image track using a single male vocalist, a synthesizer rhythm track and an oboe playing a countermelody – a very sparse, "new age" sound with a slightly upbeat rhythm midway kicking in after the opening lines; very few specifics in this jingle because the customer wants imagery.

Budget: Small

Assignment: Write a :60 full sing using the slogan as the final tag line.

Assignment #7

Name of customer: Lafayette Bank and Trust

Slogan: Let Us Earn Your Trust

Target market: The bank is trying to expand its market to pick up younger customers without alienating its older customer base.

Projected media buy: Local radio and TV, small market

Style of music preferred by customer: Middle-of-the-road, conservative

Lyric input: Jingle should provide a clear message—should sell. Sales and image are the primary considerations for the jingle. Should be able to maintain message with or without additional sales copy. Sales message should emphasize personal service, individual treatment, etc. Jingle should be able to stand on its own ("Have some meat on it" says client—the bank not the agent). Should create both image and message and have instant recognition factor. Should emphasize "Let us earn your trust" (key words here—earn and trust). Also, with bank name, downplay Lafayette or emphasize Bank and Trust. Avoid using reference to savings or national with name because of confusion with another local bank.

Hints: Having written lots of bank jingles, this one hit right down the middle—not too loud, not too soft, not a rock piece, but not a ballad. Lafayette is a small rural community adjacent to a large state university. The market base is mixed; consequently, we had to be somewhat conservative in our approach. We used a four-voice group vocal throughout the jingle. The agency gave us lots of input, part of which I've published above. The agent even told us what the bank doesn't like on our demo tape of jingles she played for the bank officers. According to the agent, "the bank prefers soft female voices, piano, horns, etc., but no synthesizers, harps, or violins."

Budget: Medium

Assignment: Write a :60 full sing for a midtempo MOR version featuring a group sing, but emphasize the female voices.

CHAPTER 5

I Need It Yesterday

The commercial music business is booming across the country. More and more musicians and songwriters have found their way into the business because it is so lucrative and because more opportunities for producing and selling their music have developed. However, before you jump into the jingle business and start calling all over town for assignments, you need a dose of reality.

Writing and producing jingles is fun; selling them is agony! After spending countless hours writing your brains out, pleading your case with an unimpressed agency rep, spending countless more hours rewriting, rerecording, and resubmitting your revision, you may get one of two responses: "OK, Stone, I like it, my customer likes it, and now I need it yesterday" or "Oh, the ABC spec? It's dead." I don't know which is worse, hearing that a spec has died with no explanation or hearing that a spec has sold and that they need the finished product "yesterday." Both answers send me racing for a Pepto Bismol bottle.

In this chapter, I will give you the tools that will help you become more competitive, faster. We'll look at the types of customers you're going to encounter. I'll give you examples of "preapproach" strategies, letters and phone calls you will use to start breaking into the business. I'll describe the initial presentation meeting during which you'll present your wares, and the jingle presentation meeting during which you'll present your spec or demo to your prospective customer. I'll also discuss how you can develop selling techniques that will help you increase your percentage of closed sales versus lost sales.

We'll also analyze typical sales conversations between the jingle seller and the customer; you'll learn what to say, how to say it, and when to stop talking. I'll give you some tips on how to "sell" on the phone and how to handle complaints from difficult customers. In short, I'll give you a punch list of do's and don'ts that should help turn you into a successful jingle writer-producer-salesperson.

Where Do I Begin?

You've studied chapters 1, 2, 3, and 4. You've experimented writing different types of jingles, slugging your way through the seven exercises in chapter 4. You feel confident and competent to jump into the jingle business. You pick up the phone and call XYZ Advertising in your hometown. The phone rings . . . and rings . . . and rings . . . and then . . .

XYZ: Good morning, XYZ Advertising.

You: Ah, well, I uh, oh, well, gee, ah . . . I'm sorry I must have the wrong number.

Click . . . dial tone!

You blew it. You messed up. You weren't ready.

Just because you may be or have become a master jingle writer/producer, the world doesn't give a damn. The world is not sitting there waiting for your call. The world is, in fact, besieged by dozens, nay hundreds of jingle writers just like you who want to make millions selling their little ditties. The world is just too busy to bother listening to another pitch.

The point is that you must shake off all your idealism about art, about creativity, about doing it "my way," and become tough-skinned, aggressive, and, most importantly, knowledgeable. You must have a plan of attack, a system that will help you get past that receptionist so that you can sit down face-to-face with someone who will listen to your music and give you an assignment. It ain't easy, but it is possible.

Back in the mid-seventies I dumped my teaching career to go full time into recording. With the help of some financial backers, I bought a large multi-track studio, hired a staff of musicians, engineers, writers, and support people. I came up with a name for my new company, ordered a sign for the building, bought a new desk for my office, and opened the doors for business.

With the exception of a couple of customers of the previous owner, no one came in to record. I was shocked. I thought that by simply setting up shop, the business would flow in. It doesn't quite work that way in the studio business.

So, one Saturday afternoon, I was sitting in my office wondering what to do about getting new business. We were surviving on the business from the previous owner and we had developed a couple of small programs that were beginning to bring in new customers, but we weren't generating enough sales to support all of the staff and the overhead of the studio.

We had a beautiful recording facility, excellent engineers, fine support people, and a good location. We could produce practically any kind of audio recording necessary, yet customers weren't flocking to our door. As I sat in front of my typewriter the thought occurred to me, "Stone, you bozo, why don't you send out a letter to everyone you can think of and tell them all about your new business and how great your facility, staff, and location are?" Brilliant, huh?

Well, that's exactly what I did. I composed a short letter that I sent out to all the advertising agencies in the state. I described our facility; I praised our staff; I extolled our location; and I promoted our services. One line in that letter began, "If you need excellent original music for radio and TV advertising . . ." I said nothing more about jingles in the letter. Instead, I went on, ad nauseam, tooting my horn about recording services, equipment, personnel, and location.

I sent out close to two hundred copies of that letter. I signed each one personally and enclosed my business card. The letters went out on Monday afternoon, so Wednesday morning I was ready for an avalanche of replies.

One week passed. Then two. Then three. No replies. Four weeks passed and, finally, about five weeks after the mailing, I got a call from an agency nearly two hundred miles away. The person said he had received our letter a few "months" ago and wanted to know if we did "jingles" and, if so, would I work with supplied lyrics? I was elated. At last, someone had answered my letter. I answered, "Of course we do jingles." The agent's response was, "Oh really. I couldn't tell from the letter, but I assumed if you were a recording studio, you probably knew someone who could write the music."

I slumped in my chair realizing that I could have accomplished the same feat had I just sent out my business card with no letter attached. The agent was telling me that only luck, not the content of my letter, had brought him to our door. Of course, had I not sent out any letter, that agent would not have produced over fifteen jingles with us during our first year working together. All was not lost.

The reason I've taken you through this rather mundane story is to let you know that what you do to represent yourself in business—sending out letters, making phone calls, dropping by to see people—reflects on how well you do what you say you can do. Too many do's in that sentence. Let's try again. If you send out a letter, make a phone call, or drop by to see someone, you'd better make sure what you have to say is of interest and clearly understandable to your potential customer. If you aren't able to tell your story about what you do, people won't take you seriously. If you're asking people to spend money with you because you "write jingles," you'd better understand why jingle writing is important to your customers. You'd better understand how jingles help your customers make more money.

Every contact you make with prospective customers is important. In the advertising business, agencies judge vendors (that's you) on many levels: the appearance you present (the look of your stationery, business cards, tape labels, etc.), the manner in which you present your work (the quality of your demo tapes and the conciseness of your presentation), and the knowledge you display about the subject. Advertising people, after all, are the people who create "preapproach" letters, stationery and business cards, presentations, and finished advertisements. They know what you should be doing to get their attention. It's similar to playing poker with someone who knows most of the cards you're holding. Since ad agencies are your primary customers for your jingles, let's design a system that will put you in front of the right people all of the time.

The Initial Phone Call. Before you send out any letters, you have to develop a list of potential customers. Who are those customers? Where do you go to find them? First, let's begin by identifying a roll-out program of advertising and promotion.

Depending on the size of your market (city), you should begin by contacting all of the local ad agencies. If you're living in a small town with only two or three agencies, you may decide to begin with a larger market nearby (an hour or so maximum distance). In most cities, you will find advertising agencies listed in the yellow pages under "Advertising," "Advertising Counselors," or "Advertising Agents." In larger cities you may find well over a hundred agencies listed. These are your primary targets for your first attempts.

Working from the phone book or a list you develop from several phone books, you simply call each one of the agencies listed. And here's what you say:

123 Adv.: Hello, 123 Advertising; may I help you?

You: Good morning! My name is Al Stone and I'm with Stone Music Company here in town. We're getting ready to send out our new demonstration tape of jingles. Who's in charge of your broadcast production?

The person answering the phone either knows exactly what you're talking about or hasn't the faintest idea. If you've reached a print-oriented agency that does little or no broadcast production, you might hear:

123 Adv.: Ah, well, that would be . . . ah, broadcast? Jingles? We don't, that is, ah, we are mostly doing artwork for advertising, you know, newspaper and magazine ads, ah, we don't use radio at all.

You thank the person for his or her time, make a note of the conversation and move on to the next call. Or, double-checking, you might ask,

You: I see. So none of your advertising customers use radio or TV, is that correct?

In your notes, you should indicate that the agency in question is primarily a print-shop (print-oriented). Place their card (see "roll-over" file later in this chapter) in a slot marked "long shots," and make your next phone call.

XYZ Adv.: Good morning, XYZ Advertising and Marketing; this is Melissa.

You: Good morning, *Melissa*. This is Al Stone with Stone Music Company Productions here in town. We're getting ready to send out our new demonstration tape of jingles. Who's in charge of your broadcast production?

Melissa: That would be Ms. Jensen, but she's on a long-distance call right now. May I take your number and have her call you back?

You: Thank you very much, Melissa. But all I need to do is verify your address and the spelling of Ms. Jensen's name, and I'll drop the information in the mail. I don't want to take up her or your time.

Getting the name of the person to contact is your primary goal in this preapproach call. If you can determine if the agency does broadcast production, fine. You don't want to spend time discussing what you do in detail with the receptionist or secretary. Be polite; be brief, and get on to the next call.

Often you will call an agency and the person answering is the person you are going to approach with your demo tape. What do you say? Basically, you go for the same information—his or her name, the correct mailing address, and a brief answer concerning the agency's involvement in broadcast production. It's important that during these preapproach calls you don't get involved in discussing your work. You want to do that in person, if possible, not on the phone. If the person answering wants to discuss your work at that moment, be prepared to drop what you're doing and drive over to the agency for your presentation. If the agency person simply wants more detail but does not want to meet with you, simply say, "I'll drop off a demo tape later this afternoon and you can listen to it at your leisure."

An exception to this "rule" occurs when the agent has a specific job in mind but won't take the time to meet with you in person. If you run into this situation, be prepared to do some quick thinking and selling on the phone. Have a copy of your contact sheet in front of you. Go through the contact sheet just as you would if you were meeting with the customer in person. Explain that you want to collect as much information about the project as possible so that you can hit the target exactly on the first attempt. Explain that you will produce a spec and would be happy to present it at a convenient time.

If the agent presses you for a price, try to avoid making a commitment. "It depends on the size of the production, the number of musicians and singers, and the licensing you need." If the customer still presses for an answer, quote a price range and then ask, "How does that compare with your budget?" The agent may be seriously concerned with the price or may be just qualifying you on the phone before meeting with you in person. The more contacts you make throughout the country, the more of this type of phone selling you'll be doing, and the better you'll become.

Once you've developed a list of potential customers—those that do broadcast production in your local market—you have a choice. You may start sending out your preapproach letters or you may continue making calls into other markets, developing an even longer list of potential customers. If you have twenty to thirty or more potential customer names on your preapproach list, I suggest you work those names first so that you get experience in how to develop your pitch. After sending out some letters and meeting with some agency reps, you may find you need to modify your preapproach phone calls to gather more information.

You may need to determine an agency's management structure. For example, some agencies have creative teams working on separate accounts. Each team may buy its own production services independent of the others. Once you get the creative director or broadcast director on the phone, you may ask if the agency uses a central purchasing system or if account managers purchase their own creative materials. Some agencies have purchasing officers who must preapprove all vendors prior to submitting bids for contracts.

Some agencies have creative directors who interview vendors and recommend companies to upper management for selection. These lower staff members have no purchasing authority, but they do represent a roadblock to getting in front of the right people. It is difficult to determine this kind of information on the phone, so after the preapproach phone call during the initial meeting with the agency, you may ask who makes the final decision on purchasing jingles. Meeting with lower staff members often reveals more information about the agency that will help you adjust your pitch prior to meeting with upper management.

The Preapproach Letter. Once you've identified the people with whom you wish to develop a business relationship, you begin sending out letters introducing yourself and your services. These preapproach letters serve as a basis for discussing your work in person and help you secure appointments with the correct people in the agency. Prior to composing your preapproach letter, you need to do a little more homework to familiarize yourself with the agencies you're pitching to.

You should read through the business section of your local newspapers and the business publications to find out which agencies are handling which accounts. You should look up all of the agencies in your market in *The Red Book of Advertising Agencies* (published by Standard Rate and Data, Chicago) for more account information. It will take some digging, but your public library should be very helpful in directing you to the right publications.

Also, you can simply ask when making your initial phone calls, "What sort of accounts do you handle? Mostly print or do you handle broadcast?" The person answering the phone may not divulge the information, but it's not really a secret, so there's no harm in asking.

Also, radio and TV stations know which agencies handle which accounts, so you might contact the sales manager of the stations on which you hear commercials and ask for the name of the agency handling the account.

Now, here's a sample of a first-mailing preapproach letter.

(Your Company Logo)

Date

(Inside address)

Dear Mr./Ms. ________________,

Rather than taking time on the phone to introduce myself, I am sending you this material to review at your leisure. (Name of your company) is introducing our custom music production services in (your city), and I would appreciate just ten minutes of your time to present our new demo tape.

I've been impressed with the quality of (agency name) radio and TV commercials, especially the (name of advertiser) campaign. It would be a privilege for us to prepare a custom music package that would give (name of advertiser) a dramatic new musical identity. Of course, we would be happy to demonstrate our musical ideas for (name of advertiser) without cost or obligation to you whatsoever.

I will be calling within the next week to ten days to arrange a convenient time for you to hear our new demo. I'd be happy to meet with you in your office or you're welcome to visit our new, state-of-the-art recording studio.

Looking forward to meeting you in person soon.

Sincerely,

(Your Name), Writer/Producer

(Your Logo)

Let's analyze this preapproach letter. In the first paragraph, you explain why you are sending the letter and other materials (out of respect for the agent's busy schedule). You also ask for a brief appointment ("just ten minutes") during which you will present your new demo tape. You also imply that your company is new to the market ("is introducing our music production services").

In the second paragraph, you demonstrate that you've done your homework. You know what accounts the agency is handling and you have an idea for their account. You indicate that there's no cost or obligation to hear a musical idea (a free spec) and you imply that perhaps the advertiser needs to develop a musical identity.

In the final paragraph, you repeat your request for a meeting and you plug the fact that you have your own production studio—a little blowing of your own horn.

By setting up your preapproach letter with these ingredients, you eliminate any fear, reluctance, or misgivings on the agent's part. It's difficult to say no to this kind of letter. Furthermore, the agent doesn't have to do anything but agree to a meeting when you call—there's no commitment to buy. Also, with your final paragraph, you're alerting the agent to expect your phone call, and you may say so to the person who answers the phone when you call: "Ms. Jensen is expecting my call."

The materials you send with your preapproach letter may include your philosophy about why advertisers should use music in their commercials, what kind of facilities (yours or the studio you rent) you're using, your personal experience in music writing and production (a brief bio), and perhaps a return post card requesting more information from you. See appendix A for examples of these materials. The purpose of this first mailing is to get your name in front of the right person in the agency. The letter does not guarantee you an appointment, but it does make it much easier to call back later to try for an appointment.

A week or so after sending out your preapproach letters you should begin your callbacks. And by the way, you should indicate every mailing you send out on your roll-over cards (see roll-over file, page 62).

Setting Appointments. You've made your preapproach calls and you've sent out your preapproach letters. What do you say when calling back for an appointment? It may seem obvious, but you might overlook something important.

When you call back for an appointment, you cannot assume that the person to whom you sent your letter ever received or read your letter. You can, however, call the agency and ask for the person by name. If the person takes your call, move to the next step. If the person is busy, out, or "in a meeting" (they're always "in a meeting"), you may leave your name and number or, better yet, ask when to call back. Here's how you can handle one kind of negative response you may encounter when calling for an appointment.

XYZ Adv.: Hello. XYZ Advertising.

You: Hello. This is Al Stone calling from Stone Music Company. May I speak with Ms. Jensen, please?

XYZ Adv.: One moment, please. (Puts you on hold.) Ms. Jensen is tied up right now. Could I have her return your call?

You: Thank you. I'm going to be away from my office. When do you think I might call her back?

XYZ Adv.: I'm not certain, sir.

You: Well, then, why don't I just try back in an hour or so, OK?

XYZ Adv.: Fine. Goodbye.

On your second or third attempt to reach Ms. Jensen you may decide to leave a message. If she doesn't call you back within two days, call her again. Here's how to handle another kind of negative response.

XYZ Adv.: Hello. XYZ Advertising.

You: Hello. This is Al Stone calling from Stone Music Company. May I speak with Ms. Jensen, please?

XYZ Adv.: One moment, please (puts you on hold). Ms. Jensen will be with you in a moment (puts you on hold again).

Ms. Jensen: This is Barbara Jensen. What can I do for you?

You: Thank you for taking my call, Ms. Jensen. My name is Al Stone and I'm with Stone Music Company here in town. I sent you some information about a week ago and I was just checking to see if you had a chance to look it over.

Ms. Jensen: What sort of information? What's the name of your company again?

You: Stone Music Company. We write and produce commercial music for radio and TV. I sent you a letter of introduction and asked if you could take ten minutes to listen to our new music demonstration tape. Could we set up a time to get together?

Ms. Jensen: Oh, ah, yeah, I think I remember your letter about jingles. Ah, why don't you send me a cassette and I'll get back to you?

You: I'd be happy to drop one by this week, and when I do, I'd like to meet you face to face so I can explain, briefly, how we work.

Ms. Jensen: Well, uh, well, yeah, OK. Just, ah, stop by, and if I've got a second, I'll try to see you. Ah, I'm usually gone from here between 11:30 and 2:00.

You: Thank you very much and I look forward to meeting you.

The turning point in this conversation occurs when Ms. Jensen asks you to send her a cassette rather than setting an appointment. Although you will mail tapes to customers in distant locations and customers who simply won't see you in person, your goal is to get your foot in the door (just like the old door-to-door salesman). No matter what the agent says, you're going to stop by. If you can get any kind of commitment from the agent to see you when you do, take it. Ms. Jensen says, "if I've got a second, I'll try to see you." With that kind of response you can and should plan to go to the agency. You tell the receptionist, "Ms. Jensen said she'd try to see me when I came by." You're telling the truth.

And here's one more approach to handling negative responses to your call for an appointment.

XYZ Adv.: Hello. XYZ Advertising.

You: Hello. This is Al Stone calling from Stone Music Company. May I speak with Ms. Jensen, please?

XYZ Adv.: One moment (puts you on hold).

Ms. Jensen: (Monotone) Barbara Jensen.

You: Good morning, Ms. Jensen. My name is Al Stone from Stone Music Company here in town. We're bringing out our new commercial music demo and I'd like to drop one by if it's OK with you.

Ms. Jensen: We do all of our jingle work with Trax Music, have for years.

You: I've heard their work. They certainly are excellent writers. Of course, we offer a different approach, no cost specs, and generous licensing that can save you money. And I'm very proud of our new demo tape. Would it be all right to drop by some afternoon this week?

Ms. Jensen: I'm going to be pretty busy all week.

You: Oh, I'm sure you are, so why don't I just drop by with the tape, and if you're tied up, I'll just leave it with your secretary, OK?

Ms. Jensen: Fine.

You: Thank you very much and I hope to see you this week. Goodbye.

This may appear to be a long shot or a no shot. The prospect has told you she does all her jingle work with your competitors. She appears uninterested, bored, maybe a little impatient. Her answers are abrupt and impersonal. Nonetheless, you keep trying. Being persistent without being obnoxious may get you in the door. After all, what have you got to lose? She's already told you she's not interested. Why not take a shot at piquing her curiosity. You applaud your competition, though not wildly, and then you offer a choice, "Of course, we offer a different approach, no-cost specs, and generous licensing that can save you money." And notice that you keep asking for the appointment even though the prospect remains impassive, somewhat negative.

Again, being persistent without offending the prospect will pay off over the course of your prospecting. You won't get in to see everyone and you probably won't be able to break down long-standing relationships with your competitors. But people do change. They move on; they have disagreements; they look for new ideas. The seeds you plant in the mind of the most negative prospect may grow, though not immediately, not overnight. But some time down the road, after you've dropped off your tapes, made your follow-up calls, annoyed your prospect with monthly letters, some time later on, she may call you in for a spec. So keep trying.

You're in the Door! Now What?

After dozens of phone calls, lots of rejection, and feeling reasonably certain you've chosen the wrong business to pursue, a miracle occurs. You've called your fifteenth agency of the day, trying to set an appointment to play your new demo tape. You've maneuvered around the receptionist on the phone. You hear the creative director's voice for the first time. You start your introduction and the creative director interrupts you in midsentence.

Ms. Jensen: Oh, yeah. Stone, Stone Music. I was gonna call you this afternoon. We've got a new account that needs music. When can you get in here?

Your stomach begins to churn; you find yourself clearing your throat to buy a few seconds. You collect your thoughts and blurt out:

You: Whenever you'd like! How's this afternoon look to you?

Ms. Jensen: Ah, today? Yeah, we need to get going on this. Today's fine. 'Bout three thirty . . . no, make that four o'clock, OK?

You: Four o'clock's just fine. I'll see you then.

Now, what's wrong with this picture? What did you forget to ask? Even though Ms. Jensen may be a fast-speaking, obviously quite busy person, you need to slow down and ask a few quick questions before you go dashing off to your first presentation meeting.

You should find out what kind of account she wants to discuss. You can do some thinking on the way to her office. You might come up with a lyric idea, a slogan, perhaps, that you could drop in at an appropriate moment during the meeting.

You might ask if you will be meeting just with her or with her staff. Walking into a meeting with an entire creative staff on a Friday afternoon just before a holiday, for example, can be rather disconcerting, if not life-threatening. It pays to know who your audience will be.

Also, unless you are sure of the location, ask for directions to her office so that you may arrive on time, find a parking space, and do a little analysis of the agency's office before the meeting. That's all. Don't try to pry any more information out of the customer prior to the meeting. In most cases, this first meeting is to qualify you, to verify that you are a jingle writer. If you pass the test, the creative director will give you the assignment.

You should plan to arrive at least ten minutes early. Introduce yourself to the receptionist and explain that you're a little early but that Ms. Jensen is expecting you. Have a seat, look alert, and pay attention to the comings and goings in the office. Make a mental note of the decor, the awards displayed, the people entering and leaving. Get a feel for the office. Is it a very formal, quiet, reserved atmosphere? Is it a zany, upbeat, wild kind of place? Soak it up without being obvious.

You've brought with you several copies of your demo tape, your promotion materials, and your business cards. You've also brought your own cassette player in case the agency has none. Make sure everything is working before leaving your office. And when the creative director approaches you in the reception area, stand, look him or her right in the eye, smile, and introduce yourself.

It's Showtime! This is the moment you've either dreamed of or dreaded. You're on! The creative director ushers you through a labyrinth of corridors, passing offices filled with laughter or occasional growls, until you reach a plush, dimly lit conference room. Much to your horror, you enter and find yourself staring into the eyes of seven rather hungry-looking people. They are not smiling. It's Friday afternoon. These people want to go home!

What do you say first?

As you place your materials carefully on the table, you smile, courteously, and in clear, strong voice, you announce:

"Good afternoon; my name is Al Stone, Stone Music Company, and I'll make this as brief as possible."

Of course, the creative director may have already introduced you to the staff, but your first words should indicate that you respect their time and won't waste it. Whether it's a Friday before a holiday or just an average Wednesday morning, let these people know that you know they are busy.

The next few moments may be difficult. Do you simply plunge in and begin your presentation or do you wait for a cue from the creative director? Once everyone is seated and ready, I suggest you wait a few moments, ten or fifteen seconds, to see if someone else takes charge of the meeting. Often, no one else will speak. If that's the case, jump in with both feet.

Prior to the meeting, you should have loaded your demo tape into the cassette player and cued it to the starting point. Use a machine that runs on batteries so you don't have to search for electrical outlets in the conference room. I usually hand out copies of my promotion material (see appendix A) so that the staff will have something to look at while the tape is playing. Even a short demo tape, three or four minutes in length, seems long during this kind of meeting, so I give the staff a list of the jingles they are hearing with a brief description of each cut.

Here's how you begin the presentation:

You: I want to thank you for inviting me in today. We're excited about our new demo and, after you've heard it, I'd appreciate your opinions. The tape is three-and-a-half minutes long, and this (hand out) is a brief description of each jingle you'll be hearing. Now, just before I play the tape, I'd like to give you a little information about our company.

At this point, you describe your background, including your experience, your company structure, your studio facilities, and anything else relevant to your ability to write and produce jingles. For example, if you're a beginner in the business, you should mention that you work with one of the city's "best music producers," someone you've contacted prior to the meeting who will help you produce your jingles. Mention the names of the studios you use and that you use the best studio musicians and jingle singers in the business. This background discussion should be quite brief, no more than two minutes.

You then play your demo tape, making sure the volume is adjusted – not too loud, not too soft. While you are playing the tape, I suggest you say nothing at all. Let the tape do the selling. If someone asks a question while the tape is playing, stop the tape, answer the question, and start the tape again.

When the tape is finished, stop the machine, rewind the tape to the front, and remove the player from the table. Say nothing at all. This is the most difficult time in the presentation. You must wait for a reaction. Don't ask, "Well, how'd ya like it?" Don't say anything.

If you've made a good impression, personally and musically, your audience will let you know. They will ask questions about the various jingles they've just heard. "Who'd ya do the 'Jarrel Flowers' jingle for?" "Was that 123 Agency's job, the White Auto track?" You might even get a little applause at the end of your tape.

What often happens after playing your demo tape, however, is nothing. Silence. No one says anything. It's an awkward moment. But be calm, wait a few seconds, turn to the creative director, and ask,

"Thanks for the opportunity to play our tape. You mentioned a project that needs music. We'd be happy to spec it for you. What can you tell me about it?"

Once again, say nothing more.

One of two things will happen next. The creative director will thank you for your time, make some vague comment about "problems that just came up with the account," and escort you to the front door. If this scenario occurs, you'll know that you failed the test. Either your tape wasn't strong enough, you weren't convincing personally, or a problem really has developed with the account and a spec is no longer an issue. Or someone will ask you more questions about your experience, your tape, your production facilities, anything related to the jingle business.

What you want to hear from the creative director is something like this:

Ms. Jensen: Well, I like your tape, Al. That 'Jarrel Flowers' track is very similar to what we have in mind for our account. We need a jingle to present to the client next Thursday. Do you think you can write one in time for that meeting?

You're in! You've passed the test! Now, you have to think fast, but speak slowly.

You: Thank you, Ms. Jensen. We certainly can produce a polished demo of a new jingle. Here's a fact sheet that I'd like to fill out right now so that we can get everything into the jingle that will absolutely dazzle your client. If I may, I'd like to record the information on cassette. Of course, I understand that this is a very competitive business, so everything you tell me is confidential.

You begin filling in answers to the questions on your contact sheet. If the creative director permits you to record this portion of the meeting, do so, but continue to fill out your contact sheet as well. Don't skip any of the questions. If you don't get answers to the questions, ask politely for more information. The more facts you get during this meeting, the easier it will be to write and produce a jingle that sells.

You should be aware of how much time you're spending in the meeting so that you don't overstay your welcome. Get the information you need, thank the staff once again for the opportunity to write for them, and exit quickly. Try to contain your enthusiasm and excitement until you're safely outside the agency. Then give yourself a pat on the back!

Now, let's suppose that you have made an appointment to present your new demo tape without knowing whether the customer is working on a project. You are simply introducing your work to a potential customer. What do you say after playing your tape? How do you ask for an assignment?

Once again, you thank the staff for the opportunity to present your tape, and then you say,

You: Is there an account you're handling that we might write a jingle for so we can show you what we can do?

Then stop talking. You've asked for an assignment. If the creative director has allowed you to come in, he or she probably has an account in mind. It may be an account the agency has been handling for years, or it may be a new account they are pitching, trying to win. They may need a jingle to accompany their presentation.

If no one offers an assignment, thank them again, remind them that you're always happy to meet with them to discuss future projects, and that, of course, you'll spec any project without charge.

When you return to your office, write a brief report (for your files) on the meeting indicating your impressions of the people you met, the agency's structure and appearance, and the potential for doing business with them in the future.

Presenting Your First Spec. You have an assignment and you've written and produced a spec or demo of a new jingle. You're ready to present your work. What do you do?

First, you call your contact at the agency, whoever gave you the assignment. You tell the person that you have a spec ready to play for him or her and ask for an appointment. Don't say much about the jingle on the phone. Just mention that "I think you'll like it."

Follow the procedures outlined above for your first meeting: arrive on time, be prepared, have your spec tape cued in your player.

When the meeting begins, you briefly explain why you've chosen the particular lyrics, musical style, and structure of the jingle. You hand out a lyric sheet and play the spec. After playing the jingle, once again, say nothing. Let the customer speak first. If he or she likes the jingle, ask for any modifications.

You: Are there any lyric changes you can suggest or have we hit it on this version?

If there are suggestions, take notes and assure the customer that you can make the changes easily or, with some modification, you're "sure we can make these changes fit."

If the customer offers no changes, you should hand him or her a copy of your Production Agreement and explain, briefly, the important sections (see chapter 8). You are not asking the customer to sign the contract at this time, and you make sure he or she understands that, but you want the customer to understand that he or she will have to sign the contract once the advertiser agrees to purchase the jingle.

Some agencies make decisions about purchasing jingles without consulting with their clients. Most others must present your jingle to their clients for approval. Your customer usually says something like this:

Ms. Jensen: I like what you've done; I'll just run it by my client and let you know what he thinks.

If you get this kind of answer, politely ask when your customer will be meeting with his or her client. You want to be able to plan for the final recording session, so it's helpful to know when that meeting will occur. It also helps you survive the wait between your presentation of the spec to your customer and a final decision on whether the jingle has actually sold.

Now, what happens if your customer doesn't like what you've written for his or her client? What if he or she says, "That's just awful! That's not anything like what I'd expected to hear!" Once again, don't panic. These things happen. Don't become defensive. Don't blame others for the problem. Simply take a deep breath and start asking questions. You may have already lost the account, but you might be able to salvage something. Here's what you might say:

You: I'm sorry, Ms. Jensen. I reviewed the tape of our meeting and my notes, and I felt we had all the bases covered. Apparently I misinterpreted something. What changes do we need to make? The lyrics? The style of music?

You want to ask leading questions to see if you can get your customer to be specific. He or she may be reacting to something very minor: the singer's voice, a noisy guitar fill, one word in the chorus. Or, your customer may be finding fault with something major, the musical style or the complete lyrics. You must do your best to calm your customer's fears, address the objections, and salvage the assignment. Listen very closely to your customer's objections and criticism. Ask for more details if the answers are vague. Here are examples of typical negative comments and how to handle them:

Ms. Jensen: Well, ah, the beat is too fast; it's too, I dunno, too rockish. This is a very conservative group of people we're dealing with.

You: I see. We need to recut the track so that it's more of an easy-listening piece (a light rock or MOR sound) rather than rock and roll. That's very easy to do. I can have that done this evening and on your desk tomorrow morning. Is there anything else we need to change? How about the lyrics?

You want to make sure that if you're still in the game and going to redo the track that you get all of the objections before leaving the office. Here's another example:

Ms. Jensen: Well, I sure don't think the words make any sense. You haven't said anything about their convenient locations, their store hours; you haven't mentioned that they're open on Sundays.

You: I see. I thought we could handle those ideas in the voice-over copy with a strong announcer. Locations and store hours change from time to time and it's easier to change the announcer than to resing the whole jingle. However, if you want us to sing the locations and hours, we can do it! Now, what about the music itself. Are we on target?

Once again, you offer a solution to the problem your customer identifies and you ask for more details to make sure you've covered everything. Here's a third and more difficult example:

Ms. Jensen: Well you've obviously missed the point entirely. I don't like anything about your jingle. It's terrible. The music's wrong; the lyrics make no sense. The singer's just awful. What were you thinking about when you wrote this? This doesn't even resemble anything you played for us on your demo tape!

Wow! This customer is really upset! How do you handle this? First, you apologize and accept the blame, even if your customer is really at fault for giving you the wrong information to begin with. Second, you ask for permission to work on a new spec, one that will be on target. Third, you try to determine which jingles from your demo your customer liked so that you can find a starting point for writing the new spec. Here's how you might answer.

You: I am sorry, Ms. Jensen. I must have completely misunderstood the information you gave me last week. Why don't we review the fact sheet and listen to our demo tape again. You can tell me which jingles on our demo are closest to what you have in mind for your client.

You are giving your customer a chance to continue the conversation (and the relationship). You are not giving up and bolting for the door, though that's how you might feel at the moment. You've got to be tough. Don't crumble under the pressure. Most people are reasonable, especially if you accept the blame for the problem and offer a solution.

If your customer gives you a second chance, make sure you ask as many questions about the failed spec as possible to define the objections in concrete terms. You don't want to miss on the second attempt.

If your customer sits back in his or her chair and glares at you, the meeting and the relationship are probably over. You might take another run at rectifying the situation by saying, "I know you're disappointed, and so am I. Why don't I give you a call in the morning and see if we can work up a new spec for you. That'll give me time to review my notes. How's that sound?"

Be ready for anything. Your customer may simply agree and usher you out the door, or you may hear, "No, I think we'd better get someone else. Thank you for your time. Goodbye." The longest walk you'll ever take is from your customer's desk to the door of his or her office.

When you return to your office, write a description of what happened during the meeting. Be very specific and keep this report close at hand to review from time to time. You want to learn from your mistakes. And, of course, send a follow-up letter to the agent with "best wishes for continued success" and your apology for missing on the assignment.

The Roll-Over File

Organizing your potential customers in a monthly roll-over sales file will help you maintain consistency in contacting these people throughout the year. A roll-over file is nothing more than a system of customer cards or computer files that you "roll over" or work through each month. Depending on your personal preference, you might use five-by-seven-inch cards on which you will keep all pertinent information about each customer. You organize your cards by city, by agency size, or by types of accounts the agency handles.

Here's a sample card (file) with appropriate notes and explanation:

AGENCY	
CCC ADVERTISING, INC.	Bob Smith
111 Main Street	555-8888
Anytown, IN 46256	Creative Dir.
Notes: Bob is a very forceful, but very likeable person. He's been with the agency for twelve years; is primarily an artist, but knows broadcast production very well. Plays golf, loves handball, and competes in local marathon. Has worked primarily with Trax Studios in the past, but is willing to listen.	
KNOWN ACCOUNTS:	
Most recent contact: [most recent date—in pencil]	

On the back of this card (or below this information in the computer file) you will keep track of all of the communication between you and this potential customer:

DIRECT CONTACTS:	RESULTS

Both sides of this roll-over file card are important. On the front side of the card you keep track of standard information about the customer's business. In this example, you note the name of the agency, the name of the contact person, address and phone number, name of accounts, and so forth. But you also keep notes on the person you are trying to work with—a little personality sketch that will help you reacquaint yourself with this potential customer month after month.

Why is it important to keep such personal information on file? It gives you something to talk about; it gives you a better picture of the customer; it gives you some common ground on which you and your potential customer may stand—a link, a bond, a shared history, perhaps. Although companies do business with other companies, in reality, people do business with people. The more information you can collect about the person you want to do business with, the better.

Next, depending on your working schedule and how much time you can devote to developing new business, you will rotate your roll-over cards on a regular basis. You might use a monthly divider system and simply move the cards from one month to the next after you've attempted to make contact. For example, you put the cards of the people you try to contact the first week in January into the first (second, third) week in February section. Each Monday morning you pull the cards for that week and begin contacting the group of potential customers with phone calls or letters.

Once a potential customer becomes a regular customer, someone who is doing business with you frequently if not every week, you can move his or her card into your "active customer" file. You may decide to contact your "active" customers on a regular though less frequent basis. Whether you're using index cards, notebooks, individual paper files, or a computer, you should organize your potential customers into logical groups and develop a system that forces you to contact each customer in each group regularly.

Persistence Pays Off

I think the hardest part of selling is finding reasons to call on potential customers month after month. How often can you say, "Hey, got any work for me?" But, in fact, that's what you have to do. Using your roll-over file, you need to come up with reasons to contact all of your potential customers, and for that matter, all of your active customers, on a regular basis. The name for this activity is sales promotion: you are promoting your business in hope of achieving sales.

Although there is nothing wrong with simply calling your prospects regularly and asking if they have any assignments for you, you might work on developing a long series of creative promotional letters that you can send to each potential account. If you can afford the cost, try to send out something to every person in your roll-over file every month to six weeks to keep your name alive in their minds and to demonstrate your creativity. In appendix A you will find a few samples of promotional pieces we've used over the years.

In addition to letters, you may find clever promotional items to send out. Calendars, novelty gifts, notepads, and other items imprinted with your name and phone number may work for some customers. The cost of these items may be prohibitive, but if you are selective in choosing who gets what promotional piece, you may find a way to absorb the expense. Moreover, the best money you spend in your business is in sales promotion.

As you think of reasons for contacting your potential and active customers with sales promotion letters and other items, here are some ideas to consider.

1. Play on current events. Although we didn't realize the tragedy of the hostage crisis back in 1979, we did send out a clever promotional piece showing one of our sales reps (my brother, Ed) being "held hostage" in the studio until he got a jingle sale. Once the seriousness of the international situation became apparent, we dropped the promotion; however, early on, it caught the attention of many customers. You certainly can think of dozens of positive current events that you can use to simply say, "Hey, we're here; we're creative, and we want your business!"

2. The congratulatory letter. Whenever you see a customer's name in the paper, send him or her a letter. "Congratulations on your promotion." "Best wishes on your new assignment." "Great job on winning the award." It doesn't have to be fancy or lengthy, but it does have to be sincere. No sales pitch.

3. Birthdays. Yeah, it may seem silly, but send a card. Again, avoid any hint of selling; just sign your name.

4. New stuff. "We just added a new 'whizbang' to our studio. We'd love for you to hear how it sounds."

5. Staff additions. "We proudly announce the addition of Sue Smith to our writing staff."

6. Sales strategies. Send a brief letter describing how using a low-cost relyric or synthesized jingle can help get a small advertiser on the air.

7. Crazy stuff. Send out recipes: "musical drum pudding . . . add two synthesized drum tracks; pour on strong electric bass and guitar; bring to a boil with a hot tenor sax; take off the heat and simmer with singers for just one hour; serve up to your client for a delightful billing period. Send quizzes with questions about jingles. Create a character, such as 'Mahvin Muzik, the hottest dude in (city),' and have the character talk about jingles; make it a monthly, one-page newsletter."

8. Have an open house party and invite everyone to "drop by from 4:00 until ? for music, suds, and snacks," and to hear your new demo tape. Hire a band, hold the event at a large studio, and play your new tape a couple of times each hour.

9. Send out press releases to all media in the area whenever you do something important. Include copies of the release as printed in the newspapers and magazines in your future promotion materials.

10. Celebrity endorsements. Produce short (two- to three-minute) cassettes with local celebrities singing (literally) your praises. Your mayor singing, "(City)'s finest jingle house is (your company name)." Be creative and be brief. Just send the tape out without explanation; see if you get any calls.

These ideas should help you come up with a variety of promotional pieces that, with time, will bring you new business. Please don't expect sales promotion to work instantly. It takes time to embed your name in the minds of your customers.

Finally, a few words about advertising. Over the years I have tried most of the traditional forms of advertising my services. I've used the yellow pages, ads in trade journals, ads in business publications, and I've even given away studio time to our local public television station in trade for publicity. None of it worked very well for my jingle business. If you decide to pay for advertising, be very careful and very conservative. You'd be better off spending your money on direct contact with your customers rather than using the "shotgun" approach of throwing an ad in a magazine and hoping the phone will ring. It might, but those are long and expensive odds.

CHAPTER 6

Red Light!

Back in the early eighties when I was producing many jingles each week in an independent studio, I developed a habit of not arriving for the recording sessions until after the rhythm section musicians had had time to set up, tune up, and rehearse. Since I used the same four players most of the time, the band became familiar with my working schedule. After months of following my rather predictable routine, I began hearing the same call from my drummer, Steve Hanna, as I entered the studio, "Red Light," the universal signal to start recording.

Instead of launching into the jingle for the day, the band would play an unrehearsed rendition of "The Al Stone Blues," a satirical, irreverent musical commentary on my apparent lack of punctuality. My engineer, my arranger, my client, and anyone else who happened to be sitting in on the session would join in the fun, and the result was that our sessions always began on a happy note (excuse the pun).

The Recording Studio

Life in a recording studio can be exciting, rewarding, entertaining, and productive. It can also be disastrous! For the uninitiated, jingle sessions differ dramatically from all other types of recording sessions.

More than anything else, the difference between a jingle session and all others is speed. Due to the high cost of studio time and talent fees and the tight deadlines for most projects, jingle sessions move at a breakneck pace. Consequently, whoever is in charge of the session—the producer—must be prepared before going in to record.

Depending on the size of the project and the type of studio you're using, you will encounter many different people with a variety of roles in professional recording studios. You will also enter a world of expensive and complicated electronic equipment. Furthermore, you will come face to face with dozens of procedures for accomplishing your goal of producing a finished jingle.

Let's begin with the people.

The Studio Owner. Owning a large recording studio reminds me of the people who used to do barnstorming and wing-walking in the twenties and thirties. As a studio owner, you're literally out there on a wing and a prayer. Large studios have astounding overhead, which accounts for the high rates they charge for studio time. In larger markets it's not unusual to pay $125 to $250 per hour for recording and mixing time.

The studio owner is usually a person who has come up through the ranks, starting either as a recording engineer, musician, or composer. In the old days most large studios were owned by the major record labels, but with the advent of affordable multitrack equipment and the rapid expansion of independent recording projects, new studios began popping up all over the country. Though major markets such as New York, L.A., Nashville, and Chicago still house a large number of big-time studios, it is not unusual to find fully-equipped analog (tape-based) and digital (computer-based) rooms in every medium to large city in the country. The competition is fierce, and studio time is almost always negotiable if the owner is realistic.

The owner's job may include any or all of the various roles in the studio: chief engineer, session player, bookkeeper, technician, traffic manager, composer/arranger, or janitor. If the owner is involved on a day-to-day basis with the nuts and bolts of recording, it's a good idea to get to know him or her so that you can deal directly with the boss if problems arise during your sessions.

The Studio Manager. More often in the larger studios you will negotiate rates and book time through the studio manager. The manager is the person who must coordinate the dozens of projects a large studio handles weekly or monthly. Though it may not be obvious, scheduling studio sessions to avoid what we call trainwrecks (sessions running into each other) is critical. The experienced manager knows what questions to ask of the customer to elicit the information necessary for a smooth-running operation. You should direct questions concerning rates, scheduling, customer privileges and amenities, outside talent, and rental equipment to the studio manager.

The Chief Engineer. The person charged with getting your music on tape is the chief engineer. In the early days of recording, engineers came from the ranks of electronic technicians, audiophiles, musicians, and composers. As the studio business expanded, the demand for highly trained, experienced recording engineers grew so that today, in most major studios, the person behind the desk (control board) usually has some sort of formal training in modern recording techniques and a ton of practical experience.

The chief engineer's primary function is to put sound on tape (or on disk) in as sonically perfect a manner as possible. The engineer's job is to record your music so that it sounds exactly the way you or your producer wants it to sound both in the studio and on the air. Consequently, most engineers have a vast knowledge of all of the tools used in modern recording: microphones, mixing consoles, tape machines, outboard equipment, computers, and synthesizers. Furthermore, successful engineers understand the dynamics of customer relations. Although they usually won't volunteer creative criticism, if asked, the astute engineer will offer expert opinion that will lead to the successful completion of your recording project.

The Assistant or Second Engineer. Large studios generally have more than one person on staff who knows how to get sound on tape. The assistant or second engineer may work your sessions as the primary recordist or as the person who helps with microphone placement, tape loading, signal routing, musical equipment set up and tear down, editing, and dubbing. If you're producing a complex jingle, using dozens of musicians and singers, for example, the assistant engineer may also handle some of the mixing of the final tape. Sometimes the chief engineer simply needs more than two hands on the console to accomplish the final mix.

The Arranger. Depending on your musical knowledge and the amount of work you have on the books at any given moment, you may require the services of a musical arranger. An arranger is a highly trained musical theorist who takes your music and develops a written score. The arranger is both your creative and technical advisor. He or she may assist you in revising your fundamental melody and chord progression and placing the music on paper for professional musicians to read.

Since I am not a schooled musician, I rely heavily on my arrangers for the "sweetening" of my jingles, adding the orchestral instruments that round out the total sound. I also encourage my arrangers to smooth out problems in my chord progessions, harmonies, and, on occasion, overall structure. Once I have finalized the writing of the jingle with my customer, my arranger takes over and creates the written score with all of the individual parts for the singers and musicians. In addition, as part of his or her fee, the arranger is present during my sessions to rehearse and direct the musicians and singers.

The Producer. Sitting beside or behind the engineer at the mixing console is the producer, the person in charge of the recording session. As a jingle writer you will often serve in this capacity; however, it's not unusual to hire someone else to handle this task. Producing requires experience more than anything else. The producer's job is to know what the final recording will sound like *before* it's recorded. Consequently, the producer must have a solid working knowledge of both music and recording techniques.

Prior to, during, and after the recording session, the producer faces a myriad of decisions. He or she is the person responsible for handling all these important details: contracting the written arrangements of the jingle, including all of the individual side parts (separate sheets of music for every musician and singer); booking the studio, musicians, and singers; coordinating the recording session schedule with the customer; securing contracts with the customer and with any unions involved in the session; ordering all materials including dubs (duplicate copies) of the final mixed jingle package; authorizing and, frequently, issuing payments to studios, musicians, singers, and announcers; issuing broadcast licenses for use of the jingle package; and making all final decisions during the recording and mixing process. Whew!

As a producer, you may also have to entertain your customer during the session, displaying not only your musical and technical knowledge—the dog and pony show—but also your ability to make good advertising decisions. Many of your customers have never been in a recording studio; consequently, you will engage in a fair amount of handholding as you build the jingle from scratch. Customers aren't always patient and don't always understand how multitrack recording works. They don't know, for example, that laying down the parts in sections is just the first step in the recording process. I have often heard, "well, that guitar (piano, trumpet, etc.) sounds too damn loud," from an inexperienced customer. You will need to develop patience!

Session Players. One of the best musicians I've ever had the pleasure of working with, John Fish, once told me, "Good players don't get in each other's way." What John meant was that good musicians understand their roles. They don't overplay and clutter up the music. Studio musicians—session players—are not only masters of their instruments but also are experienced in the vagaries of the jingle business. They understand instinctively when a session is not working musically. They have an uncanny ability to focus on the business at hand, allowing nothing to distract them from "playing the chart." They are quick to point out errors in the score and are extremely cooperative when technical problems occur during the session.

Good session players—no matter what the instrument—play in tune and in time. They own and maintain excellent instruments and equipment. They ask, when called for a session, what style of music you're recording so they will bring the right instruments. They arrive on time for the session fully prepared to record the moment you're ready for them. In every respect, good session players are professionals and are the difference between mediocre and fantastic recordings.

Over the years we have developed a short list of players who have all of these characteristics. I use basically the same four rhythm section players (drums, bass, guitar, and keyboards) on every session. I use the same four brass players (two trumpets, two trombones), the same reed person, and the same string ensemble. In most cases, these people have become personal friends as well as business associates. They know what to expect when I call them for a session, and I know what they can and cannot do for me in the studio. In the final analysis, once the chart is written it's the musicians I rely on to bring the score to life—and they always do.

Jingle Singers. Have pity on the poor jingle singers for often they must sing the most ridiculous lyrics ever conceived about unbelievable products and services. After all, the session players are playing the notes as written, and the notes may be good or bad, depending on your creative abilities. Singers, on the other hand, sing not only the notes but also the words to your song. And the words may be silly, improbable, impossible to pronounce or absurdly strung together in eighth-note bursts with nary a space for breathing.

Yet professional jingle singers dig in and do it, day after day, with nervous customers staring at them through the control room windows. They sing with a built-in smile. They sing at 8:00 a.m. or 10:00 p.m. They sing with conviction about toilet bowls and funeral homes, about brushing teeth and broiling meat, about cars and trucks and city pride. They sing and sing and sing without complaint.

Jingle singers are truly a breed apart from all the rest. Although they are most often anonymous, they perform as if they were singing on stage to thousands. They know that the customer wants to hear his or her name sung loud and clear. They maintain a positive attitude throughout the session especially when the customer is present.

Jingle singers, like session players, carry a variety of styles in their musical repertoire. They can sing in every style from Bon Jovi to Be Bop to Broadway. They know how to adjust their voices for a solid blend, eliminating vibrato, often forgetting lessons learned in formal voice training. They understand the goal of the jingle and sing with conviction, dynamics, and punch. They also understand the technical side of recording, the language of the studio. In short, jingle singers have that magical blend of professional enthusiasm, technical expertise, vocal interest, and courtesy essential for completing the project.

And the Others. Again, depending on the size and focus of the studio, you may encounter other people who may or may not participate in your project. College interns learning the ropes, various staff support personnel, secretaries, sales executives, gophers (as in "go for this or go for that"), and staff writers and musicians. As the producer of your session, you have the right, and should exercise it, to clear the studio of anyone who is not associated with the project. The work you have to do is important and, quite often, no one else's business but your own. More importantly, the quality of the work decreases as the number of observers increases. Although recording should be fun, it is a business and you should treat it as such.

Multitrack Recording

Modern recording practices include a variety of methods of getting sound on tape. The most common practice today is to record all of the instrumental and vocal parts of a song on magnetic tape or computer disk maintaining separate control over each part until you've recorded all of the parts. To accomplish this task, we use a multitrack tape or disk recorder. Whether recording to magnetic tape or to computer disk, the process is essentially the same.

A multitrack recording machine allows musicians and singers to record on individual channels or tracks, often while listening to other prerecorded parts of the same song. Multitrack recording machines permit one musician to record his or her part on one channel. A second musician may then listen to the first musician's recorded part while recording his or her own part on a separate track. Once all of the parts are recorded, the recording engineer rerecords all of the parts onto another recording machine, called the mixdown machine (either tape or disk), using a process called mixing.

Mixing the musical parts from the multitrack machine to the mixdown machine involves adjusting the sound volume level and tone quality of each recorded musical and vocal part so that the finished song sounds the way the producer wants it to sound. The recording engineer accomplishes this adjustment of volume level and tone quality of the musical and vocal parts using a mixing console, a piece of electronic equipment that permits the engineer to send and receive the audio signals to and from both the multitrack machine and the mixdown machine.

In addition to adjusting the sound level and tone quality of each instrument or voice, the recording engineer may add special effects, such as echo, reverberation, flanging, phasing, doubling, harmonizing, compression, limiting, noise gates, and others to modify the sounds of the instruments and voices. These special effects are created with electronic equipment (outboard gear) separate from but connected to the mixing console through a series of patch cords (audio cables).

To understand this process, think of the artist, the painter, with a selection of hundreds of oil paints on a table near his or her blank canvas. The oil paints are the individual instrumental and vocal parts. The artist may apply any colors he or she desires to the canvas just as the engineer may record the individual musical and vocal parts on the multitrack machine.

Once the artist chooses his or her colors, he or she may mix them together just as the engineer mixes the sounds together while transferring them to the mixdown machine. The primary difference here is that the artist accomplishes the finished product in a one-step process of creating the painting on the canvas, whereas the engineer creates the finished product in a two-step process, recording the individual parts on the multitrack machine and then transferring the mixed song to the mixdown machine.

A simple drawing showing this process appears on the next page.

The mixdown machine may be any standard re-

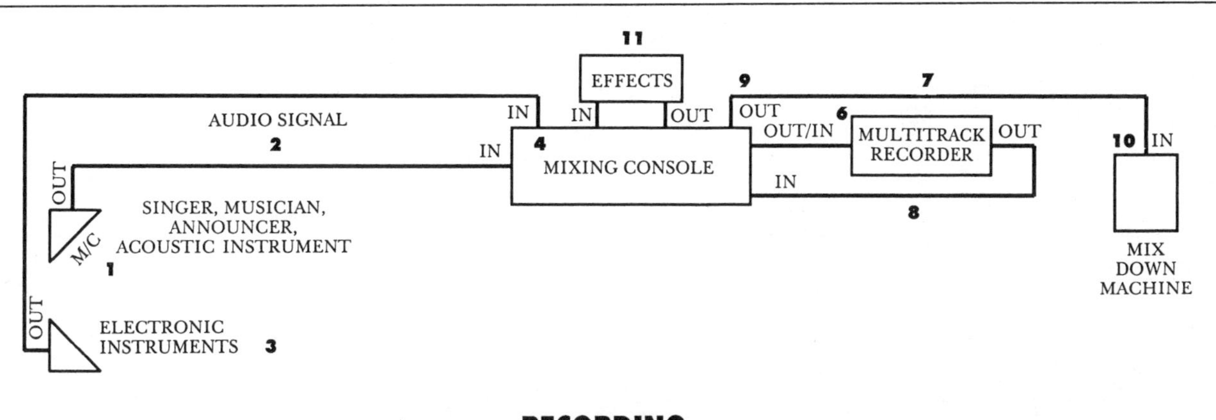

RECORDING

The audio signal (2) travels from the talent (1) or (3) into the mixing console (4), where the engineer processes the signal. The signal then travels out of the mixing console (6) and into the multitrack machine (7) where it is stored on an individual track for later processing.

MIXING

After the engineer has recorded all of the instruments and singers (talent) onto the multitrack, the engineer then mixes the audio information from the multitrack back (8) through the mixing console and out (9) to the mixdown machine (10).

During either the initial recording process or the mixdown process, the engineer may add any effects from the outboard gear (11) connected to the mixing console.

cording device, a cassette recorder, a home reel-to-reel tape recorder, or a professional half-track mastering recorder. In the jingle business, we usually mix down to a half-track recorder running at high speed to obtain the highest quality of sound reproduction. The half-track machine has two channels for stereo recording.

Track Planning. One of the critical aspects of multitrack recording is track planning—determining where to record each of the instruments, instrumental sections (groups of players), and vocalists on the multitrack tape. Multitrack recorders are usually configured in 4, 8, 12, 16, 24, 32, or 48 tracks. You may assign any number of instruments or vocalists to any number of tracks. Your goal is to record all of the instruments and vocalists allowing for the most individual control without sacrificing sound quality.

To demonstrate, let's use the middle-of-the-road (MOR) version of the ABC Flowers jingle as an example. We're using a 24-track machine. On the track log pictured on the next page we assign the drums to tracks 1, 2, 3, and 4, the guitar to 5 and 6, the piano to 7 and 8, the bass to 9. We now have 15 tracks left for everything else, right? Seems like plenty of tracks, doesn't it? Maybe. Let's continue. We record four brass instruments—two trumpets and two trombones—*twice* to fatten up the sound, so we use up tracks 10 and 11. The string section consists of three violins, one viola, and one cello. We do three passes (complete recordings of the section on separate tracks) of the strings to simulate a larger orchestral section. There go tracks 12, 13, and 14.

Now, for the reed player. We could book several reed players and put them all on one track; however, we have one fellow who owns and plays all of the reed family of instruments. We're going to use two flutes and one saxophone for the jingle. One person playing requires one track for each of the three instruments: tracks 15, 16, and 17 are now gone.

We now have seven tracks remaining. We use tracks 18, 19, and 20 for three passes of the background vocals. Track 21 is reserved for the lead vocalist, so it appears that we're safe. But what if we wanted to add a melody line played by one of the instruments, say a trumpet? Another track bites the dust. And what if we really need four passes on the

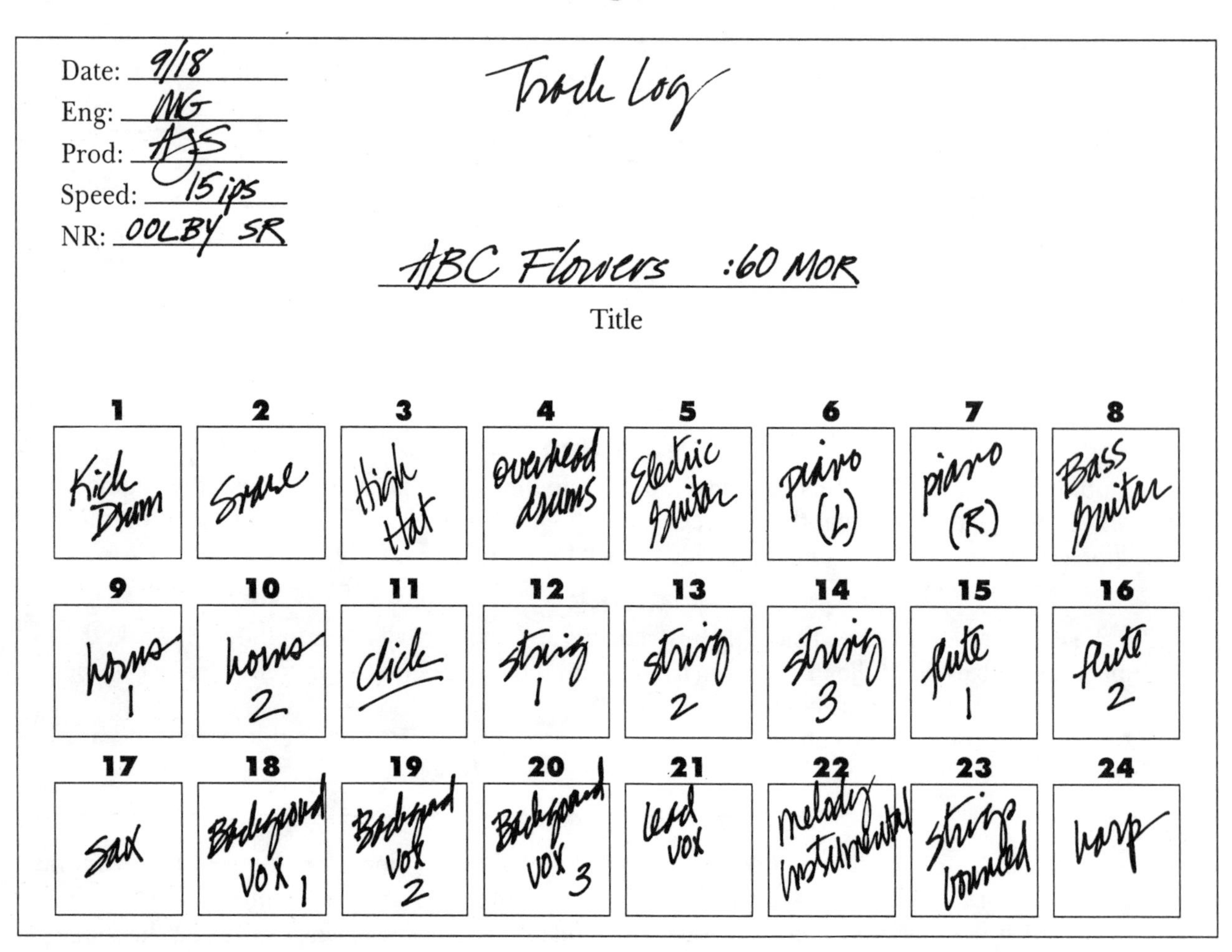

Date: 9/18
Eng: MG
Prod: AJS
Speed: 15 ips
NR: DOLBY SR

Track Log

ABC Flowers :60 MOR
Title

1	2	3	4	5	6	7	8
Kick Drum	Snare	High Hat	overhead drums	Electric Guitar	piano (L)	piano (R)	Bass Guitar

9	10	11	12	13	14	15	16
horns 1	horns 2	click	string 1	string 2	string 3	flute 1	flute 2

17	18	19	20	21	22	23	24
sax	Background vox 1	Background vox 2	Background vox 3	lead vox	melody instrumental	strings bounced	harp

strings instead of just three to give the jingle a fuller sound? And, wait a minute, I forgot the harp. Two passes for the harp? Nope, can't do it. We used track 22 for the trumpet solo and track 23 for the extra string pass. We only have one track left for the harp.

See how easy it is to use up tracks? Without careful planning you can record yourself into a corner. What if we are planning to mix down the final recording in *stereo* instead of mono and we want a better split on the drums and the strings. We might decide to record the drums on five or six tracks instead of four. We might need two more tracks for stereo flutes, who knows? That's why the statement I made earlier about the producer "knowing what the jingle will sound like before it's recorded" is so telling. Strategies for recording begin with very careful planning of all elements of the process, particularly track usage.

Planning for the Final Session. Now, to simplify and demystify the recording process for the uninitiated, let's follow the progression of events from start to finish in terms of recording. We will assume for this discussion that ABC's ad agency has approved the spec jingle, signed off on (agreed to and initialed) the revised lyrics, signed the Music Production Agreement (see chapter 8), and has delivered the deposit check (see chapter 8).

Also, for the sake of this example, we're going to assume that ABC has given the jingle writer/producer a healthy budget and wants a spectacular production, fully orchestrated, several versions—a big package. Prior to closing the sale (see chapter 8), the writer/producer has determined how many versions (different styles) of the music to create, specifically what instruments and singers to use, which studio to record in, and the date(s) for the final sessions. The producer must collect this information before determining the total cost of the project. What does the writer/producer do next?

Working with the Arranger. Dropping the name

"writer" from the title from this point forward, the "producer" contacts the arranger and discusses the final versions for the jingle package. The producer outlines the number of instruments and singers budgeted, the deadline for recording, the different musical styles for each version of the jingle, and the creative license the arranger may take with the song. The discussion might go something like this:

Producer: Got a big project for you this week, Carl.

Arranger: Oh yeah. You got it on paper or your usual dynamite cassette!

Producer: Get serious. Here's the cassette. Let's listen to the song (plays spec tape). Get the picture?

Arranger: Uh, huh. ABC Flowers. Where are they located?

Producer: (City). Got five stores and they're getting ready to expand regionally.

Arranger: Well, I like your melody real well, but "blooms for all rooms," are you kidding?

Producer: That's the agency's slogan, Carl. Hey, it rhymes!

Arranger: Sure does . . . so, what's the deal. How many versions are we talking about? Do I have a budget this time or are we "down and dirty" again?

Producer: No, you've got a genuine budget this time. We're doing three versions—MOR, country, and kind of a light rock thing.

Arranger: Really? Well, that's great. Let's get started.

Producer: OK. Let's look at the MOR track. What we're looking for is a ballad version with lush strings . . .

Arranger: Real or imagined . . .

Producer: Real strings, no synthesizer.

Arranger: All right!

Producer: Give me acoustic piano, acoustic guitar, drums, and bass—use live players—you've got room for reeds, strings, and a harp. I don't know whether I hear horns on this one or not; it's up to you; you've got the budget for it.

Arranger: (Taking notes) Great!

Producer: Now on the country track, we're looking for "class country" not really a whining steel guitar thing. A little more sophisticated with some horns, maybe a little banjo background or fiddle for sweetening. And the vocals should be straight-ahead four-part with strong "oohs and ahs," you know, "oooh-ing for bucks" stuff (background vocalists singing "oohs" and "ahs" in the popular standard country-rock style).

Arranger: Yeah, I got'cha."

Producer: And the light rock thing is wide open; just give me a strong rhythm section, maybe with some synthesizer chops. Push toward funk. You might even write it for electronic drums, too.

Arranger: OK. Anything else?

Producer: Yeah, the lead vocalist on the MOR version is an alto; on the country track, we'll use a tenor, and on the rock version we'll use a tenor.

Arranger: You want any vocal harmonies on the rock track?

Producer: Naw, let's just leave it up to the singer when he hears the track. Karl's got a lot of those harmonies in his head!

Arranger: OK. And the big question is, when?

Producer: As usual . . . I need it yesterday . . . seriously, the session's scheduled for next Thursday, so you've got a little over a week.

Arranger: You're going to try and get all this done in one day?

Producer: We're doing instruments only on Thursday; the singers will be in on Friday afternoon, starting at 1:30. Can you be there both days?

Arranger: No problem. See you then.

In the jingle business, it is very realistic to request that three full arrangements be completed in seven working days. In fact, seven days is often a luxury. Nonetheless, whenever you can grab more time for the arranger, do it. You'll get cleaner charts (fewer mistakes) and, usually, better harmonies. (See appendix B for an MOR arrangement of the ABC jingle.)

Booking the Talent. After working with the arranger, the producer's next task is to book the talent (players, singers, announcers) for the final recording session. Immediately upon getting the word from the ad agency that the jingle is sold, the producer reserves time at the appropriate studio and begins calling talent. If you're not familiar with the musicians and singers in your market, you may choose a contractor to do the booking for you. Check with your local musician's union or call the largest studio in town for a contractor.

Budgeting Time for the Final Session. Before making the calls to talent, the producer plans the entire session carefully. As I mentioned earlier, in multitrack recording, we lay down (record) tracks individually by section or player. It is easier to control each section during both the recording and the mixing steps when you're dealing with fewer musicians at one time. Also, some studios are not large enough to provide adequate isolation of instruments and singers. So, budgeting time for each section becomes essential. Using the ABC Flowers example, here's how the producer would budget time for the session.

Now, let's analyze the schedule.

ABC Flowers Jingle
Date: 9-27-90 Thursday & 9-28-90 Friday
Studio:
Music Is Us Recording
Engineer: Mike
Producer: Al
Arranger: Carl
Schedule: Thursday, 9-27-90
8:00 A.M.-10:00 A.M.—*Rhythm section on all three versions*
10:30 A.M.-12:00 P.M.—*Synthesizer on rock track; banjo on C/W*
12:00 P.M.- 1:00 P.M.—*Lunch*
1:00 P.M.- 2:30 P.M.—*Horn section on two possibly three versions*
2:30 P.M.- 3:00 P.M.—*Pad for problems*
3:00 P.M.- 4:00 P.M.—*Strings and harp on MOR version*
4:00 P.M.- 5:00 P.M.—*Reed instruments on all three versions*

Friday, 9-28-90
1:30 P.M.- 3:30 P.M.—*Singers on all three versions*
3:30 P.M.- 5:00 P.M.—*Announcer voice overs*
5:00 P.M.- 7:00 P.M.—*Mix*

First of all, this schedule assumes that we're using top-of-the-line, professional musicians, singers, and announcers. The less experienced the players, the more time you will have to allow for each section. Second, we are assuming that the studio we are using is also top of the line, probably a 24-track (analog studio with the capability of recording on twenty-four separate channels at the same time) or digital (computer-based studio with virtually unlimited tracking capability) studio. We also are using an experienced broadcast-jingle-oriented engineer who understands the time limitations for a project of this size.

Third, we are budgeting time based on the knowledge that our arranger is experienced in writing charts for jingles, which means the orchestration is relatively sane—challenging but realistic. Our arrangers know the players we use and write parts to fit the talents.

We have budgeted two full hours for the rhythm section on all three versions of the jingle. On the MOR version we'll be using acoustic piano, acoustic drums, acoustic guitar, and electric bass. On both the country and the rock versions we'll use an electronic piano or synthesizer, acoustic drums, electric guitar, and electric bass. The same four players will cover all the parts on all three versions and will know what to expect before coming to the studio.

If you are unable to arrange a visit to a studio or talk with an engineer to learn about budgeting time for sessions, you can use this simple system: for every musician or singer involved in the session, compute a half-hour of studio time for set up, rehearsal, recording, and down time. If you hire professionals, you should be safe. Here's an example:

4 rhythm section players
4 brass players
3 string players
1 reed player
4 singers
16 total players divided by 2 (for a half-hour each) equals
8 hours budget for the recording session.

If you can group sections together in the studio with adequate isolation, you may subtract an appropriate number of hours. For example, if you can cut the rhythm section and horn section together, subtract one hour. If you can cut the rhythm section, horn section, and reed player together, subtract two hours. However, the more musicians and singers playing at the same time, the slower the recording process goes. You may find in our last example that you still need the extra hour you subtracted by cutting three sections at once to accommodate the increased number of people trying to achieve a clean recording.

Another way to budget time is simply to compute on the basis of the number of sections for each version of a jingle. In our ABC example we are using a rhythm section, horn section, string section, vocal section, reed section, and three overdubs—banjo, synthesizer, and announcer. Since we are recording three versions of the ABC jingle, I am allowing two hours for each section playing on all three versions, an hour and a half per section playing on two versions, only an hour per section playing on one version, an hour for the three overdubs, and two hours for mixing. Keep in mind that for each *musical version* we will record at least a :60 and a :30, and perhaps a :10.

Here's how this budgeting process looks:

Section	*Number of Versions*	*Budgeted Hours*
Rhythm	3	2
Horns	3	2
Strings	1	1
Vocals	3	2
Reeds	2	1.5
Banjo	1	1
Synth	2	1.5
Announcer	3	2
	Total Hours	12

Now, with some simple addition, we compute that the singers are going to record 27 tracks of background vocals and 9 tracks of lead vocals to complete the jingle package: 3 passes of background vocals on each of 3 versions of the jingle for each of the 3 time lengths = 27 background tracks; 1 pass of lead vocals on each of 3 versions of the jingle for each of the 3 time lengths = 9 lead tracks. Again, track planning is critical. More importantly, hiring professional jingle singers who read music is almost mandatory if we are going to get all the singing finished in our allotted two hours.

The Announcer Track. As a jingle writer/producer you won't often have to contend with cutting the announcer voice-over; however, in an attempt to give you as much information about this business as possible, I've included an announcer session along with the jingle session. For our mythical jingle package for ABC Flowers, the customer has requested that we cut a permanent announcer voice-over track inside the jingle *prior* to the mix. Usually, agencies cut announcer voice-overs *after* the mix so they can change the copy as needed.

In this case, the announcer voice-over, which consists of one line on each mix of each version (excluding the :10s), will become a permanent part of the package. The line the announcer will speak is "With stores all around town, call 555-9999." We have budgeted a whopping hour and a half for the announcer to accomplish his part; however, given the amount of time it takes to find each cut on the master tape and record the announcer, we may not have overestimated the time requirements by much.

An alternate way to proceed is to cut the announcer on a wild track (a separate piece of tape cut on the half-track machine) and bounce the track up to the multitrack machine later. Nonetheless, the engineer may spend about the same amount of time searching for the correct places at the end of each version in which to place the prerecorded announcer tracks. Later, after mixing the jingle, the agency will call announcers as needed to record other voice-overs for future use.

Down Time. In addition to track planning, a producer must understand time requirements for down time (nonrecording functions). It takes time for the engineer to set up microphones, run headphone cables, find and hook up direct boxes (electronic devices into which musicians connect the audio output of their electronic instruments to send the audio signal to the control board), and load the tape machines. It takes time to switch from a rhythm section setup to a horn section setup. It takes time to rewind tape, to adjust volume levels for different players and singers, and to allow the musicians who are finished to tear down their equipment and leave the studio. The best ways to learn about these seemingly innocuous but time-consuming matters is to visit a recording studio and watch several sessions or discuss budgeting studio time with a studio manager or recording engineer.

Technical Difficulties. Another problem that is difficult to control is technical difficulty—equipment failure. No matter how new, how expensive, how perfectly maintained studio equipment may be, it still breaks down. And it seems to happen only when your customer is attending the session! Microphone cables break, input channels fail, headphone amplifiers crash, and tape machines simply stop running. If the problem is severe and there's no way around it, you may have to reschedule the session. However, major studios usually have contingency plans and extra equipment that will get you going if only temporarily until the problem is solved.

It's in the smaller studios that you often encounter insurmountable problems. When the one-person studio's monitor speakers blow, that's usually it—you're finished for the day. So, be prepared, no matter where you record, for technical difficulties.

On to the Studio!

The big day has arrived and we're ready to record the final version of our new jingle. We've booked our talent, reserved studio time, commissioned an arrangement, and notified our customer to meet us at the studio.

We arrive at the studio about a half-hour early to make sure everything's ready. We meet our engineer in the control room and discuss the session. The engineer assigns each instrument a track on the multitrack tape machine following our track planning sheet. Using microphones for the acoustic instruments and direct boxes for the electronic or electric instruments, the engineer or the assistant engineer routes the audio signals from each player through the mixing console (control board) to the multitrack machine so that the engineer will have separate control over each instrument at all times.

About fifteen minutes before the call (start time), our arranger and the rhythm section players arrive and unload their equipment. Once the players are tuned and ready to go, the arranger hands out the charts and instructs the players on style and feel. After a few run-throughs, the section (band) is ready to record the first take (attempt at recording) of the first version.

The producer speaks to the players and the arranger through a "talk-back" microphone in the control room feeding their headphones. Each player can hear the producer and each other's instruments in their headphones. During the run-throughs, the musicians may ask for more or less volume from the individual instruments in the headphone mix. The drummer may say, for example, "Give us a little more piano in the phones, please."

During the run-through, not only are the musicians practicing the music, but also the engineer is busy setting volume levels, adjusting the EQ (tone quality), and adding any outboard effects (compression, limiting, flanging, phasing, gating, echo) desired for the initial recording.

The engineer slates the beginning of the tape: he or she records the name, date, time, and place of the session and the name and length of the version. The drummer gives a count off and the band plays the song all the way through. The producer and engineer listen to a playback and decide if another take is necessary. Frequently, the musicians will confess to errors in the playing that only they seem to hear, and even with the best players, a take may fall apart before completion.

The goal of the initial recording is to capture as many of the instruments as possible cleanly (without mistakes) on tape. If, for example, the drummer, pianist, and guitarist play all the way through the chart but the bass player misses a couple of notes, it is possible to save the three good instruments and rerecord the bass by itself with the bassist listening to and playing along with the recorded tracks. Because we record each instrument on a separate track, simultaneously, we are able to save the clean tracks and repair the problem tracks. As the music approaches the spot where the error occurred, the engineer "punches in" (puts the bass track into record) and the bassist records over his mistake.

At the end of the repaired section of the track, the engineer "punches out" the bass and rewinds to check the punches for accuracy. This punching in and out process occurs frequently throughout the recording of all instruments, singers, and even announcers. It's a fast, efficient way to record and save time.

Once the producer and engineer agree that a take is a keeper, the band moves to the second version of the jingle. The musicians switch instruments if necessary, retune, adjust headphone levels, and practice the chart. At the appropriate moment, the drummer shouts "red light" and off we go recording the rhythm section for the second, and eventually the third, version of the jingle.

After the producer listens to and accepts the

rhythm section recordings of the three versions, he or she hands out talent releases (forms the musicians, singers, and announcers sign agreeing to the terms and conditions of payment and use of their performances) to those players who are finished. Our practice for the past ten years includes paying the talent as they leave the studio: they appreciate not having to wait months for their checks. The engineer resets the studio for the next step in the recording process—overdubbing (recording additional instruments).

As you may recall, on the ABC jingle we budgeted two hours for the rhythm section to record the three versions of the jingle. If all has gone well, we are ready to overdub the banjo track on the country version and the synthesizer track on the rock version. Since we're already set up to record acoustic instruments, we record the banjo first. The guitar player from the rhythm section happens to double (also plays) on banjo, so once the engineer has set up the microphone and the banjo player tunes to the track (checks to see that his instrument is in tune with those already recorded), we're ready for a rehearsal.

Listening to the prerecorded rhythm section, the banjo player plays along following his chart. Since the chord progression is the same for banjo as guitar, the musician should be able to go to red light after only a couple of practice runs. Once the banjo track is finished, the musician signs his talent release, picks up his check, and leaves the studio.

The producer ushers in the keyboard player who has been on a break waiting for the banjo track's completion. The keyboardist has already used his synthesizer as a piano for the country and rock tracks, so he and the producer simply discuss what other synthesizer fills (additional musical passages) he will play on the rock track. The engineer rewinds the tape to the rock track, sets the volume level from the synthesizer, and plays the prerecorded tracks through the headphones to the keyboardist. The overdub process continues exactly as with the banjo player. It's 11:50 a.m.; we're on schedule. It's time for lunch.

During the lunch break, the assistant engineer resets the studio for recording both the horn section and, later, the string section with harp. On the ABC track we're using four horn players: two trumpets and two trombones, but to make the section sound fuller, we're going to have the musicians play through the chart two times resulting in the effect of eight horn players. Later, we'll do the same thing with the strings, actually tripling the number of players with three passes.

The overdubbing of horns and, later, the strings and harp follows the same procedure as with the banjo and synthesizer. The players listen to the prerecorded tracks in their headphones and play along following their charts. If mistakes occur during these acoustic recordings, we usually rerecord the whole section since individual mistakes would be difficult to eliminate. Consequently, the producer and arranger must check the tracks very carefully for both accuracy and balance of instrumental passages.

Following the recording of the horns, strings, and harp, the engineer resets the studio for the solo reed player. The musician overdubs each reed instrument on a separate track in the same manner as the banjo and synthesizer. Since we're working with a single player rather than a group, these reed overdubs go quickly.

It's 5:00 p.m. and we're finished for the day. Three fully recorded instrumental tracks in :60, :30, and :10-second lengths are on tape awaiting the singers and the announcer who will be in tomorrow afternoon. Before leaving the studio, the producer checks each version of the jingle and, if there's a little time left, the engineer might do a quick mix (a simple mixing of the recorded parts without much attention to relative volume levels, tone quality, or special effects) onto cassette for the producer to study prior to the next day's vocal session. If the producer hears anything unsatisfactory in the quick mix, he will still have time prior to the singer's session to correct the problem.

The Vocal Session. Though recording singers is not unlike recording musicians, I have found that working with singers requires even more attention to style and overall effect because most advertisers and listeners notice the singing on jingles more than the playing. Also, I prefer working with singers during the afternoon when their voices are warmed up rather than in the morning when they may be overcoming a late night gig in a club.

As I mentioned earlier, professional jingle singers are a breed apart. They are able to sing complicated lyrics in any style at practically any speed. They know that what they are singing may seem silly or nonsensical on the surface, but they rarely let their personal feelings about the commercial affect their performance.

Background Group Singing. In recording background singers (group sings or BG Vox), as we are doing on the ABC jingle, I usually use a soprano, an alto, and a tenor. Occasionally, I'll use a bass-baritone in the group to give the vocal track some bottom; however, most of the tenors we use can add that baritone line after we finish recording the group. In most group sings, which we use for background vocals, I have the singers placed within two feet of the vocal microphone. This close-miking technique gives us a more intimate, up-front effect that allows for clearer diction and a brighter-sounding vocal rendition.

What we listen for most in recording group vocals is the blend—the balance among voices that creates the effect of one harmonious sound. We want the final effect of the group sing to be anonymous—we don't want one voice to dominate the others. To achieve this effect, we usually record at least two passes of the same vocal parts, in this case, resulting in the sound of six singers instead of three. Occasionally, I'll add a third pass with the singers standing several feet away from the microphone permitting them to belt out the song. This technique creates an interesting blend of tight, close-up harmony overlaid with voices singing with more punch, more character.

Lead Singing. Recording the lead singer (LD Vox or soloist) differs from recording background singers in that we record the lead singer on only one track, one pass. We choose our lead singers carefully so that the voice fits the style and character of the music. Depending on the style of music, the lead singer may work the microphone closely or may step back and belt out the song.

As with recording the other instruments and vocalists, we are trying to capture one sparkling performance from the lead singer with all the notes in tune, the vocal expression consistent, and the interpretation of the lyrics perfect. The lead singer's part is the performance the customer listens to most attentively. The lead singer is telling the story, selling the product or service, singing the customer's name. Though we certainly don't shortchange any element of the jingle, we pay particularly close attention to the vocals, especially the lead vocals.

The Mix. Once all of the recording and overdubbing is finished, the producer and engineer begin setting up the control board for the final mix. Prior to the recording session the producer has met with the customer to determine precisely what mixes the customer will need. For the ABC Flowers jingle package, the producer and customer have identified the following mixes for all three versions:

:60 Full Sing
:60 Open-Close (short instrumental bed)
:60 Open-Close (long instrumental bed)
:60 Tag
:60 Instrumental
:30 Full Sing
:30 Open-Close
:30 Tag
:30 Instrument
:10 Full Sing
:10 Tag
:10 Instrumental

The engineer begins by cueing up the master tape on the multitrack machine to the first version he plans to mix (in this example, the MOR version). The engineer plays the tape and listens to only the drum tracks—each one separately at first. Using the tone controls (EQ) and the various pieces of outboard equipment, the engineer develops the sound for each instrument in the drum kit. He also balances the volume levels of the drums and cymbals before moving on to the next instrument, usually the bass guitar.

Most professional engineers know as they are recording how to get the sound of each instrument on tape so that a minimal amount of work is left for the mix. As he completes the processing of each instrument or section, the engineer moves on to the next until the entire instrumental section is complete.

The producer listens throughout this process, approving or modifying the engineer's decisions. Then the engineer begins the vocal mix.

Mixing vocals is basically the same as mixing instruments. The engineer listens to each pass of the background vocals adding EQ and other outboard effects, such as reverb or echo, until the producer is comfortable with the mix. Finally, the engineer balances volume level of the vocal tracks and the instrumental tracks so that the listener will hear every word of the vocals clearly. In studio jargon, we refer to this balancing of vocals to instruments as "pushing the vocals out front" of the music. Should we mix the vocals as if we are doing a hit record, we might lose some of the lyrics to the instruments. So, in jingle mixing, we push the vocals up front a little further than normal.

Once all the instrumental and vocal tracks (including the announcer) are in place and ready, the engineer rolls the quarter-inch tape on the half-track machine and begins laying down the mixes. We usually proceed in the order of the mixes, as outlined above, with the :60 full sing. After laying down the :60 full sing of the first (MOR) version, we move on to the :60 open-close (short bed).

To accomplish our goal of mixing the open-close, we simply follow the chart and bring the singer's recorded tracks in and out at the appropriate moments during the jingle. As we take the singers out, we bring in the melody line instrument so that in the final mix the listener hears the following parts in this order: instrumental introduction, singers with instruments, instrumental only with melody instrument, singers with instruments on the tag, and the announcer tag line spoken over the final :02 seconds.

Using our lyric sheet, the :60 open-close looks like this:

ABC FLOWERS
:60 OPEN-CLOSE (SHORT BED)

[Instrumental introduction]

Every week, every day, every minute, every hour,
Make your life so special with beautiful flowers,
In the hallway, in the kitchen, in the bedroom, by the stairs,
Using your imagination, put flowers everywhere.

[Take out the singers on the first chorus and the bridge. Bring the singers back in on the final chorus.]

Why not live it up a little bit and brighten your day
It's so easy, you can do it, we're a phone call away!"
Fill your rooms with blooms from ABC Flowers!

[Announcer tag line]

With stores all around town, call 555-9999

For the :60 open-close long bed mix, we simply take the singers out sooner and bring them back in later in order to create a longer musical bed for future announcer voice-overs. Here's the lyric sheet showing this example:

ABC FLOWERS
:60 OPEN-CLOSE (LONG BED)

[Instrumental introduction]

Every week, every day, every minute, every hour,
Make your life so special with beautiful flowers,

[Take out the singers on the last two lines of the verse, the first chorus, the bridge, and the final chorus. Bring the singers back in on the final singing tag line.]

Fill your rooms with blooms from ABC Flowers!

[Announcer tag line]

With stores all around town, call 555-9999

The :60 tag might be instrumental all the way down to the last chorus or down to just the tag line. The :60 instrumental is just that, no singing whatsoever, but in this case, we keep the announcer voice-over tag in at the end.

We mix the :30s and the :10s in basically the same fashion, bringing the singers in and out as needed throughout the mix.

Once we have mixed all twelve mixes for each of the three versions, the engineer prepares the master tape for delivery, pulling out everything not part of the mixed jingle (e.g., slates, tuning chords, count-offs, false starts, etc.). The engineer places leader tape (nonrecordable plastic or paper tape used as a spacer between recorded material) between the various jingle mixes and records the titles of each cut on the tape box or label. If requested, the engineer also runs cassette copies from the mixed master.

Over the years, we have followed the practice of not giving the mixed master to the customer. Legally the customer owns the master tape, but it's rarely a good idea to let it out of your hands. Tapes get lost and customers find it difficult to understand why they must pay for an expensive remixing session simply because they lost their master. Instead, we give the customer (usually the agency) a high-speed (fifteen inches per second or ips) dub (copy) of the master that the agency may use to produce future commercials without coming back to us for a tape.

Also, before finishing the mix, I always have my engineer pull off the various instrumental copies I will need for future relyrics (selling the same music with different lyrics to another customer in a different market). These copies include the tuning chords and drummer count-offs but do not include the melody line instrument. If the customer decides, against my better judgment, to take his master tape with him, I put my instrumental mixes on a separate reel. Once again, by keeping these special instrumental mixes set up for relyricing, we can avoid the expense of multitrack studio time for future singing assignments. We can take the mixed instrumental master and use it in our own small eight-track facility.

Once we've finished the mix, made our copies, and labeled our multitrack master tape, we're ready to deliver the finished jingle to our customer. If you follow the business plan outlined in chapter 8, you know that before you hand the jingle package to your customer, you either pick up your final check or submit your invoice due for your customer's signature of acceptance. Don't let the tapes out of your hands until one or the other happens! Either you get your money up front or, if you know you can trust the customer to pay you on your terms (net 30 days or less), you get a signature on the invoice that says you will get your money.

No matter how well you know your customer, always, *always* get all of your costs for studio time, tape, and talent *up front*. You are not a bank, so don't act like one.

Here are a few other tips that will help you during the recording process for large or small projects, in large or small studios.

The Click Track. Most people would refer to the click track as a metronome. I'm not sure where the term "click track" came from, but it probably derives from the literal sound from an electronic metronome fed to the musicians' headphones.

As you write jingles you are conscious of time constraints. No one wants to produce a :61-second jingle. You may use a metronome as you write, or you may simply plan the chart so that a quarter note equals so many beats per minute resulting in a certain number of measures for a :60-second jingle. Once you go into the studio, however, it's wise to consider using a click track to keep the musicians on time and in time. By sending a predetermined pulse from the click track through the headphones to at least the drummer, if not all the musicians, you avoid the problem of coming up short or long at the end of the song and the problem of speeding up or slowing down during the song.

Most studio drummers have worked with click tracks; some like them; but most hate them They are helpful because using a click keeps the band together. Some musicians and producers hate the click because it causes a mechanical feel. Most purists would object to this artificial aid; however, jingles are jingles and business is business. If a click track saves time during the session, use it. By the way, your engineer should record the click track and save it as long as possible before erasing it. The overdubbing musicians need it as a guide. Later, the engineer may dump (erase) the click to free up a track for recording other instruments.

The Tuning Chord. Since multitrack recording involves recording different musicians and singers at different times (another point the purists rail against), it is a good idea to have your keyboardist play a tuning chord just prior to the count-off for the jingle. Here's the sequence of events at the start of the recording process.

The engineer rolls tape and hits the record button for the appropriate number of tracks. Next, the engineer or producer slates the tape. The producer then tells the keyboardist to "lay down a tuning chord" that other players and the singers use later in the day or, in fact, any time in the future. After the tuning chord is down, the drummer starts the count-off.

If you follow this procedure—slate, tuning chord, count-off—at the beginning of every jingle you will help yourself immeasurably later in the day and even months or years down the road. Nothing is more frustrating than trying to find an unmarked (unslated) track on a reel two or three years after the original session. And once you've found that unmarked track, nothing is worse than trying to add new instruments without having a tuning chord or count-off recorded in front of the jingle.

The Count-Off. A few more words about the count-off. Most studio musicians know this point already, but the uninitiated may not. When giving the count-off—"one, two, three, four"—or whatever number of beats you need, make sure the drummer leaves the last count silent. If it's a two-bar count-off (4/4 time), for example, the drummer would say, "one, two, three, four, one, two, three" and then only *think* "four." Since you don't want the drummer's voice counting on the final mixed version of the jingle, leaving out the last count makes it easier to edit out the drummer's voice during the final mixdown and edit session, especially on uptempo jingles.

More about Mixes. Remember that when you do a jingle for one customer, you may be using the same track over and over again for future customers (relyrics). No matter what the requirements for the original customer, you should always plan to cut a :60, a :30, and a :10-second length, even if your original customer only wants a :60. You may resell the track dozens of times around the country and you might need that :30 or :10 in the future.

Also, you can save some studio time if, as you are writing the jingle, you plan for an edited :30 or :10. If, for example, as you write the :60, you plan that the first thirty seconds of the :60 can become a :30-second mix and that the last ten seconds of the :60 can become the :10-second mix, you can save yourself hours of studio time and talent fees. You record the :60 jingle on the multitrack machine, using all of the instruments and singers. During the mixdown process, you mix the :60s you need and then lay down (record) just the front half of the :60 for your :30-second edits. After mixing the :30s, you lay down just the last ten seconds of the :60 for the :10-second edits. You may be able to save as much as two or three hours of studio time. Once you've mixed the :60-second jingle, laying down mixes for the :30s and :10s is quick and simple.

Melody Line Instruments. Another small but important point on mixing—if you're using a solo instrument to play the melody of the jingle during segments when the singers aren't singing, you should be sure to mix a separate cut that you'll label :60 (or :30 or :10) instrumental *without melody*. Again, for future use (relyrics), you will need instrumental mixes without the melody instrument playing so that you can have vocalists sing new lyrics to the track for new customers. Once the relyric singing is complete, you may hire another solo musician to put the melody line back on the jingle. You may have to modify the melody line on the written score to match subtle changes you've made in the melody of the relyric; however, in most cases, playing the original melody works.

Some jingle houses go a step further in setting up mixes for future relyrics. Some producers create what they call "safety copies" during which they mix down the jingle on a 4-track machine with one track for rhythm section, one track for melody, one track for singing, and one track for sweetening. If they decide to use a track for a relyric, they simply pull out the safety copy, rerecord the four tracks on the 8, 12, 16, or 24-track machine, erase the old singers, and resing the track for the new customer. The producer may even send out just the rhythm section with one singer as a demo and then record new singers and add the prerecorded orchestration for the final.

Storing Your Mixes. One last bit of housekeeping. When you put together your master reel of the mixed jingle package, make sure the engineer stores the tape "tails out" (on the take-up reel rather than supply reel). Storing tape played out (not fast forwarded) onto the take-up reel helps protect the tape from damage.

Also, put your :60 full sing version *last* on the master reel so that it will be the *first* cut on the storage reel (tails out). Put your instrumental mixes on next to the last. You may have to use these mixes frequently in the future. Storing the cuts in this order will save you an enormous amount of time and aggravation.

CHAPTER 7

Rockin' and Rollin' at Home

Now that I've taken you through a recording session in a professional multitrack studio, you might be better able to evaluate your need for some kind of a small production studio of your own. You can use your small studio for cutting jingle specs and demos, for doing relyrics, and even for recording low-budget finished jingle packages. Furthermore, depending on your interest, abilities, and budget, you can even earn additional nonjingle income with your own small studio.

Building your own small recording studio is not difficult nor does it have to be terribly expensive. You can set up a very functional studio in your home, for example, for under a thousand dollars. For over ten years I've been operating a small 8-track facility from my home doing nearly all the pre- and postproduction work (spec recording and dubbing and editing) for my jingles as well as producing voice-overs and nonbroadcast tapes, such as long narrations for sales presentations, for my nonjingle customers. However, before you even consider setting up a small studio, you need to determine precisely what abilities and needs you have.

Evaluating Your Strengths

If you decide you want to set up a commercially viable recording business, you should go through a fundamental analysis of yourself, your market, and your competition in order to find your niche. The same is true for entering the jingle business and setting up your own small recording facility. You should write down both your strengths and weaknesses and your likes and dislikes to determine how and where you fit into the jingle business.

It's important to understand what you think you're good at and not good at doing. For example, I am not particularly good at writing harmonies. I often use the same basic chords and patterns over and over again. Consequently, I rely heavily on my arrangers to improve my harmonies. On the other hand, I have enjoyed great success with melodies and lyrics for jingles, and I have a good ear for producing vocals. Also, since I am just a marginal musician, I almost always employ a master musician to handle all of the instrumental parts on my specs and demos.

As you evaluate your strengths and weaknesses, you will discover what kind of studio you should build and how you will use it. The choices are mind-boggling. You may choose to set up one of the following types of small studios.

1. A small, cassette-based multitrack (a 4- or 8-track recorder with small, built-in mixing console using a standard cassette as the master tape) permits you to record specs and demos on cassette with little possibility for any postproduction work. You won't be able to do any editing or dubbing of finished jingle packages, but you will be able to create excellent specs and demos.

2. A larger, cassette-based multitrack provides you with better-quality recordings for specs, demos, and some low-budget finals.

3. A semiprofessional multitrack facility with better monitoring capabilities (more expensive speakers and amplifiers) allows you to produce broadcast

quality (suitable for broadcasting on radio and TV) tapes.

4. A professional multitrack studio enables you to cut broadcast quality work including singers and announcers as well as some of the instrumental tracks.

5. A MIDI studio with or without multitrack equipment and a mixdown machine enables you to cut synthesized instrumental tracks and add vocals to finals. Even if you are not a musician, it is possible to learn to operate this sophisticated equipment.

Keep in mind, the more flexible your studio is, the more expensive it is. However, with a better studio you'll be able to do more business in-house and spend fewer dollars outside. But let's consider what you might want to do even if you're not a musician or a recording engineer.

Suppose you're primarily a writer—not a composer—but a wordsmith. You have learned how to write jingle lyrics and have even come up with a few hummable melodies, but you have no music or technical background. Why do you need even a small studio, much less a MIDI set-up?

Assuming you're following the suggestions I've made about collaborating with a local musician/composer, you'll need to record your specs and demos somewhere. Unless you've tied in with a person who has his or her own studio or a MIDI set-up, you're going to spend money recording. Although I am not a believer in acquiring overhead, I do believe that anything that helps you be more creative, worry less about how you're going to create, and do your work more quickly is good. Having your own small studio will help free your creative energies.

You should keep in mind, however, that the recording industry has been going through a dramatic revolution since the midseventies. The technology has developed rapidly and the age of specialization is upon us. You may discover that working with a musician who already owns and understands the sophisticated equipment available today will give you a better shot at competing in the jingle business. These synthesists have spent years learning about and following the changes in technology. Furthermore, the buying public, your customers, have become more selective in their tastes. No longer will they accept boring, repetitious, mechanical-sounding rhythm tracks that just a few years ago were the norm. Nonetheless, you can set up a studio that will improve your ability to create and compete. So, what do you need?

Choosing Your Equipment

Again, as a nonmusician/nonrecording engineer writer, you might consider setting up a studio with a small multitrack cassette recorder/mixer. Tascam Corporation's "Porta 05" 4-track cassette unit would be perfect for recording your rough specs that you could then give to a musician friend to arrange and write out in musical notation. Just as with the large reel-to-reel multitrack machines, these small cassette multitracks allow you to record on one track, then overdub on additional tracks. The primary differences are that the cassette format is normally limited to four or eight tracks and it does not reproduce broadcast-quality recordings, so your work with a cassette multitrack is limited to spec or demo quality.

Along with the cassette multitrack, you'll need a good microphone, such as a Shure SM–57, and a pair of headphones, such as the AKG K45. It is not necessary, however, to invest in large studio monitor speakers, amplifiers, and fancy mixdown tape decks. You can use your home stereo for monitoring and your home cassette deck for mixing down.

You'll also need to dedicate a room in your home or office to your new studio. With a minimal amount of soundproofing, you should be able to eliminate outside noise interference and create a viable acoustic environment in which to record. Using commercially available soundproofing materials, you can cover the walls, windows, and doors in the room and eliminate most of the sound transfer from the outside as well as from within your studio. You may also want to build a small isolation booth in the room in which your singers and announcers perform.

If you are more ambitious, you may decide to build a room within a room, leaving approximately two feet of air space between the walls of your studio and the existing walls of the room. You then fill the new walls with insulation material, seal off any spaces that might allow sound to enter or escape, add a solid core door covered on both sides with soundproofing materials, and you're ready to record.

If you decide to build this type of room, you

would be well-served to purchase a set of plans from a professional studio design firm. Without spending a fortune, you should be able to set up this type of small studio in your home and greatly improve your ability to produce high-quality specs and demos. The diagram below illustrates a typical small studio set-up, including an isolation booth for recording a few musicians, singers and announcers.

If you're a little more serious about doing broadcast-quality work in your own small studio, you might take the plunge into a more sophisticated studio package. You might choose to stick with the multitrack cassette format, but move up to a much better quality machine, such as the Tascam 238 8-track deck. Or you might choose a more traditional reel-to-reel multitrack such as the Tascam 388 ¼″ 8-track with built-in mixing board. With either choice you will add better microphones, such as the Shure SM 81 or the Electro Voice RE–20, better monitoring with professional-quality studio speakers, such as Tannoy PBM 6.5 or JBL 4408 monitors, driven by a high-quality amplifier, such as the AMR PMA 200 or the Carver PM175, and some type of professional mixdown machine, such as Tascam's 32 ¼″ half-track machine.

With a more sophisticated equipment package, you may want to operate in a more professional environment, perhaps a small space outside your home or at least a couple of rooms dedicated exclusively for studio use in your home. You can expect to invest from six thousand to eight thousand dollars in this type of equipment package, not including the acoustic treatment for your control room and studio.

If you have some recording experience or if you plan to get some professional training in recording engineering (which isn't a bad idea for all jingle writers), you might plan to set up a more commercially viable studio in which you may record your own work and sell studio time to outside customers. Going into this type of set-up frequently though not always requires moving out of your home into a commercial location. You should check with a good local zoning attorney to determine if you may operate a commercial studio legally from your residence.

Your choices for a small but professional multi-

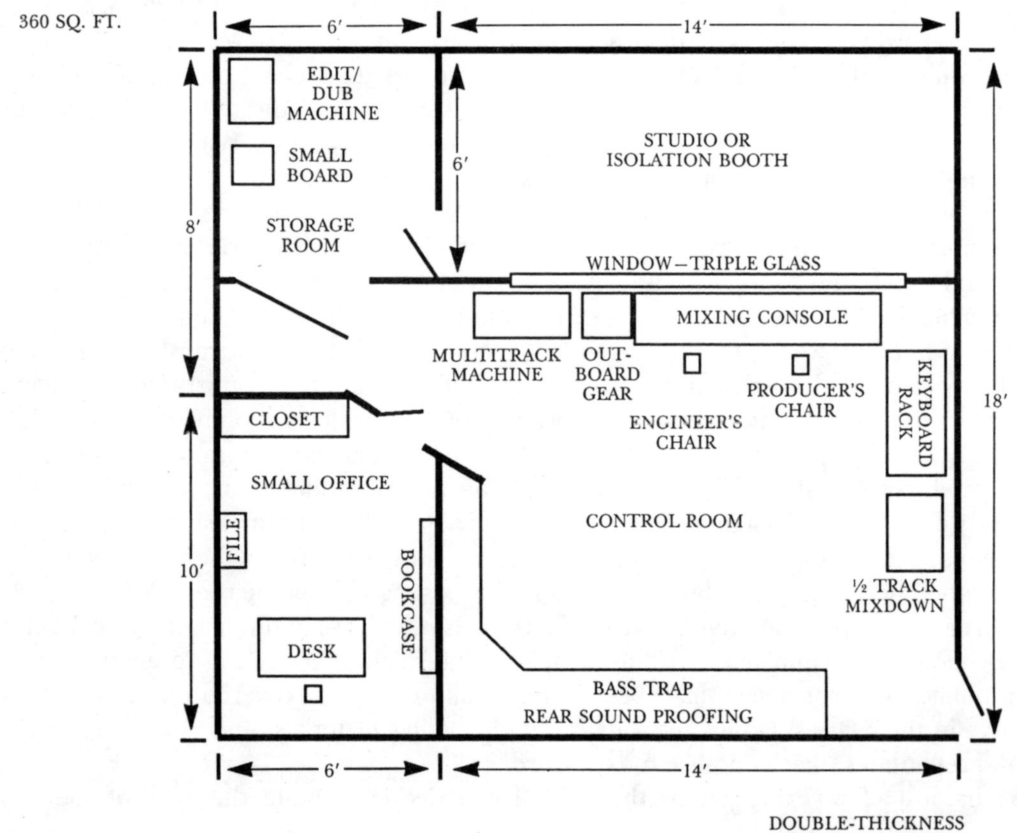

track studio are virtually unlimited; however, here are some examples of the equipment you will need.

You might consider the Tascam TSR–8 reel-to-reel 8-track or the Tascam MSR–16 reel-to-reel 16-track for your multitrack machine. You'll need a flexible control board (mixer), such as the Tascam M312B or the M520, with plenty of input and output channels. You'll want top-of-the-line monitor speakers, such as a pair of UREI 809s or KEF 103/3s driven by an appropriately rated power amp, say a Carver PM175 or a Carver M4.0+. Your microphone selection might include any of the microphones I've mentioned earlier, depending on what you're planning to record (just voices or voices and some acoustic instruments). You might add an AKG 414B–ULS or an AKG C414B–ULS to allow for even more flexibility with vocalists.

In a more elaborate small studio you'll need a professional mixdown machine, a half-track such as the Otari 5050B–II. You'll also obtain high-quality headphones for the singers and musicians, direct boxes for connecting instruments to your control board, microphone cables, a patch bay, some outboard effects units and other signal processing equipment. The price tag for this type of small studio can easily exceed twenty thousand dollars.

To MIDI or Not to MIDI. Again, depending on your abilities and your interests, you may consider setting up a combination analog and MIDI studio. Even if you're not a musician, you can learn to operate most of the digital equipment on the market today. Your set-up would include some type of synthesizer-controller, probably a digital synthesizer with sequencing or sampling capability. Or you may purchase a separate sequencer, a dedicated computer that serves as a recording and playback device in which you can store and retrieve musical sounds. A sequencer allows you to write and record songs of virtually any length (depending on the sequencer's memory) using a synthesizer to input the digital information.

Along with your synthesizer you would add a digital drum machine such as the Alesis HR 16, a computer with music-writing software, and a small analog set-up such as the first or second package I described above. The price tag for this combination digital/MIDI/analog studio—from six to ten thousand dollars.

For the nonmusician, digital equipment with MIDI capability combined with a personal computer (PC) and a small analog package gives you an enormous step forward in competing with the "big guys." Here's why. With some concentrated study (though not nearly as much as required to become an excellent musician) you can learn to operate this type of equipment and produce excellent music.

You hook up all the equipment with cables via MIDI, which stands for "musical instrument digital interface." MIDI allows you to use your PC as a sequencer or to hook up any number of pieces of digital equipment to each other as well as your computer. You connect your synthesizer and drum machine to your PC and load your sequencing software program (or you may be using a dedicated computer called a sequencer). You connect the digital equipment back through your mixer and then to your multitrack recorder (either cassette or reel-to-reel).

With everything hooked together, you can literally write your jingles by simply playing the notes you hear in your head on the synthesizer, in any key or at any speed you wish. You don't have to be a good technical player. You simply have to be able to push down on the right keys, much like the old hunt-and-peck method of typing. Some programs allow you to input the music via the computer's typewriter keyboard.

Depending on the software you purchase, the computer will store the notes you are playing and play them back when you ask it to. You can play a melody as slowly or as quickly as you are able, make mistakes, and the computer can play back the melody through the synthesizer in the correct time, at the correct speed, *without* the mistakes!

Now, consider for a moment the possibilities. With a good-quality sampling keyboard (a synthesizer capable of recording, storing, and playing back thousands of musical sounds) and with a versatile drum machine, you can lay down all of the music for your spec jingle without hiring another musician. And if you're a decent singer, you can sing the spec yourself. You become, literally, a one-person orchestra.

Obviously, if you have absolutely no experience in music and recording whatsoever, you're going to have to experiment and learn to operate this equipment. It won't be easy, but it will be possible. Also, you will find dozens of sources for help in learning to use computers and synthesizers through your local music stores, musical equipment manufacturers, computer software manufacturers, computer-accessible bulletin boards, and public seminars. Furthermore, there are a number of publications on the market that address the subject on a regular basis.

Secondly, if you are not a musician, you will have to study existing music closely to learn how musicians do what they do. Specifically, you'll need to train your ear to hear drum patterns, bass lines, chord changes, solos, and harmonies. On the market today are a number of excellent ear-training courses as well as individual instrument teaching aids on cassette. Otherwise, you'll have to use the services of musicians until you can handle the various instruments yourself.

A Closer Look at Synthesized Tracks

Now, let's look a little closer at the subject of using the technology to produce excellent specs and demos without hiring a large number of musicians. Let's assume you've pulled together a basic MIDI studio package with some analog gear for singing and mixing down your specs. The salesperson from your local music store has helped you get the equipment set up and running in your converted basement control room, measuring a whopping eight feet by ten feet.

Let's also assume that you either play an instrument or that you have studied music enough to know what parts the various instruments play. Or, you have connected with a musician who can translate your musical ideas to the equipment for you. Even marginal players like myself are capable of adding the various instruments to accompany melodies from nonmusicians.

Either as a musician or as a nonmusician, you would have written the jingle in basically the same way as if you didn't own a small studio. You would have begun with the general idea and followed the process of shaping the lyrics, timing the passages, and roughing out the melody. However, with the help of your new studio set-up, the fun begins.

The Drum Machine. With your rough chart in hand (or perhaps just your lyric sheet and a rough cassette of you warbling the melody), you sit down in front of your new drum machine or your synthesizer work station that contains drum sounds. Let's assume you're writing a light-rock piece. You select the tempo that fits the time requirements for the jingle, let's say 120 bpm (beats per minute). You listen to the metronome or click track from your drum machine and begin experimenting with a bass (kick) drum beat. If you've never played drums or studied how drummers play, you could spend hours just finding a sensible rhythm for your drum pattern. That's why you either need to become familiar with what parts all instruments play or connect with someone who is already conversant.

You then continue building your drum kit (full set of drums) pattern adding the snare, perhaps on beats two and four, high hat, ride and crash cymbals, and any other percussion sounds you think fit the piece, for example a shaker, tambourine, bells, hand claps. You can add intro's, fills, pick-ups, breaks, anything a live drummer can and would do.

As you follow your rough chart from introduction to verse to chorus to bridge, you actually "write" the drum kit pattern on the drum machine as slowly or as quickly as your ability allows. Remember that you can change any beat in any measure at any time. You can move parts around, add or subtract measures, speed up or slow down, error correct, erase, and start over. You can even add a more human feel to the drums once you're finished so that it doesn't sound so mechanical.

Most of the modern digital drum machines give you a wide selection of drum sounds. You should experiment with different sounds for each instrument (drums, cymbals, and percussion pieces) until you find the sounds you like. Once you have your kit together, you simply store the pattern in the memory. This pattern will dictate the overall structure for the entire jingle, so you should double- and triple-check the timing to make sure you have your :60, :30, and :10-second lengths covered.

The Synthesizer. Most synthesizers have factory preset sounds covering every imaginable (and sometimes unimaginable) sound. Some synthesizers allow you to modify these sounds and create your own original sounds. Some synthesizers (sampling synthesizers) can record any sound and reproduce it digitally. You can even "play" sound effects as if they were musical instruments.

As you move from programming your drum kit to adding the other instruments for your spec jingle, you must be selective. Time is your enemy, though many synthesists enjoy spending time looking for sounds and experimenting for hours. After you've got the drums in the can (programmed and stored), you build the rest of the rhythm section just as if you were working with live musicians. You'll add the bass, the piano or keyboard, and perhaps a guitar pattern.

You have a choice of dozens of basses from traditional string bass to electric Fender bass to electronic synth bass sounds. Just as you choose the sounds for your drum kit, you select the type of bass sound you think will be appropriate for the style of the jingle you've written. Just as composers write chord progressions and patterns for harmony instruments, bass players play patterns for bass lines. The notes fit the chord pattern and the style of music, and the bass line supports the entire instrumental movement. Again, the beauty of working with a synthesizer is that you can experiment with the bass pattern and sound much more quickly (and much less expensively) than with a live player.

The same is true for the piano and guitar tracks. You can lay down a piano pad (a simple rhythm pattern that supports the melody of the jingle) and then add some synthesized guitar fills to round out the rhythm section. You'll find the choices for piano and guitar sounds are as varied as the bass sounds. As I mentioned in chapters 3 and 4, think simplicity when producing the rhythm section. Establish the feel of the jingle with the drums and bass and then add the piano and guitar to harmonize the melody. The newer synthesizers and programs allow you to "humanize" the feel of the track to eliminate the old mechanical effect so common with the earlier tools.

Adding Scratch Vocals. Once you've experimented with your rhythm section parts and have chosen sounds that best fit your musical idea for the jingle, it's best to transfer the music to tape. Rather than adding all of the sweetening instruments, (the horns, strings, reeds) at this time, you should shift your emphasis to working on the vocals while listening to see how your melody fits with the music you've produced thus far.

For most specs, it's better to keep the instrumental track simple and put emphasis on the vocals. If you feel the need to add sweetening, do so after you've finished working out the vocal harmonies so that your sweetening instruments don't get in the way of the vocals.

If you're doing head arrangements (making up vocal or instrumental parts on the spot rather than writing the parts out), you will find that transferring the instrumental parts to tape will save you time and help expand your creativity. When you can hear yourself (or your vocalist) singing the melodies and harmonies against the track on tape, you can work on parts more easily.

Once you've nailed down all the vocal parts, you can simply save these scratch vocals (rough vocal parts recorded only as a guide for future singing) and return to the synthesizer to program the remaining sweetening tracks.

Sweetening the Spec. Again, the emphasis here is on simplicity. Although you want your spec or demo tape to sound as polished as possible before presenting it to your customer (see chapter 5), you don't want to overload the track with so many sounds that the song gets lost in the shuffle. Overproduction accounts for as many lost jobs as poor melody and lyric writing. If a track sounds busy—too many things going on at once—the listener may miss the point. So, take your cue from the hit songs of the past twenty years. Add the instrumental parts that support, not detract, from the melody.

If you're writing a light-rock piece, a rhythm section with a few tasty horn punches is sufficient. If it's a country jingle, perhaps a steel guitar slide here or there or a classy harmonica line will work. For ballads you'll undoubtedly use a soft string section, and for strong rock, a screaming lead guitar line pulled back in the mix will add the flavor you need. Again, don't overdo it!

The beauty of working in your own small studio is that you have complete control. No one is looking over your shoulder and you don't have to watch the clock as closely as if you were renting time in someone else's facility. However, the downside of working from your own studio is that you can become immersed so deeply in projects that you lose sight of the objective—making money.

Turning Your Small Studio into a Money-Maker

If you've invested hundreds or thousands of dollars into your own production facility you should consider the possibility of using it for projects other than your own jingle work. Depending on how much time you can devote to running your business (full time or part time), you can advertise your services to the general public and actually sell time in your studio. Be sure to consult with your attorney to determine the legalities of operating a commercial enterprise from your home.

Let's return for a moment to your studio set-up and add some ideas that may modify your equipment selection.

Voice-Overs. One of the most lucrative areas for making money in the small studio business is doing commercial voice-overs, recording announcers for radio and TV commercials. If you have set up your studio with a small multitrack reel-to-reel machine, a mixing console, some good monitor speakers, and a high-quality mixdown machine, you can compete for this business.

You will need to add an isolation booth for the announcers and you'll probably have to invest in a better headphone monitoring system than you would need for just doing spec jingles. Also, since most voice-over business comes from advertising agencies – those same people you're selling your jingles to – you should be available to work during regular business hours instead of part time at night or only on weekends. Consequently, you should consider adding a little more sizzle to your set-up, even if it's at home.

For example, if you're operating from your basement or garage, you should add a private entrance so that when your customers arrive they are not walking into your home to get to the studio. Secondly, you should make the environment look as professional as possible. Instead of folding chairs and a card table, buy or rent office furniture and set up a conference room. Add the typical office decorations – potted plants, fancy pictures, a comfortable sofa and matching chairs, new carpeting – anything that says, "We're professionals even though we work at home!"

Once you've made these modifications, you can begin pitching ad agencies and other businesses for their production work. Doing voice-overs is relatively easy work, much easier than doing jingles. Here's how it works.

An advertiser wants to produce a radio or TV commercial with or without music and sound effects (SFX). The advertiser writes the copy (script), hires an announcer(s), and books studio time. Upon arrival at the studio, the producer (representing the advertiser) gives the copy to the announcer(s) who reads the script for time and interpretation. Once the producer is satisfied with the read, the recording engineer rolls tape and the announcer records the copy. Sounds familiar, huh? If the producer requests it, the engineer adds needle-drop music (prerecorded music leased through production libraries) or sound effects and mixes the spot down to the half-track machine. That's it. It's that quick.

Now, please understand that many voice-over sessions are more complicated. Multiple sound effects, multiple voices, intricate edits, synchronization with video, all these elements add to the complexity. However, most of the day-to-day recording of voice-overs is fairly straight ahead: an announcer, some copy, a little music, and you're done.

Nonbroadcast Recording. We live in a world in which people use cassette tapes to sell and promote almost anything. Companies describe the features and benefits of their newest gizmo on cassette. Motivational speakers expound for hours about "being the best you can be" on cassette. Religious groups sell sermons, furnace manufacturers sell furnaces, and even the people who deliver your phone books have listened to cassettes to learn how and where to put your directories so you don't break your neck tripping over them on your porch. I call this mass production of cassettes "disposable audio." Tapes that serve primarily one purpose, one play, and goodbye.

Over the years I have recorded an amazing number of nonbroadcast programs. You can find this type of business fairly easily. You can contact manufacturers who are introducting new products and need to communicate specific product information to their dealers around the country. Any sales-oriented firm that trains its representatives can use cassettes. Any company doing work that requires a consistent performance of tasks are potential customers, such as medical equipment technicians, hospitals, computer software manufacturers, industrial material handling, educational services, real estate training, sales training, equipment operations, and personnel management.

Any company or organization that needs to tell

its story to a large number of people to attract new business, new members, or new associates can use your services. You can contact local, state, or federal government agencies that produce "how to" pamphlets or promotional materials and convice them to put their information on cassette. The list is endless!

Finding Nonbroadcast Business. How do you find these companies, agencies, and organizations? A good place to start is a reference you probably have in your home right now—the telephone book. Look up "associations" in the yellow pages. You'll find medical, governmental, manufacturing, fraternal, religious, service, sales, and social groups listed. Look under "athletic," "business and trade," "clubs," "environmental," "fraternities and sororities," "human services," "labor," "political," "professional," "veterans," "youth," and "social service" organizations. They're all there waiting for you to contact them with a letter or a phone call.

Contact attorneys, architects, builders, and chiropractors. Send a letter to every manufacturer listed in your state's "industrial manufacturing directory" that your state department of commerce or your local Chamber of Commerce should have. Use your imagination and think about what companies might be able to increase their sales, improve their productivity, or inform the public about their good works through simple cassette recordings. Don't forget professional public speakers, comedians, freelance writers, and announcers looking for a new radio job.

But What Do I Tell These People? If you have set up a small recording studio and want to make money while you build your jingle business, you tell your potential customers that you can provide them with the best recording service in town for the best price. You show them how they can make more money, spread their message, accomplish whatever it is they want to accomplish simply by recording their messages in your studio. You show them how easy it is, how inexpensive it is, and how much fun it is to record. In short, you sell them on yourself, first, and on the concept of recording, second.

A sample preapproach letter you might send out to generate some sales leads for your studio appears at the top of the next page.

An even better idea is to produce a short cassette tape demonstrating exactly how your potential customers can use cassette tapes. It's a little more expensive to send out cassettes, but it makes sense, doesn't it? If you're trying to sell businesses on using cassettes to improve their businesses, and you're in the recording business, why not show them what you mean with a cleverly written script? Here's an example of a script you might produce, complete with sound effects, to attract new business for your studio.

Sample Script

(Opening music: hard-hitting, big-sounding)

Announcer: (big, booming voice) From out of the Midwest . . . the sound of the nineties! Rock Solid Productions presents . . . (music fanfare) "The Solution to Every Problem You've Ever Encountered!" (fanfare again).

SFX: (Telephone ring)

Character Voice: (Typical, annoying operator) Hello . . . hello . . . ah, who'd ya wanna talk to, huh?

Announcer: Ah, no one anymore, Goodbye. (SFX: telephone hangs up).

SFX: (Busy office sounds)

Announcer: (frustrated, pleading) . . . but all I want to do is get an estimate on repairing . . .

Character Voice: (Interrupting) . . . I'm sorry. That's not my department, you'll have to come back next week . . . (fades out)

SFX: (Factory sounds)

Character voice: So, ah, you see, ah, I've got, I mean, we've got the best equipment at the lowest price, and besides that, I can get you a discount if you'll order three today.

(Vignettes end abruptly. Complete silence.)

Announcer: (Sincere, convincing) If you need to communicate to your customers, your staff, your employees, whether at your home office or around the world, put your message on cassette and watch your sales grow (SFX: slide whistle), improve your employee's telephone skills (SFX: telephone ring), help your retail sales force improve customer relations (SFX: applause), in short, accomplish any goal you would normally have to write about. Do it effectively with cassettes.

(Light music fades in)

Announcer: It's sad but true; people don't read as much or as carefully as they used to. But they do listen to cassettes—at home, in their cars, in the office, on vacation. People listen and learn. (Insert

Date

(Inside address)

Dear Mr. ________________,

Have you ever wondered why people just don't seem to understand your business (group, club, organization, message, etc.)? Did it ever occur to you that today, unfortunately, people don't read. Now, I don't mean they can't read; they simply don't take the time to read everything they should read carefully.

There is a solution to both of these problems: your need to increase sales (membership, donations, etc.) and the public's lack of attention to reading material.

The answer is: put your message on tape!

That's right. Technology has given us the means to record practically anything on cassette tape and deliver it to your potential customers (members, associates, donors, etc.) quickly and inexpensively.

People *do* listen to cassette tapes—in their cars, at home, while they're jogging or mowing the lawn. They listen and learn.

And they become your customers (members, associates, donors)!

Let me show you in fifteen short minutes how we can put your message on cassette tape for you. I'll be happy to stop by your office, at your convenience, or you're welcome to visit our studio to discuss how cassette tapes can help your business (club, group, organization, church) really grow.

Looking forward to hearing from you soon!

Sincerely,

xxxx

short excerpts of sales training, product explanations, motivational speakers, etc.)

Announcer: At Rock Solid Productions, we specialize in creating exciting, dynamic, and effective cassette programs on any subject, for any audience, for every budget. Contact us today and put some punch (SFX: fist hitting a punching bag) into your next program. Rock Solid Productions (phone number).

If you owned a business that needed to reach out to more customers and explain your products, services, and ideas, wouldn't a letter or a cassette like one of these intrigue you? Wouldn't you at least want to hear a little more about the subject? Out of a hundred contacts who receive your letter or tape, you should be able to sit down with at least three or four and discuss a recording project. So, the more contacts you make, the more leads you'll get. The more leads you get, the more sales you'll make.

In chapter 5 you learned how to present your jingle-writing services. You learned what to say, what not to say, and what to do during the preassignment meeting and the presentation meeting. Pitching your studio services is similar; however, when talking with nonadvertising customers, you should assume that they know little if anything about the recording business. This fact can work to your advantage.

I will not rehash all the selling techniques I discussed in chapter 5, but I will point out some important information you should present to your nonadvertising customers when selling your recording studio services.

Selling the Sizzle. The old sales pro's maxim, "Sell the sizzle, not the steak," still applies today, especially when you're pitching a customer who is unfamiliar with the studio business. Selling the sizzle means stressing the novelty of recording, showing the customer how he or she can participate in the production, and doing a little razzle-dazzle about the technology.

Once you have an appointment to present your ideas for doing a cassette program for a new customer, you should start doing your homework. Find out as much about your customer's business as possible. Go to the library; do some research. If you're going to talk with a manufacturer of furnaces and air conditioners, learn as much as you can about the products before the meeting. Pick up the jargon of your customer's industry. Try to imagine the audience your customer shoots for every time the cassette rolls.

Here's a typical preassignment meeting with an industrial account. You have a studio, you have connected with an experienced announcer who will work through you on a per-job basis, and you are a competent writer. Your preapproach letter has generated a sales lead with the public relations officer of a major furnace and air conditioning system sales organization. You've done your homework and you arrive at your customer's office five to ten minutes early to get a feel for the place.

Your customer, Mary, ushers you into her large, tastefully decorated office, offers you coffee, which you accept, and indicates a comfortable leather chair in front of her spacious, very expensive, mahogany desk. You soak up all of the surroundings and take note of the various advertising and public relations awards displayed prominently on the paneled walls.

The conversation begins.

Mary: Thank you for coming in today. Your letter intrigued me and I wanted to see what you had in mind that could help us, to use your words, "increase our sales dramatically." Frankly, I've never considered using cassette tapes before, so, well, let's just say I'm curious.

(What Mary is saying is, "You got my attention; now, sell me!")

You: Well, thank you for seeing me, and I appreciate the opportunity. We've been doing some research into what we in the recording business call, "the industrial market," because we believe, and our studies have shown, that companies such as yours can really take advantage of the new technology. For example, I think we can put together a dynamite sales presentation tape for all of your reps in the field . . . you have over a hundred and fifty around the country, don't you?

Mary: Why, ah, yes, that's right . . .

You: Well, what if these hundred and fifty sales reps could give the identical presentation to every single customer they encounter, every time, without fail, so that they cover all of the information you've been trying to get them to cover for years, wouldn't that be great?

Mary: It sure would. You can't imagine how many letters and phone calls I have to make every week to these people just to get them to try new ideas, to try and use the sales aids we give them. Which brings up the question, how is anything you give me going to change that?

You: I'm glad you asked. Suppose you bring all your sales reps in for a big meeting, wine and dine 'em, and then show them your new sales presentation manual, complete with flip charts and your new dynamite cassette. You make the meeting mandatory, and you really pull out the stops, go first class. After the meal you explain that the new approach *simplifies* the process of selling so that they can see more customers and make more money.

Mary: How do they do that?

You: Simple. We write and produce in our studio using one of our professional announcers a powerful cassette tape that goes step by step through both your furnaces, like your new Z95 high efficiency model, and your air conditioners. We describe the features and benefits exactly the way your top salesperson would, exactly how you folks here in the home office want them presented, and the field representative simply points out the features on full-color photographs of the units. The pitch is timed out to run no longer than ten to fifteen minutes and has a built-in close, something like, "now, if we can show you how, for as little as $62 a month, you can have the Z95 in your home, wouldn't you want to know?" That's how we can increase your sales dramatically.

Mary: That's good stuff. I see you've done your homework. Well, suppose we do this, this, ah, cassette, and the flip charts, and, uh, suppose the sales reps have little pet things they say, that they always say; what do you do about that?

You: Good point. Before we finish writing the script, it would be great to have the sales reps send in their ideas, you know, "your sales ideas can become part of the new (company) sales presentation tape." You might even offer them a bonus for every idea that makes it into the tape.

Mary: I see. That's good.

You: Furthermore, after the tape is done and out in the field, nothing stops the sales rep from adding information after he or she has played the tape. What we stress is that the tape supplements the sales rep's job, helps him or her. It doesn't replace the sales rep; it just makes him or her better. If you can, you might even supply each rep with a portable cassette player emblazoned with your company logo!

Mary: I like it! But, ah, how much is all this going to cost?

You: Probably a lot less than you're spending on long distance phone calls. Let's take a look at the cost items for this type of project. Oh, and so I don't forget, here is our sample tape that you may listen to at your leisure that demonstrates our announcers, our writing, and our production facility. And by the way, it would be great for you to come to the recording session. It's kind of like entering "Star Trek" control, but it's a lot of fun and I want to produce the tape exactly the way you want it.

You and Mary then discuss budgetary items based on your rates for studio time, announcer talent, master tape, and duplicate cassette copies.

Successful salespeople do several things extremely well. They know their products or services thoroughly, they do their research on new customers, and they listen very carefully to their customers. Let's analyze the conversation for the key ideas you should try to work into your pitch. Notice particularly how you try to pick up on Mary's questions, objections, and, at times, negativity.

Your first comments indicate that you have been doing some "research" and have determined that Mary's company can "take advantage" of the "new technology." This statement establishes credibility and includes intriguing words such as "take advantage," everyone loves to take advantage, and "new technology"—Ah, something new, huh? Furthermore, at the end of your first statement, you make a very specific reference to Mary's "hundred and fifty sales reps" that should indicate, as it does in this example, that you have done your homework.

Also, you use strong words when describing what you want to produce for Mary's company, i.e., a "dynamite sales presentation tape." You end the first statement with a question for which you already have an answer just to get Mary to nod her head in agreement.

Your second statement is both a question and the presentation of your "solution" to the problem of increasing sales for Mary's company. You ask, "what if . . .?" describing what you believe is a very favorable change in Mary's company's sales effort. The solution, of course, is for Mary to hire you to do the cassette tape.

Mary, being the astute professional she is, asks a question that she's been asking of herself or that she's been asked by her superiors, i.e, how are you going to fix this problem?

Listening carefully, you respond to Mary's question with the disarming, "I'm glad you asked that," and continue discussing in detail your solution to the problem, namely, call a "meeting, wine and dine 'em," and so forth. You then finish the statement with "they can see more people and make more money."

Here's the turning point in the sale. Mary either likes the idea or she doesn't. She either continues to pose objections or she sees the value in what you're saying and asks for more details. In this example, Mary takes the bait and asks for more details, "How do they do that?"

At this point, you're moving quickly toward your closing statement. Just prior to asking for the order (as we discussed in chapter 5), you use your research information to nail down your credibility and to personalize the project for Mary. "We write and produce . . . a powerful cassette tape that goes step by step through your . . . Z95 . . ." You use as many specifics as you can and point to the advantages of having the home office input as well as the top sales reps' input on the project.

Now, just as in the jingle presentation, you end your preclosing statement and stop talking. You haven't tried a trial close or a final close, but you've done enough to establish your credibility and to outline the project you have in mind for Mary's company. Your only task now is to field any final questions Mary may have, which she does in this example, and then move to the closing statement.

When Mary asks, "How much is all this going to cost," you know you're close to a sale. Mary isn't saying, "No, I don't think this will work," or "Yeah, but . . ." rather, she's saying, in effect, "If your price is fair, we'll do it."

Don't give a figure off the top of your head, even if you have one in mind. Instead, pick up on something Mary said earlier in the conversation, that she spends countless hours calling her sales reps around the country. Your initial answer to her question: "probably a lot less than you're spending on long-distance phone calls."

Prior to moving to the close and discussing the cost items, you inject one trial close, ". . . it would be great for you to come to the recording session." A little razzle-dazzle, but more importantly, you're talking past the sale.

Obviously, in real-life situations, Mary might ask dozens of questions, some of which you may not be able to answer. But in most cases, if you've sent out a clear preapproach letter, if you've done your homework, and if you listen closely, the sales meeting shouldn't take hours. It should go fairly smoothly. Either the customer likes you and what you have to say or he doesn't. Either he's interested in the project or he isn't. You'll know early in the conversation, and you can continue battling for the sale or simply leave your car and demo tape and exit quickly.

Just as with selling jingles, you won't close every nonbroadcast sale. But the more presentations you can make, the better you'll become at selling and knowing when *not* to meet with an account. It takes courage to say "no" when you think that going to a meeting is a waste of time. But after you've been burned by a few flaky noncustomers, you'll learn.

Selling Time to Other Musicians. Another market to consider approaching for business for your small studio are musicians. Though most synthesists have invested something approaching the national debt in equipment, many of them do not have recording facilities in which to work once they've programmed all their music. Also, depending on how much synthesizer equipment you decide to purchase, your studio may offer the nonsynthesizer player both the recording facility and additional instrumentation with which to complete a project.

Your competitive advantage as a small studio owner is that you can offer a high-quality service at a reasonable rate. You approach the musicians with the notion that recording does not have to break you—you don't have to mortgage the farm to get your songs on tape. You offer to work with them on a "personal basis" to "help them achieve their goals." Of course, before you roll tape and definitely before you let tape out of your studio, you collect your fees. I'm not cynical; I'm realistic.

How Do I Find Musicians to Use My Studio? Musicians are everywhere. Finding them is easy. Get a notice on all school bulletin boards and church bulletin boards, in school newspapers, church bulletins, local musician publications. Send a letter to each local night club inviting the musicians in to see your set-up. Put announcements on local music store bulletin boards. Here's a sample announcement:

> Attention All Serious Musicians
> Finally, you can get your music on tape without all the hassle and expense . . . get that *Big Studio Sound* at a *Small Studio Rate*.
> (your logo)
> We take your music seriously and we can help you produce the finest quality demo tape or finished product.
> (insert your equipment list here)
> Call us to discuss your next recording project.
> (your phone number)
> Professional recording for serious musicians.

Unless you don't mind people showing up at your home at all hours of the night unannounced, you should leave your address off your advertising materials. Force the people to call you for an appointment so you can qualify them on the phone before inviting them over.

When quoting rates, try to avoid selling on the phone. If possible, get the musicians to come in so that you may talk to them on your turf. You can also get a better feeling for how serious they are about recording their music and paying their bills. Once both sides feel comfortable with each other, you can begin to put together a package of services for their demo tapes, including studio time (set-up, recording and mixing, and editing and dubbing), outside talent (that you may be supplying), master tape, cassette copies, and any other requests the musicians have, such as extra equipment that you must rent for the session.

Most local bands prefer to think in terms of cost per hour or cost per cassette dub, so if possible, quote your rates for the whole package in terms of these smaller increments. It's easier for the band members to deal with.

Songwriters. Songwriters are another excellent potential market for your studio, especially those nonmusician songwriters. Even if you too are a nonmusician, you can produce demo tapes for songwriters that includes a fee for your friend, the synthesist, as well as your time and tape.

In most major cities you can find songwriter associations. Most of the groups publish some kind of a newsletter. A simple ad in the publication will bring you leads from songwriters trying to get their songs on tape and out to publishers.

Here's a sample ad:

> Songwriters' Special
> Demo three of your songs
> for less than $ ________.
> Price includes studio time, master tape, five cassette copies, and engineer. Comfortable, low-key professional studio. Call: ____________ for more information.

Once you establish your fee for this type of package, rather than selling time by the hour, you can add on musician fees, extra tape copies, extra time charges, and anything else that the writer requests above your advertised package. What you don't want to do is mislead the writers in any way. If you're setting a time limit on the production of the three songs, and you should, specify that time limit in the ad. When the potential customer calls and you determine that he or she is not a musician, you should be very open about what musicians charge for their demo services (even if you are the musician).

Once you begin a concerted advertising and promotion effort for outside business, your studio time will begin to dwindle. Make a point of setting aside enough hours in the day to continue your sales and production efforts on behalf of your jingle company. Don't overbook yourself. It's better to hire a freelance engineer to handle that late-night session so you can get some sleep prior to your big jingle presentation in the morning. You won't make as much money hiring freelancers, but you'll make something. If and when you're booking your own studio so solidly that you don't have time for outside projects, you'll either expand your operation or discontinue accepting outside work. And that, my friend, is a tough decision.

CHAPTER 8

The Check's in the Mail

Building a jingle business is like building any other business that sells intangibles. Since you are selling a product and service, writing and producing music, you should be ready for an extreme range of criticism. You will find people who are brutally honest about your work and those who hide their true feelings behind vague platitudes. You'll encounter people who will abuse your spec policy, who order dozens of tracks without qualifying their customers in advance and then fail to tell you why the jingle didn't sell.

You'll also encounter competition, often known, more often not. In the early seventies only a handful of people were producing jingles as the main thrust of their business. Today, literally thousands of people are active in this lucrative field. Consequently, prices have fallen for most local and regional projects. But that's not all bad. What the competition has created, however, is even more of a need to look and sound as professional as possible. The way the business community perceives you includes not only the way you sound on tape, but also the way you look on paper and the way you handle yourself in person.

In this chapter we will consider several important elements that will help you manage your own jingle company. We'll examine the questions of incorporating your company and choosing a name for your company. We'll uncover sources for new business and explain how to work with direct accounts. I'll take you through our Musical Production Agreement that helps guarantee payment and nails down all of the important details of the deal between your company and your customer.

Another important skill you'll need to develop is the ability to talk with your customers. In this chapter I'll give you some examples of techniques I've used successfully over the years. We'll also consider what you should charge for your services, how to license and copyright your work, and how to sell the music you've written for one customer to another customer in a different market.

To Incorporate or Not to Incorporate

To compete effectively in the marketplace today, you must have a plan of attack, and part of your plan should include establishing a business structure through which you will operate. If you're going it alone, a sole proprietorship may be the answer. If you're teaming with other people, you might consider a partnership arrangement. But if you're really serious about getting into the business, you might want to establish a corporate structure.

In the jingle business, as in any other, problems occur that you cannot foresee and that may result in litigation—a lawsuit. You may be completely innocent of any wrongdoing; nonetheless, when you open your mail one afternoon, you might find waiting for you a notice of action. Someone is suing you!

If for no other reason than to avoid being sued personally, I recommend you set up a corporation under which you operate as a jingle writer/producer. You should retain an experienced attorney to draw up and file the paperwork for you, and, unless you're going into business with other people, your partners, you should hang on to all of the stock in your new corporation.

Your attorney will explain in detail sole proprietorships, partnerships, and corporations and which structure best fits your personal situation. Each structure has advantages and disadvantages, particularly with regard to tax and other liabilities. Establishing a corporation, for example, can help you protect your personal assets in the event someone does sue you. With the corporation between you and the public, you can shield (protect) your personal assets. When you operate as a corporation, a disgruntled customer or other aggrieved party must sue your corporation, which is a separate entity. They may also file against you personally, but if you have been operating as a corporation, you limit your liability to the assets of the corporation.

On the other hand, if you choose to set up a partnership, each of the partners may be liable for the actions of the other partners. It is often the case, for example, that if one partner incurs a debt on behalf of the partnership, even without the knowledge of the other partners, the others may still be liable for the debt.

Even if you have employees, you may operate as a sole proprietorship and simply file a Schedule C on your personal federal tax return. A sole proprietorship is an individual running a business in its own name or as a d/b/a (doing business as). As a sole proprietor, you may be liable personally for anything you or your employees do in the name of your company, but if you are the only employee, this structure may be the easiest for you to manage.

An alternative to sole proprietorships and partnerships is the corporate structure. A regular corporation is a separate entity. It has its own tax reporting requirements. A subchapter S corporation differs from a regular corporation in that the profit or loss from the business flows back through the stockholders' personal tax returns. The subchapter S corporation does not pay taxes; the stockholders do. Also, subchapter S corporations provide the stockholders with the corporate shield and many of the accounting advantages of regular corporations.

You should not make the decision about which structure to use for your business hastily. It will be one of the most important business decisions you make with ramifications years and years later. I urge you to follow the advice of your attorney and accountant before you start operating your business.

What's in a Name?

Before you hang out your shingle as a jingle writer/producer, you must have a name for your new business. You might opt for the simple "use my own name as the company name" decision, as I have, using Stone Music Company as a d/b/a under our corporate name, Sundiblu, Incorporated. Or, you might try to position yourself in the marketplace by choosing a name that says more about what you do. I apologize up front to any existing companies who may be using any of these suggestions: "The Jingle Factory," "(City) MusicWorks," "Budget Music Projects," "Ad-tunes," "Monster Tracks," "Award Winning Jingles," "(Nickname of your city) Jingles," "Fasttracks." The possibilities are endless.

Here are some questions you should consider when choosing a name:

Is the name easy to remember?
Does the name tell the audience who I am and what I do?
Is the name creative in and of itself?
Is the name distinctive?
Will the name be appropriate in five or ten years?
Will customers corrupt (shorten) the name?

Choosing a name for your jingle company will be another important but difficult decision; therefore, try *not* to make the decision in haste, as I did years ago. I had to make a decision expeditiously when I dismantled a large recording studio and became a small production company with a very small studio. Without giving it much thought, I chose the name Stone Music Company, a rather unimaginative appellation. "Oh, I get it Stone. All you could think of was your name. That's real imaginative," my potential customers must have been thinking. The name is easy to remember, but it doesn't reveal much creativity.

Also, the name of my company did not and does not define precisely what we do. It doesn't give potential customers much to go on when they hear the name or see it in print. Do we sell musical instruments? Do we sell records? Do we give guitar lessons? Do we sell sheet music? These are some of the questions people have asked when calling our office for information.

The name, Stone Music Company, doesn't tell our customers that we write and produce commercial music. If your forte is writing hard-driving, contemporary music, perhaps your name should reflect your talent. "Killer Tracks," "Monster Music Production," or "Contemporary Musical ID's" might work. But keep in mind that you may have to live with the name you choose for a long time. Just think how silly "Groovy Tracks" or "Dynamite Disco Jingles" would sound today.

Finally, you should be careful to avoid choosing a long, complicated name. "The Music Emporium Song Crafters and Jingle House Recorders" might be a creative and interesting name for your business, but can you imagine answering the phone with all of that? And will your customers remember all of your long name? No, they'll probably shorten it (corrupt it) to "song crafters" or "music emporium" out of necessity. The advertising community shortens and abbreviates nearly everything. So, be careful.

Sources for New Business

In chapter 5 you learned how to find customers for your jingles and how to sell them. I mentioned that one of the best and most accessible sources for finding your customers is the phone book, the yellow pages. In addition to the yellow pages, I also mentioned that you should visit your local library and look at the publication, *The Red Book of Advertising Agencies*, published three times a year by Standard Rate and Data of Chicago, Illinois. You'll find this book in the business section or reference section of the library. The *Red Book* contains detailed information on hundreds of ad agencies around the country. You'll find listings that include the names and phone numbers of broadcast producers. Some agencies list the names of their accounts; others simply identify the percentage of business they place in print, broadcast, billboards, and direct mail.

The *Red Book* provides a wealth of information on larger agencies around the country, but be aware that not all agencies are listed. Usually the agency must handle at least one regional or national account to qualify for inclusion in the book. Also, the information you'll find in the book is supplied by the agency, not by the publisher. Due to the rather hefty price tag, check out the *Red Book* in the library before subscribing.

Another excellent source for new business is your state's Department of Commerce. Most state departments publish various directories about companies doing business within your state. The listings are varied and you'll be able to find important information about companies that could become your customers. What you're looking for is a company that has a large number of employees, that holds regular large-group meetings or conventions, and that believes in promoting itself to its customers, dealers, or agents. These are those nonbroadcast or industrial accounts I mentioned earlier.

Any company that holds large meetings to introduce products or services to its staff, its dealers, or its agents could use your services as a jingle writer, or more precisely, a composer. Your understanding of commercial music will help you convince the marketing director or promotion director of a large company to hire you to compose a corporate theme song for the company's next convention.

For example, we had a call a few years ago from a national moving company. Their advertising director wanted us to produce a theme song for his annual agents convention to be held in Lake Tahoe. He wanted a two- or three-minute song promoting a new service his moving company was introducing to its agents. He was going to hire dancers and singers to perform the song to an instrumental version played on tape at the opening ceremonies of the convention, but he also wanted a singing version of the song to play at other times during the convention to emphasize the new service to the agents.

We wrote and produced both versions of this convention theme song and his show worked perfectly. The singers and dancers rehearsed with our tape and charts (printed music), and the customer played our full sing version of the song through the hotel's PA system at various times throughout the convention. It was such a success that the following year this same customer came back to us to do another convention theme song and a complete jingle package for broadcast use.

There are literally thousands of conventions and meetings going on *every week* in this country. Local and state convention bureaus know who these groups are and will be happy to provide you with names, addresses, and phone numbers of the people in charge. All you have to do is contact them well in advance of their meeting dates.

Your search for businesses that hold conventions or large group meetings may take you out of your city to larger metropolitan areas that have large convention facilities. Once again, checking with your local library, you should look for business publications for large cities, the weekly or monthly tabloids geared specifically to business. In these publications you'll find listings for most of the large meetings and conventions being held in the various cities. A few phone calls to the publication or the specific organization should lead you to the right contact person.

Radio station account representatives (known as time salesmen in the trade) are another excellent source for jingle assignments. Station reps are always looking for new accounts to get on the air. You might offer a special deal on doing spec tracks these reps can use to help land their new accounts. The station rep approaches a potential advertiser and offers an "introductory package" of spots (commercial announcements) on his or her station. Then the rep says, "and we've even got this dynamite jingle for you!" Nothing sells better than the advertiser hearing its own name sung on the air.

So, contact the sales manager of each local radio station and work out a deal to provide spec jingles for all the sales reps' new accounts. You might work up a sliding scale for pricing your work that encourages the reps to sell more of your tracks. For example, if you normally charge $2,500 per original jingle, consisting of a rhythm section and one singer, you might work out a deal that allows the station to buy five tracks from you at an average cost of $1,750 per track—a quantity discount. Depending on the cost of the track, the station may use the jingle as an enticement to get the advertiser on the air. Therefore, they simply throw in the jingle at no charge. Once you've developed a large library of jingles that you can use as relyrics (instrumental mixes to which you can add new lyrics), you can really wheel and deal with the stations.

Direct Accounts

Working directly with an advertiser rather than through an agency can be frustrating. I've done it dozens of times and it's always difficult. A local or regional direct account is usually a very small business that cannot afford to hire an ad agency or a very large company that wants to save the cost of an agency and do the work in-house. In either case, you usually encounter people who think about the dollars first and the service you're offering second. They don't all want you to work "cheap," but they are not always familiar with the cost of production because they are involved in only one account—their own.

Nonetheless, you should contact as many direct or in-house accounts as you can find. Some will not pan out, but others can be quite profitable. Finding these accounts is not difficult. Simply watch, listen, and look at all the advertising going on in your market. You'll see TV ads with the owner or manager of the company acting as talent on the spot. You'll hear them on the radio. You'll see less than professional ads in the newspaper and magazine. As you begin building your account list—potential customers for whom you hope to work—you will identify which agencies handle which accounts. When you find an account without an agency, you create a new card for the "direct accounts" section of your roll-over file.

You approach these direct accounts in exactly the same manner as you would approach any agency with one exception: most agency people understand the game; most direct account people do not. I've had owners of small businesses expect me to select, place, and pay for their air time as part of the cost of their jingle! They assumed that that was part of the deal which, of course, it wasn't. I've had direct accounts expect two, three, often four different versions of music for the price of one version. I've had accounts ask me to change the music entirely—the arrangement, the melody, the rhythm, even the lyrics—*days after* the recording session. As you discuss the jingle project with a direct account, you should be very careful to explain precisely what they are getting for their dollars.

What to Say to Potential Customers

In chapter 5, I discussed the research you need to do to build your files of potential customers. I took you through some sample phone calls, an initial demo presentation meeting, and your first spec presentation. What you learned was that being successful in the jingle business means not only being able to write good jingles, but also developing effective selling skills.

Selling is both an art and a skill. You can develop selling skills by reading about selling, practicing techniques, and listening to other good salespeople in action. Developing your artistry as an effective salesperson, however, will take months, if not years. Selling is both presenting yourself and your services and asking for the order. If you do a good job of presenting yourself and your services, asking for the order should be easy. Let's take a closer look at selling yourself and your services.

Returning to the ABC Flowers account, let's assume you want to approach XYZ Advertising, which has just won the ABC Flowers account. You found out that bit of information by keeping up with the business activity in your town, reading the business publications, the business sections in the local papers, and following the business gossip you hear all of the time from agencies, producers, musicians, singers, and announcers. You want to go in and pitch XYZ on using your jingle house for the new ABC jingle.

Again, assuming that you've never met with XYZ to discuss jingle production, you have an immediate opening statement. You've done your homework, so you know who is in charge of buying jingles at XYZ. You call the agency and ask for the broadcast producer by name.

When the producer comes on the line, you introduce yourself and offer congratulations on XYZ's winning the new account. Here's how the conversation might go.

Bob: This is Bob Smith; may I help you?

You: Mr. Smith, thank you for taking my call. My name is Rick Jones and I represent Triple Threat Jingles. I just wanted to call and congratulate you and the agency on winning the ABC Flowers account. I know you must be pleased.

Bob: Thank you. It's a very nice account for us.

You: I may be a bit premature, but I've been working on a musical idea for ABC Fowers and if you have just a couple of minutes, I'd like to stop by and play it for you. Do you think you'll be using a jingle for the ABC radio and television spots?

Bob: Possibly. Ah, we've talked about it. Ah, what's the name of your company, again?

You: We call it "Triple Threat Jingles" because we try to offer three times the service the other houses offer. Would you have a few minutes tomorrow morning, Mr. Smith?

Bob: Ah, well, what'da'ya have? . . . ah, you've already written something for ABC?

You: It's just an idea that I think you might like. I've got a terrific musical hook and a great slogan that might fit ABC. Of course, it's just an idea, but it would be a good way for me to show you how we work and what we can do for you. What's a good time to stop by?

Bob: Well, OK. Why not? Why don't you come by, oh, say, ten o'clock tomorrow morning? That OK?

You: Perfect. Let me give you my phone number in case you need to call. It's 555-4444. My name's Rick Jones, and I'll see you at ten tomorrow morning!

Bob: OK, fine. See you then.

Obviously, you may run into roadblocks. Bob may already have a jingle. He may have used one to win the account. Or he may be doing all of his production work with another jingle house. Or he may simply not be receptive to seeing you. You must be able to think fast and answer any objections the customer may throw at you. Here are a few examples:

#1 Bob: Well we aren't ready to talk jingles right now. Call me back in a month or so.

You: Fine. I'll be glad to. So that you'll have your own copy, why don't I drop off a demo tape tomorrow so you can hear what we can do. Would that be OK with you?

#2 Bob: Well, ah, we always use Bellow Productions out of (city) for our jingles.

You: They're a fine company; I'm familiar with their work. I think you'll be pleasantly surprised at our originality and our pricing structure. It'll just take a couple of minutes and I promise I'll be on my way.

#3 Bob: This is not a good time to talk about music. We've just landed the account and we just started to put together the campaign for next year. They're not doing any broadcast till next year.

You: I certainly understand. Would it be OK with you if I simply dropped off one of our new demo tapes so you'll have a copy of your own when you're ready to talk jingles? Would that be all right?

#4 Bob: We contract all of our music production through Jim Johns; he's a local contractor who handles everything for us. Let me give you his number; hold on.

You: Thank you very much for Jim's number. I'll drop a copy of our new demo tape off at your office so you'll have your own copy.

It's difficult to know in advance every reaction you'll get, especially as an unknown vendor calling on a potential customer. What you don't want to do is become a pest. If the customer isn't responding to your questions, thank him for his time and move on to the next customer. You won't get in the door every time. However, if you offer your potential customer an idea, something different, something provocative that no one else has offered, you might break through and get the appointment.

Staying on top of the market is the best way to beat the competition in the door. If you know what's going on, what agencies are handling what accounts, you'll be ready to spring into action the moment the time is right. And the more calls you make, the more quickly you'll know when the time is right.

The Production Agreement

In chapter 5 you learned how to present your jingle demo, how to ask for assignments, and how to present your spec jingle. You also learned about what happens when the customer rejects your spec. But what happens when you hear those magical words, "It's a 'go' for final!" You've got a sale!

Without exception, you should always get a signature on the dotted line of your contract before you spend a dime producing a jingle. Having all the details of your agreement spelled out prior to the recording session will save you untold headaches down the road. Our lengthy production agreement has been quite useful throughout the years in heading off any problems due to miscommunication. It also contains a section that helps you get your money faster. Let's examine the production agreement, section by section.

Music Production Agreement

(Your company name) (hereinafter "Licensor") hereby agrees to produce and record a musical composition (hereinafter "Jingle") for licensing to (advertiser's name), (hereinafter "Customer") in each version circled below:

1. ballad	9. R/B
2. bluegrass	10. MOR
3. big band	11. pop
4. classical	12. march
5. country-rock	13. polka
6. country-western	14. jazz
7. dance	15. hard rock
8. dance band	16. other__________

and customer agrees to accept, pay for and limit use of the Jingle all in accordance with the terms and conditions of this Agreement of which this first paragraph is also a part.

This first paragraph of your agreement explains that you are responsible for producing and recording the jingle for the customer in the musical style(s) indicated and that the customer will pay you for your work. It's important to identify the musical style(s) so that there is no question of what kind of music you were going to produce for the customer. This definition helps eliminate the "I thought you were going to do a country-western jingle for me" comment from a customer who tries to avoid payment.

Article I: PAYMENT

1. The Total Price for the production, recording and the license to use the Jingle is $ __________.

2. Customer shall pay without notice the Total Price to (name of your company), (address of your company), (or at such other place as Licensor may direct in writing) in installments as follows:

a) One-half (½) of the Total Price upon Cusotmer's execution of this Agreement;

b) One-half (½) of the Total Price upon delivery of the Jingle.

3. Past-due installments shall accrue interest at the rate of eighteen percent (18%) per annum, compounded monthly.

In the event of default in payment of any said installments when due, the entire unpaid balance of principal and interest shall become due and payable immediately, without notice, at the election of the Licensor. No delay or omission on the part of the Licensor in the exercise of any right or remedy shall operate as a waiver thereof, and no single or partial exercise by the Licensor of any right or remedy shall preclude other or further exercise thereof or of any other right or remedy. Acceptance by Licensor of any partial payment shall not constitute an extension of the time periods herein set forth nor shall it constitute a waiver of default.

The maker(s) and endorser(s) jointly and severally waive demand, presentment, protest, notice of protest and notice of nonpayment or dishonor of this note, and each of them consents to extensions of the time of payment of this note.

Article I covers the question of how much and when your customer will pay you. Notice that the very first point in the article is the Total Price. This figure represents every dollar you plan to spend producing the jingle and your entire profit, including your licensing fees. Before you set your price, be sure you've covered all possibilities.

Also, notice that in point two, the customer agrees to give you one-half (or whatever percentage you choose) of your money up front, "upon Customer's execution of this Agreement." It's a polite but firm way to ask for your money. Also, the balance of the Total Price is due upon delivery of the jingle, not thirty, sixty, or ninety days later. Some customers may balk at signing your agreement because of this rather tight payment policy; however, if you want to make sure you'll have a chance of getting paid, stick to your guns, keep the clause in the contract. Fight for it.

Article II: PRODUCTION AND RECORDING OF JINGLE

1. Customer acknowledges that prior to signing this Agreement it received and reviewed a "Spec. Tape" or a "Demo. Tape" that provided a sample of how the Jingle in its unfinished form would sound. Customer's execution of this Agreement constitutes acceptance of the words, style, and version of the Jingle as set forth on the Spec. Tape or Demo. Tape, whichever was last received, except for the following changes

____

____

____

____

and that to complete the Jingle in a form acceptable to Customer, Licensor need only record the musical instrumentation and vocalization and produce the music mixes hereinafter specified.

2. In producing the Jingle, Licensor shall utilize the following instruments and vocalists:

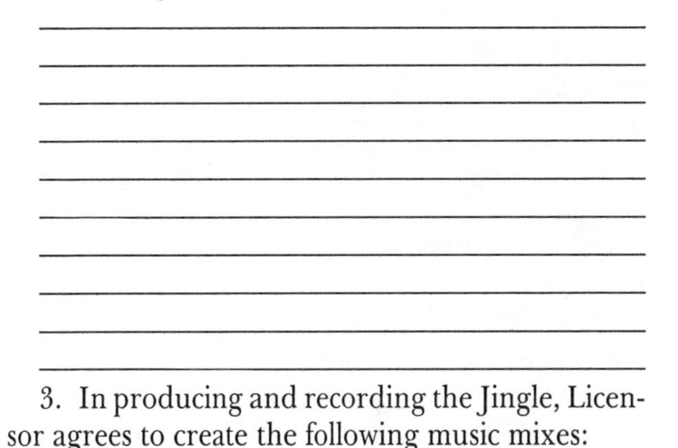

3. In producing and recording the Jingle, Licensor agrees to create the following music mixes:

____

____

____

____

4. Licensor shall provide ten (10) day notice to Customer of the date and place in (State) (as solely selected by Licensor) where the final recording of the Jingle is to occur. Customer shall have the right to attend the final recording session and may require reasonable minimal changes of the instrumentation, vocalization and music mixing of the Jingle. CUSTOMER AGREES THAT IF IT DOES NOT APPEAR IN PERSON OR BY AGENT AT THE FINAL RECORDING SESSION IT CANNOT AND WILL NOT REJECT ACCEPTANCE OF THE JINGLE FOR BEING NONCONFORMING TO THE TERMS OF THIS AGREEMENT.

5. Customer agrees that its acceptance of the Jingle at the final recording session *or* its failure to appear at the final recording session shall constitute acceptance of Licensor's tender of the Jingle in its final complete form.

6. Customer acknowledges that Licensor's obligation under this Agreement is limited to the production and recording of the Jingle for license to Customer. Customer agrees that it alone, and not Licensor, shall be responsible for entering into requirements for television and radio advertising in the designated market area.

Key points in this article include the notice that the

customer has heard and accepted the spec or demo tape as the rough version of the track and that you're simply going to record it in final form. That's important. If the customer wants to make changes in the jingle, he or she should do so prior to signing the Agreement so that everything is settled before moving on to the final. The spaces at the end of point one are for minor changes in lyrics or arrangements.

Point two identifies what instruments and singers the customer may expect to hear on the finished jingle. Point three identifies the number and kind of mixes you will produce for the customer as part of the jingle package. If the customer starts requesting dozens of extra mixes, you should not hesitate to bill for the extra time and tape.

I've found that points four and five help eliminate the possibility for nonpayment more than any other clause in the contract. By requiring attendance at the final recording session, you are able to get your customer's approval on the spot. If he or she doesn't show, he or she forfeits the opportunity of rejecting your final product. As long as you do what you're supposed to do under the terms of the Agreement, you should have a strong legal position from which to operate in the event problems arise later.

Article III: RIGHT TO USE OF JINGLE

1. Licensor hereby grants to Customer a license solely to use the Jingle for radio and television advertising in the following designated city, state, or national advertising market area:

____
____
____
____
____
____
____

2. The right to use the Jingle within the designated market area shall be exclusively with the Customer. Provided that, if the market area is designated by the name of a city, the use of the Jingle shall be limited to an area within a seventy-five (75) mile radius of the center of the specified city; that if the market area is designated by the name of a state, or states, the use of the Jingle shall be limited to the lawful boundaries of the specified state or states; and, that designation of a national market area shall limit use of the Jingle to the lawful boundaries of the contiguous forty-eight (48) states of the United States of America and the states of Hawaii and Alaska.

3. Customer acknowledges that Licensor specifically retains all copyrights, phonorights and publishing rights in and to the jingle.

4. With respect to any and all areas outside of Customer's designated market area, Licensor shall have the unrestricted right to sell, utilize or otherwise grant rights, licenses, interests or privileges in or to the Jingle.

5. Customer agrees that the license herein granted shall not become effective unless and until Licensor has received full payment of the Total Price heretofore set forth in this Agreement. Customer further agrees that none of its rights or interests in or to the Jingle may be voluntarily or involuntarily assigned, transferred or otherwise conveyed or encumbered, without the prior written consent of Licensor, and that the occurrence of any such event shall automatically revoke the license herein granted and Licensor shall retain all right, title and interest in and to the total price set forth in this Agreement.

6. Cable television and satellite television waiver. Each party acknowledges that due to the current practice and usage of cable television systems and satellite transmission of television programming it is possible that, beyond the control of either party, the Jingle may be broadcast from the designated market area to another market area that has not been licensed to Customer or that the Jingle (or substantially similar version thereof) may be broadcast from a market area for which Licensor has granted a license to another customer into the designated market area that has been herein granted to Customer. Each party hereby expressly agrees that the occurrence of either such events will not constitute an infringement by Licensor of the license herein granted to Customer nor a violation of the copyrights or other reserved rights of Licensor by Customer. Nor will the occurrence of either such events cause the designated market area to be either increased or decreased from the area specified in this Agreement.

This entire "right to use" article is loaded in your favor. What you're establishing is that you own the rights to the music you have created and that you are licensing the right to use this music in a specific area of the country for a specific fee. You are notifying your customer that you are retaining all other rights to the music and that you may choose to license the same music (though undoubtedly not the same lyrics) outside your customer's defined market area. Establishing this structure allows you to resell (relyric) your tracks in markets outside those already leased to your customers.

Article IV: ADDITIONAL WORK

This Agreement covers only the services, work product and license specifically described herein and the amounts, costs and fees specified herein cover only such described services, work product and license. If, after Customer's execution of this Agreement, any additional services or work product are requested or if any requested deviation from the described services or work product requires or results in additional work product or services, then an amount, as solely determined by Licensor, shall be added to the amounts, costs or fees originally specified herein with such amount of increase to be based upon the then prevailing standard rates of Licensor for such additional services or work product. Any such additional amount shall be added to and become part of the Total Price hereinabove set forth and shall be paid in equal installments at the time and in the manner specified for the unpaid installments set forth in Article I of this Agreement.

Article four is an attempt to reduce the amount of extra work your customer may request from you as part of the deal though the extra work is clearly not a part of the Agreement. If a customer asks for an extra dub or an extra mix, I usually go ahead and give it to him or her. However, if the customer starts requesting five or six extra mixes, perhaps another singer or a second set of lyrics, I draw the line, refer to the Agreement, and quote a price for the additional work. Once again, it's a tough call. If you are certain you'll get repeat business from a particular customer, you may decide to ignore the clause and do whatever it takes to satisfy him or her. I don't advise this kind of behavior, however tempting it may seem.

Article V: NOTICES

All notices provided for in this Agreement shall be in writing and shall be deemed to have been delivered upon deposit in the United States Mail, certified or registered, postage prepaid, to the last known addresses of the parties.

Article VI: ATTORNEY FEES AND COSTS

In the event that any party fails to comply with the provisions of this Agreement it shall pay or reimburse the party successfully enforcing this Agreement, the reasonable attorney's fees and costs incurred in seeking or obtaining compliance with this Agreement.

Article VII: COMPLETE AND BINDING AGREEMENT

1. Each party acknowledges that no representations of any kind, other than the representations set forth in this Agreement, have been made to it as an inducement to enter into this Agreement and that this Agreement constitutes all of the terms of the Music Production Agreement hereby entered into by and between the parties.

2. This Agreement shall be binding upon all of the parties and their estates, successors or assigns (if any) and heirs or legatees.

Article VIII: MODIFICATION OR WAIVER, APPLICABLE LAW, VOLUNTARY EXECUTION

1. A modification or waiver of any of the provisions of this Agreement shall be effective only if made in writing and executed with the same formality as this Agreement.

2. This Agreement and the rights of the parties hereunder shall be interpreted in accordance with the laws of the State of ________________________.

3. Each party, by the execution of this Agreement, acknowledges it is entering into this Agreement of its own free will and volition and that no coercion or undue influence has been used to cause him to enter into this Agreement.

Dated this ________ day of ________, 19________.

(Name of company)

By: ____________________________________

(title)

ACCEPTANCE

The customer hereby accepts and agrees to be bound by the foregoing Music Production Agreement on the terms set forth therein and, concurrently with the delivery of this Acceptance, is paying to Licensor the one-half (½) payment of the Total Price.

Dated the ______ day of ______, 19______.

____

(Name of Customer)
By: ______________________________
Title: ______________________________
Customer's Address: ______________________________
____
____
____

Customer's Phone Number: ______________________________

Articles five through eight are the standard clauses most attorneys include. They are rather self-explanatory. Notice that when the customer signs the Agreement, he or she is once again indicating that he or she will be delivering a partial payment to you. You should not have to ask for this payment; nonetheless, if it doesn't arrive with the signed Agreement, call the customer's attention to the problem. Don't roll tape until you have the payment in your hand (or better yet, until the check clears your bank).

What to Charge for Your Services

Probably the most often-asked question I get from customers and, unbelievably, from competitors is "what do you charge for your services." Though the simple answer is "as much as I can get," realistically, I have researched the local and national markets over the years, appraised my talent and facilities, and have simplified the business of establishing rates.

Since I have a small recording studio, I charge by the hour for studio time I sell to non-jingle customers. I quote a rate of $50.00 for one hour with a one-hour minimum. Depending on the project, I may choose to offer a discount for blocks of time booked. Through research I have found that comparable studios in my market average roughly between $20.00 and $30.00 per hour. The larger studios charge between $75.00 and $125.00 per hour. Despite our small set-up and limited amount of space and equipment, we've determined that positioning ourselves as the cheapest studio in town made no sense at all. Our experience in the business and our comfortable working conditions certainly account for something, and that something is a higher rate.

Furthermore, we do not want to cater to the struggling musician market; consequently, we charge what may appear to be a high rate for a studio of our size. But we operate under a very explicit principle: we do good work and we charge for it.

Since time, tape, and talent are our primary products or services to sell, we expect to make a profit on our tape sales. Simply put, we buy wholesale and sell retail. The markup is appropriate and consistent with both retail stores and other studios in our market.

Our charges for composing music range from very inexpensive to very expensive depending on the nature of the assignment. For small, nonbroadcast music projects we have charged as little as $500 for a :30-second synthesized bed. For large, national jingle packages in multiple versions with buy-out licensing (see Music Production Agreement), the figure quickly jumps into the five-figure area.

When pricing your jingle packages, establish a creative fee, an amount of money you want to earn on every project after you've paid all of your production expenses. For example, for every piece of commercial music you write and produce you may try to net (earn after expenses) no less than $1,500. Whatever your creative fee, you must add on all of your production costs including studio time, talent, and tape.

Here's an example of how to price a local jingle package that you write and produce in one musical version:

Creative fee	$1,500.00
Eight hours studio time	400.00
Six (6) musicians @ $100	600.00
Tape, reels, boxes, cassettes	75.00
Total Cost of Job:	$2,575.00

So, you might bid the job at $2,950.00 to give yourself a little extra budget for problems. As you prepare your bids for every project, the important ingredient is "how much do you want to net" per job or per hour? Once you've established that figure in your mind, the rest is relatively easy to compute. Be sure to add some extra dollars for those problems that may and often do develop in production. You'll find it's easier to explain how you saved your customer a few hundred dollars than to ask your customer for more money because of production problems.

If you are a nonmusician jingle writer, you will act in a capacity somewhat similiar to an agent. You will hire a composer, perhaps on a fee-per-project basis. You will hire musicians to do the work and you might act only as a producer on the project itself. It is perfectly acceptable for you to mark up (add in a percentage of the cost for yourself) everything you buy: the composer's fee and the musicians' (talent's) fee. If the composer charges you $1,000 for the composition, you should mark it up according to what you want to net and what your market will bear. If the musicians charge you $75.00 an hour or per jingle version, you should not hesitate to mark up their fees to your customer.

Your markup is your fee for all of the services you render. It's just like an agent's commission. Your customer simply agrees to the total price as you indicate it in your Production Agreement. He or she does not need to know the specifics. As a nonmusician you may make less money on each project, but you may be able to do more projects by jobbing out the composing to several different people.

A few other areas you need to consider when establishing a price for your work: travel time, meeting time, long-distance phone calls, shipping/handling charges, duplication costs, possible add-ons by your customers (see Production Agreement Article IV), and licensing (see Production Agreement Article III). For each of these areas you should not hesitate to charge a fee.

For example, if your customer wants you to make a series of long-distance phone calls on his or her behalf to talk with his or her client about the jingle project, don't hesitate to add these charges to the bill. If you have to make special trips to and from your customer's office for endless meetings with his or her client, add an amount to the total price as part of your creative fee. Determine what you think your time is worth and estimate the number of hours for such trips, phone calls, and meetings.

Licensing

In Article III in the Production Agreement, you see the "Right to Use" clause. As the creator of the jingle, you automatically own the copyright to what you've written. When "selling" the jingle to your customer, you are actually granting a license to use the jingle in a specific area of the country. You are actually not selling the music but rather leasing the jingle to your customer.

As you compute the total price for the jingle package, you should include a fee for additional market licenses that will become part of the total price. You should include a local buy-out license as part of the total price for the jingle without extra charge; however, if your customer wants to use the jingle in other markets outside his licensed local area, for example, for a chain of retail stores located in five cities, you should add a fee for each additional market. You can develop this market licensing fee on the basis of cities or ADIs (Areas of Dominant Influence). For instance, we currently charge $500 per ADI for additional market licenses.

Licensing is very important because it establishes ownership of the jingle, your customer's right to use the jingle, and your right to resell the jingle as a relyric outside your customer's license area. It's important to establish ownership of and right to use the jingle as part of your written agreement because federal copyright laws suggest that without such definition, in writing and in advance of production, your customer may rightfully claim ownership of the words and music under the "work for hire" provision of the statute. "Work for hire" means that your customer has hired you to write the jingle and owns the copyright on the work.

Registering Your Copyright

According to the law, the moment you create the jingle, you own the copyright, but to protect yourself, you should register your copyright with the Copyright Office at the Library of Congress in Washington, D.C. You should write to the Copyright Office and obtain form SR, which you will use to register the copyright for your jingles. There is a nominal registration fee and the form includes complete instructions on filing your copyright registration.

Licensing Organizations

The three major licensing organizations, ASCAP, BMI, and SESAC, collect and distribute royalty fees for songwriters. In recent years, these organizations have developed royalty schedules for jingles. If you are not already a member of one of these licensing organizations, you should contact each one and decide which offers you the most attractive programs.

The Relyric

I've saved the best for last. Throughout this book you've encountered the term "relyric" many times. I briefly describe the word in several places, but now I want to explain how lucrative the relyric concept can be.

Let's assume that you've written and produced the ABC Flowers jingle. Your customer, XYZ Advertising, is elated. Their customer, ABC Flowers, is so thrilled with the new jingle that they have increased their advertising budget to get the jingle on the air more often. Increasing the budget means more commission dollars to XYZ—that's why they're so happy!

You've issued a local buy-out license to XYZ Advertising as part of your Production Agreement (Article III). XYZ Advertising has the right to use the jingle in your city only for an unlimited time (in perpetuity).

One week to the day after delivering the ABC Flowers jingle, you get a call from an advertising agency in a distant city (outside the licensing area for the ABC jingle). The creative director describes a new account his agency has just landed. As he is talking, the ABC Flowers melody is running through your mind.

The creative director asks you if you can do a jingle for a small business with a very limited budget. You answer, "Of course we can!" The director begins describing a flower shop that needs to increase its in-town sales. The shop has moved to a new location near a large mall and is ready to go after new business. The owners want to . . . well, you get the picture. It's the ABC Flowers account all over again, on a smaller scale, certainly, but essentially, the same assignment.

You whip out your contact sheet and begin asking questions. While listening to the creative director's answers, in your mind you begin to fit the new flower shop's name into the ABC jingle.

You are on your way to producing your first relyric. Hanging up the phone, you race to your tape library, throw the :60 full sing mix of the ABC Flowers MOR version on your tape player, and pull out the original lyrics.

Writing feverishly, you substitute words and phrases from the new contact sheet for the ABC lyrics that you decide to drop. In less than fifteen minutes you've got: a new set of lyrics ready for singers! Of course, you can use any track for any customer as long as the music fits the customer's target audience. You don't have to use the ABC Flowers jingle just for flower shops.

Relyrics can be the most lucrative part of your jingle business. There are thousands of businesses that, for a variety of reasons, will not or cannot spend the money necessary to produce an original jingle. But they will spend a smaller amount of money for a relyric if you can create lyrics that fit the original melody.

Since you retain the rights to your jingles for all markets outside the original customer's area(s), you can and should market these tracks as often as possible. Though some agency people abhor "retreads," their term for relyrics, most astute advertising people understand the value of using an existing piece of music for a customer with limited resources.

If, for example, the original price for the MOR version of the ABC Flowers jingle (one of the three versions only) was $3,500 (your $1,500 creative fee plus $2,000 in production costs), you can save your new customer roughly 50% by resinging the track. You can price your relyrics much lower than your originals because you have limited production costs: singers, perhaps a musician or two, a little studio time, and tape. And keep in mind that you can relyric a track dozens of times and sell it all over the country, as long as you own the rights to music, protect each customer's market license, and have paid your talent on a buy-out, nonresidual basis.

GLOSSARY

A CAPPELLA: Singing without instrumental accompaniment.

ACCOUNT EXEC, ACCOUNT REP: Account executive or representative; the person in charge of sales on a particular account, working either for an ad agency or a radio or TV station; salesperson.

ACCOUNT: A customer or client represented by an advertising agency; or any customer or client of a jingle house (see also DIRECT ACCOUNT).

AD AGENCY: An advertising agency; a company that coordinates the creative development, preparation, placement, and review of advertising, promotion, and public relations for other companies (see also IN-HOUSE and HOUSE agency).

ADI: Literally, "area of dominant influence"; a geographic area that a radio or TV station's broadcast signal clearly covers; used to define geographic areas for determining advertising and licensing rates (see also MARKET and TERTIARY MARKET).

AIR TIME: Available time on a radio or TV station that an advertiser may purchase for commercial announcements.

ANALOG, ANALOG RECORDING: In simple terms, recording information on magnetic tape rather than into a computer's memory (see also DIGITAL).

ANSWER: In lyric writing, a line that repeats another lyric line or in some way expands upon an idea established in another lyric line; usually sung by background singers (see also ECHO).

ARRANGING, ARRANGEMENT: Creating various instrumental and vocal harmony parts to accompany the melody and lyrics of a song or jingle in any desired style of music (see also ORCHESTRATING and SCORING).

ARTCARD: A printed or typeset piece of artwork used in TV production, usually white lettering on a black background or black lettering on a white background; used to superimpose printed information on a TV commercial.

AVAILS: Literally, "availabilities"; specific increments of time (e.g., :30, :60, :90) available for purchase by an advertiser on a radio or TV station to promote the advertiser's products or services.

BACKGROUND VOCALS, BACK-UP SINGERS, BG VOX: The supporting vocalists or vocal background harmonies sung by several vocalists.

BED: The part of the jingle containing only the instruments, not the singers (see also OPEN-CLOSE, DONUT, and TAG).

BOOK, BOOKING: Hiring a performer for a recording session or reserving time in a recording studio, e.g., "I need to 'book' time in the studio for next Wednesday" or "make sure you 'book' a tenor for the session."

BOUNCE, BOUNCE TRACKS: Combining musical or vocal parts by rerecording two or more recorded tracks on a multitrack machine onto one or more tracks of the same machine; this process enables an engineer to use more tracks than originally scheduled without losing a significant amount of audio quality; also called "Ping-Ponging" tracks.

BPM: Beats per minute.

BREAK, BREAK POINT: Commonly used to describe the note at which a female singer switches for "chest voice" to "head voice" (see also CHEST VOICE and HEAD VOICE).

BRIDGE: In jingles, the part of the song offering a change in melody (countermelody) and lyric, allowing the listener's ear to rest; the section that breaks the monotony of the verse-chorus-verse-chorus structure; often is the first part eliminated in the mix to create longer instrumental beds.

BROADCAST QUALITY: Any recorded material suitable for broadcasting over commercial stations or networks.

BUMP: A short vocal line injected into the mix of a jingle to create a dynamic vocal effect (see also SPIKE).

BUTTON: A short, usually three-to-five-second, instrumental and/or vocal performance, usually a slogan or musical ID (see also STINGER).

BUY-OUT: An agreement indicating that a customer has paid the full amount for the use of a product or service and that no other payment shall be due (see also RESIDUALS).

CALL: Hiring a performer for a specific job; also refers to the specific time for a recording session, e.g., "you have a nine o'clock 'call' tomorrow morning" (see also BOOKING).

CAMPAIGN: An advertising campaign; a fully defined advertising program designed to promote a company's products and services through various media; a total advertising effort as opposed to a single advertising schedule of, e.g., radio and TV commercial announcements or newspaper ads.

CASSETTE-BASED MULTITRACK: A cassette recorder capable of synchronizing multiple tracks of material recorded at different times (see also MULTITRACK).

CHART: Music and lyrics for a jingle written out in musical notation; also, an individual instrumental or vocal part written out (see also LEAD SHEET, PARTS, SIDE, SCORE).

CHEST VOICE: Commonly used to describe the sound produced by a female vocalist when singing in the lower part of her vocal range; a fuller-sounding voice with most of the sound being produced from the chest rather than from the throat and heat (see also HEAD VOICE).

CHORUS: In jingles, the part of the song that contains the most important lyric information, e.g., the slogan, the musical and lyrical hook.

CLICK, CLICK TRACK: An electronic metronone that musicians and singers hear and follow but that the engineer erases from the final recording of the jingle; usually just the drummer hears the click track in his or her headphones so that he or she can keep the rest of the musicians in time and on time.

CLONE: See MULT.

CO-OP MONEY: Funds supplied to an advertiser by a manufacturer of a product to help defray part of the cost of advertising the manufacturer's product.

COMMERCIAL ANNOUNCEMENT: An advertisement on radio or TV, purchased in time increments of :10, :15, :30, :60, :90, or :120 seconds (see also SPOT or SPOT ANNOUNCEMENT).

CONTACT SHEET: A form that a jingle salesperson fills out with a potential customer collecting factual and creative information regarding the production of a jingle.

CONTROL BOARD: Mixing console.

CONTROL ROOM: In a recording studio, the talent performs in the "studio" and the producer and engineer do their work in the control room that houses the mixing console, tape machines, outboard effects, and other pieces of recording equipment; the two rooms are isolated from one another.

COPY: Written advertising material; the words an announcer says during a radio or TV commercial announcement; the words rather than the artwork in any advertisement, electronic or print.

COUNT-OFF: The band leader's or section leader's method of getting all musicians to start playing at the same moment; the count-off is usually a two-bar or single-bar count in the meter of the song; e.g., in a 4/4 time signature, the drummer would count two-bars of four, "one, two, three, four, one, two, three, four," and the musicians would start playing on the next beat.

COUNTERMELODY: An alternate melody used to break the monotony of repetitious themes or motifs or to accent and expand upon a musical theme; countermelodies are often used in background singing or as the melody of the bridge (see also BRIDGE).

COVER: Simply, the ability of a singer, musician, or announcer to sing, play, or speak the parts as written; e.g., "can you 'cover' that?" Also, a term used to define the performance, either live or recorded, of another artist's work.

CREATIVE DIRECTOR: The person in an ad agency responsible for management of all creative work in the agency.

CREATIVE FEE: An amount of money a jingle writer earns above all other costs of production; the writer's net profit (see also NET).

CUT: Record.

D/B/A: Doing business as.

DEMOGRAPHICS: Defining people in terms of socioeconomic status, age, interests, occupation, neighborhoods, or any other identifiable characteristic that enables an advertiser to tailor its message accordingly.

DESK: Mixing console.

DIGITAL, DIGITAL RECORDING: In simple terms, recording information into a computer's memory rather than on magnetic tape (see also ANALOG).

DIRECT, DIRECT BOX: A device that permits a musician to connect his or her electronic instrument into the mixing console; as in "going direct" rather than connecting the instrument into an amplifier and miking the amplifier; this process reduces the amount of noise transferred during the recording process.

DIRECT MAIL: Advertising materials sent to potential customers defined as a group demographically; any type of mass mailing of advertising materials.

DIRECT ACCOUNT: A customer or client not represented by an ad agency (see also IN-HOUSE and HOUSE agency).

DONUT: A jingle mixed so that the singing is heard at the beginning and at the end only, with an instrumental section in the middle; the instrumental section is called the "bed" (see also OPEN-CLOSE).

DOUBLE: 1) A single musician who plays two different instruments, as in, "he plays clarinet but he doubles on sax"; 2) also, to duplicate an exact instrumental or vocal part (see also MULT, STACK, and CLONE).

DRIVE TIME: Morning and afternoon time periods on radio stations during which commercial announcements cost the most amount of money because the stations have the highest numbers of listeners; usually identified as 6:00 a.m. to 9:00 a.m. and 3:00 p.m. to 6:00 p.m.

DRUM KIT: A set of drums usually containing a combination of snare, bass, floor toms, ride toms, cymbals, and high hat.

DUB: 1) The process of making copies of recorded material; 2) a copy of a master recording (see also DUPE).

DUMP: Erase.

DUPE: A dub.

ECHO: 1) In lyric writing, an echo is a line that repeats a lead vocalist's line but is usually sung by background singers; 2) technically, an electronic or physically delaying of an audio signal to produce a doubling effect of an instrumental or vocal part.

EDIT: To cut and reassemble pieces of recorded information; often editing is a physical cutting and splicing together of magnetic tape, but electronic editing occurs without such physical movement.

EQ, EQUALIZATION: Simply, tone control; more precisely, the process of cutting or boosting the various frequencies of any sound.

FALSETTO: Commonly used to describe the sound produced by a male singer when he sings above his normal voice range; the falsetto voice is artifically high and thin, but often serves to add a distinct flavor to background vocal group harmonies.

FATTEN: The process of making an instrumental or vocal part thicker sounding by doubling or tripling the parts either with additional musicians or singers or by recording several passes of the same musicians or singers performing the same parts (see also DOUBLE).

FEED, FEEDS: Sending an audio signal from an instrument or a microphone to another piece of electronic equipment, e.g., to a mixing console, recorder, outboard effect, etc.

FILL, FILLS: Short instrumental passages, often improvised, to round out an arrangement; a producer or arranger may ask professional studio musicians simply to "fill at bar 18" instead of writing out a part.

FINAL: The finished recorded project ready to broadcast (see SPEC and DEMO).

FLAM: A drum beat performed by hitting both sticks on a drum at roughly the same instant with one stick slightly delayed from the other.

FLIGHTS: Buying blocks of advertising time for commercial announcement on radio, usually grouping spots together rather than simply running commericals on a daily basis.

FORMAT: The type of programming a radio station uses, e.g., Top-40, MOR, Easy Listening, AOR, Adult Contemporary, Country-Western, R & B, Beautiful Music, etc.; usually refers to the type of music the station plays.

FREE-LANCE, FREE-LANCER: A person who works on a "per job" basis not as a regular employee of a company, as in "free-lance writer" or "free-lance artist."

FULL SING: A jingle mixed so that the singing is heard throughout the entire piece of music.

HALF-TRACK MACHINE: A professional two-track or stereo recording machine that records its two tracks on the full width of the quarter-inch tape; differs from consumer machines (quarter-track) that frequently are designed to record two tracks in one direction and two tracks in the opposite direction.

HAT: High hat cymbal.

HEAD VOICE: Commonly used to describe the sound produced by a female vocalist when singing in the upper part of her vocal range; a thinner, brighter-sounding voice with most of the sound being produced in the throat and head rather than from the chest (see also CHEST VOICE).

HEAD ARRANGEMENT: Making up vocal or instrumental parts on the spot, in the studio, not prior to the recording session.

HEADPHONE MIX: The balance of instruments and singers as heard through the performers' headphone in the studio; e.g., talent may request to hear a different "headphone mix" than the producer is listening to.

HOOK: Both lyric and a melody; the hook is the main lyrical and musical theme of the jingle; it is short, memorable, and, ideally, quite original; when all else is removed, the listener should be able to recall the hook.

HOUSE AGENCY: An advertising agency or advertising department established within a company serving only that company's advertising needs (see also IN-HOUSE AGENCY).

ID: Identification, as in "musical ID."

IN-HOUSE AGENCY: An advertising agency or advertising department established within a company serving only that company's advertising needs (see also HOUSE AGENCY).

IN THE CAN: Recorded.

IPS: Inches per second, the speed at which a tape recorder/player is running; in professional studios, most recording is done at high speeds, 15 or 30 ips; most mixdown is done at either 15 ips (masters) or 7½ ips (dubs).

ISOLATION, ISOLATION BOOTH: For the purpose of controlling individual recorded information, the separation of various musicians, singers, and announcers from one another; also, the separation of control room and studio; an isolation booth is simply a small, soundproof room in which an individual or small group performs.

KEEPER: A good take; an acceptable recording, as in "it's a keeper!"

KICK: Bass drum.

LAY DOWN, LAYING DOWN: Recording.

LEAD VOCAL, LD VOX: The solo vocalist's part, usually singing the melody of the jingle.

LEAD SHEET: The music of a jingle written out including the melody notes, the accompanying chords, and the lyrics; lead sheets do not include instrumental and vocal arrangements.

LEADER TAPE: Nonrecordable plastic or paper tape used to separate individual mixes from one another on a reel; sometimes imprinted with timing marks.

LICENSE: The right to use a copyrighted piece of music granted by the owner of the copyright (licensor) to the user of the music (licensee) for a specified period, in a specified market (geographic area), in a specified manner (broadcast or nonbroadcast).

LOGO: An insignia for a company; a piece of artwork symbolizing a company's name, often a trademark.

MARKET: A city or town; a geographic area; an area of a state or region of the country, often defined in terms of "the area of dominant influence (ADI)," which means a geographic area clearly covered by a radio or TV station's broadcast signal (see also ADI and TERTIARY MARKET).

MEASURE: A division or section within a piece of music marked by vertical bars.

MEDIA BUYER: The person in an ad agency responsible for buying advertising time on radio and television stations and for buying space in newspapers, magazines, trade publications, and billboards for the agency's customers.

MIDDLE C: Not only the actual note on a piano keyboard, but also a reference point from which various instrumental and vocal ranges are identified, e.g., "she sings two octaves above middle C."

MIDI: Musical instrument digital interface; the facility for connecting various electronic instruments together enabling one musician to control a vast number of instruments at one time.

MIX: To blend recorded instrumental and vocal performances together to achieve a desired balance of all musical parts. .

MIXING CONSOLE: An electronic device that permits a recording engineer to control and distribute the flow of audio signals to and from various pieces of equipment, such as microphones, recording machines, electronic musical instruments (see also CONTROL BOARD and DESK).

MODULATE: Changing the key of a song within the song; e.g., modulating from A up a half-step to B flat.

MULT: Precise duplicate recordings of the same instrumental or vocal parts, used to "fatten" or thicken the sound of the part (see also DOUBLE, STACK, and CLONE).

MULTITRACK: A recording machine that permits the storage of audio information on individually controlled channels or tracks; often, configured in 2, 4, 8, 12, 16, 24, 32, or 48 tracks, each separate and controllable by a recording engineer; permits the recording of music and vocal performances at different times rather than only at one time.

NAME DROPS: The process of singing new customers' names into an existing jingle for relyrics or syndication (see also RELYRIC and SYNDICATION).

NEEDLE DROP: Prerecorded music used for producing commercials, as in "dropping the needle" on a recording as opposed to composing and recording a new piece of music for the commercial.

NET: Simply, profit, as in "how much did you net on that job?"

OPEN-CLOSE: A jingle mixed so that the singing is heard at the beginning and at the end only, with an instrumental section in the middle; the instrumental section is called the "bed" (see also DONUT).

ORCHESTRATING, ORCHESTRATION: Creating various instrumental and vocal harmony parts to accompany the melody and lyrics of a song or jingle in any desired style of music (see also ARRANGING and SCORING).

OUTBOARD, OUTBOARD GEAR: Individual pieces of electronic equipment used for audio signal processing; usually connected temporarily to the mixing console by the recording engineer.

OUTDOOR, OUTDOOR ADVERTISING: Billboard advertising.

OVERDUB: Recording additional instrumental or vocal performances to previously recorded material.

OVERHEAD: The total amount of money needed to pay all fixed costs of business on a monthly or yearly basis, including rent, utilities, salaries, and any other ongoing, identifiable costs.

PAN, PANNING: The placement of all parts of a recorded program in a stereo perspective, from far left to far right; e.g., the engineer may pan the strings far left and far right to give the effect of the strings surrounding the rest of the band.

PARTS: Individual instrumental arrangements taken from the complete musical score, e.g., a "part" for the first violin.

PARTS: Separate musical arrangements for individual instruments or singers; also for instrumental sections or vocal groups (see also SIDES).

PASS, PASSES: The number of times a part or a section is recorded; one recording equals one pass; two recordings equal two passes, etc.

PIANO PAD: A simple piano chord pattern played as accompaniment for other instruments or singers.

PICKUP: Beginning a song or jingle, or a section of a song or jingle, prior to the downbeat of a measure; e.g., beginning on beat four of the preceding measure.

PING PONGING TRACKS: See BOUNCE.

PITCH, PITCHING: To present a sales message to a potential customer; as a noun, the "pitch" refers to the presentation (see also PRESENTATION).

PLAYING THE CHART: Playing the music as written without improvisation or ad libbing.

POSITIONING STATEMENT: A slogan; a concise, public pronouncement of an advertiser's competitive advantage over its competition; an attempt to create in the customer's mind a uniqueness about a company's products or services (see also SLOGAN and POSITIONING).

POSITIONING: To analyze an advertiser's products or services and to define a competitive advantage, a uniqueness, something that sets the advertiser's products or services apart from its competitor's products or services (see also POSITIONING STATEMENT and SLOGAN).

POSTPRODUCTION: 1) Additional work or use of recorded material after the final recording session; e.g., using a jingle package as the soundtrack for a television commercial is postproduction; 2) in video production, the term "post" refers to all work done to a film or video after the initial shooting schedule is completed – e.g., editing, animation, postproduction scoring (adding music after the film is shot).

PREPRODUCTION: Planning for all facets of the recording process – composing, revising, making copies of charts, arranging for talent and studio time, etc. (see also POSTPRODUCTION).

PRESENTATION: The meeting during which a salesperson offers his or her company's ideas and materials to the customer (see also PITCH).

PRINT SHOP: 1) A printer; 2) an advertising agency specializing in creating printed advertisements rather than broadcast advertisements.

PRINT: Newspaper and magazine advertising, as in "print advertising."

PRODUCER: The person in charge of controlling all elements of a creative project, including hiring talent; booking studio time; collecting the creative parts, e.g., musical scores, artwork, storyboards, etc.; coordinating schedules with customers; filing contracts; paying talent and studio fees; making final decisions on the acceptability of creative performances; and delivering finished projects to customers.

PUNCH IN: Allowing a performer to begin recording a part at any place other than the beginning of the song; PUNCH OUT, logically, means ending the recording of a part at any place other than the ending of the song; "punching in and out" is used to correct small errors in performances when all other performers have finished recording their parts without error.

QUALIFY: Analyzing potential customers to determine legitimate interest in and ability to pay for a production.

QUICK MIX: A blending of recorded instrumental and vocal tracks for study by the producer prior to the final mix for use on the air (see also MIX).

RECORDING ENGINEER: A person responsible for placing instrumental and vocal performances on magnetic tape or disk; a recording engineer operates all of the studio equipment such as microphones, mixing consoles, tape and disk machines, and outboard effects gear.

RECORDIST: Recording engineer.

RELYRIC: Writing new lyrics to fit an existing jingle for sale to a new customer in a different market.

RESIDUALS: Payment of fees for services or products on an ongoing basis; usually applies to payments made to musicians, singers, actors, and announcers for use of their recorded performances beyond a specified period.

RESOLVE, RESOLUTION: The sense of completion of a melody line; the feeling that the line or song has concluded.

RHYTHM SECTION: A small ensemble of instruments, usually comprised of a bass, a guitar, a keyboard, and drums; in multitrack recording, the rhythm section is normally recorded first; the sweetening instruments are recorded after the rhythm section (see also SWEETENING).

RITARD: Ritardando (Italian), meaning to hold back or slow down the tempo of the song.

ROLL TAPE: The command given by the producer to the engineer to start the recording process.

ROLL TIME: The amount of time required for videotape machines to achieve full speed; usually one-half to one second.

ROLL-OVER FILE: A simple method of organizing customers and potential customers into groups to help a jingle salesperson maintain regular sales contacts.

SAFETY COPY: 1) A backup duplicate of a master recording; 2) a special mixing of recorded parts so that additional recording may occur in the future.

SAMPLING SYNTHESIZER: A synthesizer capable of recording and reproducing any sounds in digital format; highly dependent upon the on-board computer memory.

SCORING, SCORE: Creating various instrumental and vocal harmony parts to accompany the melody and lyrics of a song or jingle in any desired style of music (see also ARRANGING and ORCHESTRATING).

SCRATCH VOCALS: Recording a vocal track to use only as a guide for musicians or singers, not to be used as a final recording; scratch vocals are usually erased prior to or immediately after the final vocal recording sessions.

SECTION: A grouping of instruments from the same family, e.g., trumpets and trombones, violins and violas, all the reed instruments; also, refers to any group of related instruments being recorded at the same time.

SEQUENCER: A dedicated computer that stores audio information digitally for use in producing songs and jingles; usually connected to or controlled by a synthesizer.

SESSION PLAYERS: Musicians who have experience playing in recording studios.

SIDES: Another term for individual instrumental arrangements taken from the musical score, e.g., a "side" for the trumpet.

SIDES: Musical parts.

SIGNED OFF: Having a customer initial or sign a document indicating the customer's acceptance of the contents of the document, e.g., "signing off," or accepting, the lyrics of a jingle.

SLATE: Recording identifying information at the beginning of jingle indicating the name of the project, the date, the take, the position of the jingle on a specific reel of tape, and anything else the producer wants to include; also, the electronic means for recording such information, e.g., a microphone which, when activated, sends a signal directly to all tracks of all recording machines.

SLOGAN: An advertiser's motto, summary statement of products, or services; statement of competitive advantage; a short, cleverly worded expression about an advertiser's business that an advertiser hopes becomes universally associated with its products or services (see also POSITIONING STATEMENT).

SOCK: High hat cymbal.

SPEC: A speculative assignment, one for which there is no financial compensation for work performed; applies to writing, instrumental, vocal, arranging, or any other talent performing work on a project without compensation; also, "spec" refers to the actual speculative recording itself as in "here is our 'spec' for the project."

SPIKE: A short vocal line injected into the mix of a jingle to create a dynamic vocal effect (see also BUMP).

SPLIT TRACKS: Mixing instrumental parts of a jingle onto one or two tracks and vocal parts onto one or two other tracks for the purpose of creating additional mixes outside the original recording studio; often used in syndication jingles when vocal parts must be modified frequently with name drops.

SPOT, SPOT ANNOUNCEMENT: An advertisement on radio or TV, purchased in time increments of :10, :15, :30, :60, :90, or :120 seconds (see also COMMERCIAL ANNOUNCEMENT).

STACK: See MULT.

STINGER: A short, usually three-to-five-second, instrumental and/or vocal performance, usually a slogan or musical ID (see also BUTTON).

STORYBOARD: An artist's rendering of the various scenes in a TV commercial indicating visual and audio information to be created.

STUDIO: 1) A recording studio; 2) the room in which the talent performs (see also CONTROL ROOM).

SWEETENING: Adding additional instrumentation to a previously recorded song or jingle; usually the addition of orchestral sounds to a four-piece rhythm section (see also RHYTHM SECTION and OVERDUB).

SYNC, SYNCH: To link up various parts of a performance to other parts of a performance as in "in sync."

SYNDICATION: Simply, the process of selling the same advertising program, with minor changes, throughout the world.

SYNTHESIZER: An electronic device capable of producing musical and nonmusical sounds; often controlled by a piano-style keyboard.

TAG: A jingle mixed so that the singing is heard only at the end of the song; the instrumental portion of the song is heard from the start; the instrumental section is called the "bed"; also, a short part of the jingle, separate from the verse, chorus, or bridge, that often contains the advertiser's slogan or the musical hook.

TAKE: An attempt at recording.

TALENT RELEASE: A statement indicating that payment has been made for a performance, signed by singers, musicians, announcers, actors, arrangers, or anyone else who performs on a recording session (see also TALENT).

TALENT: Anyone hired to perform on a recording session, e.g., singers, announcers, actors, musicians.

TALK-BACK: A microphone located in the control room through which the producer or engineer speaks to the talent performing in the studio.

TARGET, TARGET AUDIENCE: A defined group of people for whom an advertising message is developed (see also DEMOGRAPHICS).

TELEMARKETING: Direct telephone solicitation of business using "live" operators or recorded messages.

TERTIARY MARKET: A secondary or less dominant geographic area in which an advertiser's message may be broadcast or delivered. "Tertiary markets" are those geographic areas immediately outside "primary" markets or those areas surrounding an ADI (see also ADI and MARKET).

TRACK: An individual channel on a recording machine onto which information is stored. Also refers to a finished jingle: "That track is really hot."

TRAFFIC DEPARTMENT: Radio or TV personnel responsible for scheduling spots on the air.

TUNE TO THE TRACK: The act of tuning one's instrument to a prerecorded piece of music, usually accomplished by having the piano player on the session record a single chord to which all other musicians and singers may tune at any time in the future.

VENDOR: Anyone selling goods or services to anyone else; in advertising, vendors are suppliers, such as printers, artists, announcers, actors, and jingle writers, who sell their work and materials to the agency for the agency's customer.

VERSE: In jingles, the part of the song that establishes the theme, the setting, the mood, and the story; often, the part that is eliminated in the mix to create longer instrumental beds.

VERSIONS: Related primarily to jingles, different musical styles, not different mixes of one musical style.

VIBRATO: Rapid but slight variations of a tone sung or played adding warmth, emotion, and expressiveness to the note.

VOX: Vocal, vocals.

WEAVE: A jingle mixed so that the singing is heard at various points throughout the song, alternating with instrumental portions, literally "weaving" the vocals in and out of the mix.

WILD TRACK: 1) The recording of a part during the final mixdown session of a jingle; wild tracking usually occurs because the producer has run out of tracks on the multitrack machine; 2) a wild track is also any single part, instrumental or vocal, that is recorded separately, usually on a separate two-track machine, and later is rerecorded onto a multitrack machine to line up with other parts.

APPENDIX A

Sales Promotion Materials

Here are a few sales promotion ideas. You may use materials like these to contact your customers on a regular basis—primarily to keep your name in front of them. Some of the materials may become part of your own company "promotion kit" that you give to each new customer at your first face-to-face meeting. Any material you send out or hand out should be printed professionally.

Promotion #1

(handwritten on the front of the envelope)

Here's that information on the $2,500 you can put in your pocket.

(the letter)

> Dear :
>
> Why spend $2,500 more for your next jingle package than you have to? Put that money back in your pocket! We can save you at least $2,500 on your next jingle package with our new [brand name] computer-based synthesizer. We can create fully orchestrated, dynamic new jingles for your clients for thousands less than you're used to spending.
>
> For your small-budget accounts or for your million-dollar spenders, check out our new demo "Sizzling Synthesis: Demo #1."
>
> You won't believe your ears! Call today for your free copy!
>
> [Your name and phone number]

Promotion #2

(Use preprinted three-by-five recipe-type cards, mailed in a small manila envelope imprinted with "Your Recipes for Success" or "Dieters Beware: Dangerous Recipes Inside!")

> Rocky Road Homemade Dessert
>
> Ingredients:
>
> 10 gallons of solid drums
> 32 bars of chocolatey bass line
> 1 cup of electronic piano pad
> 2 licks from electric guitar
>
> Directions: Mix ingredients in [name of studio] for two hours; blend in strong male or female singer; bring to a boil and dump eight mixes into the jingle package; place on client's cassette player for :60 seconds and be ready to dance.
>
> Serves millions
> Cost per serving: extremely competitive
>
> Call [your name/phone number] for details

Promotion #3

(on outside of envelope)

The Best Music in New York or L.A. . . .

(at the top of the page inside the envelope)

> . . . Is in [Your City]!
>
> If you think you have to go to New York or L.A. to get that "national" sound in production music, think again. [Your company] offers national-quality jingles at competitive pricing . . . much more competitive than you would imagine.
>
> Our new demo will open your ears to the possibilities right here in town . . .
>
> For Your Free Copy
>
> Call: [your name/phone number]

A Typical Follow-Up Letter

(sent after a demo presentation meeting with no assignment)

[Date]

[Inside address]

Dear :

It was a pleasure meeting with you and your staff on [date]. I was thoroughly impressed with your organization and the professionalism I sensed.

I just wanted to thank you again for the opportunity to present our new jingle demo. When one of your clients needs a dramatic, exciting, and memorable new musical identity, you know who to call. We're always ready to jump in and write our brains out for you!

Continued success!

Sincerely,

[Your name]

Follow-Up Letter #2

(sent to confirm a spec)

[Date]

[Inside address]

Dear :

Just a quick note to thank you for the opportunity to write a new jingle for [name of account]. We're excited about this assignment and we will be contacting you by [date] to arrange a convenient time to meet with you and your client.

In the meantime, we will work on the lyrics and music based on the information you supplied. If you think of anything else that will help us write the "perfect" jingle for [name of customer], don't hesitate to call.

Again, thanks for the assignment, and we'll be contacting you soon.

Sincerely,

[Your name]

Sample Bio

(experienced)

Sammy Sweettunes has been a performing musician for nearly fifteen years, and during that period he has written and produced hundreds of jingles for all types of customers.

Trained at the Quarter Note School of Music, Sammy majored in composition and performance, graduating with a 3.75 GPA on a 4.0 scale. While attending Quarter Note, he worked as a free-lance musician and as a copywriter for XYZ Advertising (Minneapolis, MN).

Of particular interest is Sammy's recent composition for BetchaCan Motors of Detroit, a new dealership that used Sammy's jingle to become the number one dealer in the Metro Detroit area in its first year in business.

Also, as a performing musician, Sammy brings continuity to his production, playing all rhythm section instruments as well as adding synthesized orchestral parts. His specs sound like finals!

To date, Sammy has written and produced nearly five hundred jingles for local, regional, and national accounts. He has won several first-place awards from the Ad Club and continues to produce all of his jingles in his own fully equipped 24-track studio known as "Sammy's Place."

Sample Bio

(inexperienced)

A 1985 graduate of Noteworthy University (Seattle) with a major in Mass Communications, Rachael Keys has spent most of the past five years working as a free-lance writer for the Noteworthy Press Newspaper. Her interest in advertising and her skill in composing excellent music and lyrics have led Rachael into the jingle business. RACHAELTUNES was founded on May 1, 1990, as a full-service commercial music production company.

Since graduating from Noteworthy, Rachael has completed courses in radio and TV writing, marketing, advertising, direct sales, media management, and creative writing. Also, she is a member of the [local Ad Club] and will serve as Treasurer next season.

Tom "Mr. Keyboards" Smith, an associate writer and producer with RACHAELTUNES, provides the musical accompaniment for Rachael's lyrics and melodies. Working from POSIT-TRACKS RECORDERS—a fully equipped MIDI studio—Rachael and Tom present an exciting, dynamic approach to music composition and production. Tom holds a degree in music composition from HalfRest College and has been the musical director for over thirty musical theater productions.

Sample Return Postcard

Include a postage-paid card along with your preapproach letter.

FREE! Yep, it's FREE. Our new demo tape is hot off the press, or, actually out of the duplicating machine. If you're looking for an incredible new sound for your customers, just fill out and mail this card.

Yes! I'd love to hear your new demo tape.

Name: ____________________
Company: ____________________
Address: ____________________
City, State, Zip: ____________________
Phone Number: (   ) ____________________

Handout or Mailer

Why Jingles?

If you need reasons to explain to your clients why they need jingles, these eight might help:

1. Jingles add instant identification. Throughout the entire commercial, the music is playing, hammering home the identity your customer is spending so much money to achieve. As the listener becomes more and more familiar with the music, hearing the jingle is enough to cause your client's name to jump into the listener's mind.

2. Jingles are "hummable." Everyone hums a tune now and then; and everyone will be humming your client's new melody, thinking about your client's store, products, and services. Jingles can be the most memorable part of any broadcast advertising campaign.

3. Jingles are attention-getting. With thousands of commercials airing daily, a dynamic new jingle will get the listener's attention quicker than any other element in the campaign.

4. Jingles are fun. Everyone loves music and your client's jingle could be the next local "hit song."

5. Jingles add consistency to your client's advertising. With the right jingle, your client will build name recognition, store traffic, and customer loyalty, faster, using any promotion you create. The jingle gives you a consistent vehicle with which to build your campaign and keep it going.

6. Jingles have a long shelf-life. Your clients will get more mileage out of their new music package than any other advertising tool, except their logos. Jingles live on and on even when other advertising materials get stale. If the musical style changes, updating the track is easy and relatively inexpensive.

7. Jingles are creative. You can really get your creative juices going when you work with us on developing a new musical identification for your clients. You can write the lyrics yourself or have us do it; if you're able, you can even write the song!

8. Jingles are affordable. With modern technology, having a fresh new jingle is no longer out of reach of even the smallest advertiser.

Let us show you how easy and inexpensive it can be to produce a new jingle package for all of your broadcast accounts.

Call: [your name and phone number]

APPENDIX B

Arranging

For years I've been using arrangers to translate my rudimentary approach to writing music into playable charts. I rely heavily on the expertise of these schooled musicians to improve my fundamental melodies and add harmonies that make sense and that give the jingle a more appealing sound.

For the past dozen years, Carl Smith, my arranger, and I have used the system I've just described: I "write" the melody and the lyrics for a jingle and supply Carl with a cassette recording of my warbling the song and banging on a guitar or piano. Here's what Carl does next.

First, he listens to my tape carefully several times, copying note for note the melody I'm singing. He even writes the "mistakes" I sing on this first draft of the melody. Drawing on his vast experience as a music educator in both instrumental and vocal music performance, Carl sings the melody to determine the most comfortable vocal range and adjusts the key of the song accordingly. For example, on the ABC Flowers jingle, Carl determined that an alto lead vocalist, singing in the key of A-flat would be best.

Next, Carl writes out a lead sheet in the original key (C Major), numbering the measures beginning with zero for the pick-up bar. He also creates another lead sheet in a comfortable key for orchestration (A-flat—see p. 118). Since each musical style has its own harmonic language (types of chord progressions), Carl pays close attention to style as he accepts or modifies the chords I have played on my rough cassette recording. Along the way, Carl calls me to verify the key change to avoid any talent booking problems, such as not being able to find the right singer for the voice range Carl has selected.

In our discussions, I've indicated to Carl that I would like to hear a solid brass section, a light string section with harp, two or three reed instruments, and, of course, our standard four-piece rhythm section. He knows that we will be doubling the four brass players, so he is able to write parts for four trumpets and four trombones instead of only two of each. Carl also knows that we will triple or quadruple the string parts, so he writes for a much larger section of players than we're actually booking.

Carl then lays out the score with the numbered measures working in concert pitch, nontransposed. Concert pitch is the actual sound of an instrument or voice. Certain instruments require transposed parts because the players do not read their parts in concert pitch. They read their parts in transposed pitch. So, to avoid mistakes in writing the arrangement, Carl writes in concert pitch and then transposes the parts for individual instruments. For example, in order for a B-flat trumpet to sound the note B-flat, the player reads the note C, a whole step up; therefore, all the other notes written for the B-flat trumpet must be transposed up a whole step from concert pitch. He pays close attention to details that could become serious and expensive problems in the recording studio. For example, because it is possible to change key and change rhythm from measure to measure or within measures, he notates key signature on all staffs, noting changes if and when they occur from page to page. He labels instrumentation (and vocal parts) on all pages making it easier to find parts during the hectic recording session.

Creatively, Carl tries to capture the flavor of the song as I have written it. He knows the style of music I've written and which instruments best fit the style. He also has become familiar with most of the players and singers we use, so he understands their strengths and weaknesses.

As you examine Carl's score for the ABC Flowers jingle, notice the simplicity yet the diversity of the harmony parts; the punchy brass parts to grab the listener's attention at the beginning of the jingle; the tasteful string lines, moving but not overpowering; and the gentle harp fills, sparse but effective in pulling the jingle into the MOR style we're shooting for.

Notice also the changes in the lead vocal part—the melody. Carl listened to my rough cassette recording and caught the subtle shifts in rhythm that transcend my simplistic stressed-unstressed notation. Also, notice the change of key in measure 29, the final chorus and tag. Carl modulates a full step from A-flat to B-flat to add excitement to the final ten seconds of the jingle.

Finally, find the background vocal parts and notice how Carl has improved upon my original ideas regarding placement of the answers and echoes as well as the specific notes (and harmonies) the background vocalists will sing. Again, the goal is to produce a full-sounding jingle without clutter from singers or instruments. We want our jingles to breathe; in advertising terms, we want some "white space" (the absence of any color, artwork, copy, photograph, etc., in print ads) in the song.

As you listen to jingles on the air, first study them in terms of melody and lyric. Then listen closely to the arrangement. The more you study other jingles, the easier it will be for you to develop your own skills as a composer.

ABC FLOWERS
:60 Full Sing
Key of A♭
Fast
A.S., arr. CES
Eve - ry week, eve - ry day, eve - ry min - ute, eve - ry hour, make your
life so spec - ial with beau - ti - ful flowers. In the hall - way, in the kitch - en, in the
bed - room, by the stairs, us - ing your im - ag - in - a - tion put flow - ers eve - ry - where.
Why not live it up a lit - tle bit and
bright - en your day? It's so eas - y you can do it, we're a 'phone call a - way.
Fill your rooms with blooms from A - B - C Flowers! No mat - ter
where you live get on the line call five fif - ty five, nine - ty
nine, nine - ty nine. A - B - C Flowers makes it eas - y for you to get
flow - ers to - day just a 'phone call a - way. Fill your rooms with blooms
from A - B - C Flowers. Why not
live it up a lit - tle bit and bright - en your day? It's so eas - y you can do it we're a
'phone call a - way! Fill your rooms with blooms from A - B - C Flowers!
© 1990 Al Stone

ABC FLOWERS (MOR)

Original Key, C

Al Stone, arr: CES

:60 full sing

2
Lead Vox
bed-room, by the stairs, us-ing your im-ag-in-a-tion put flow-ers eve-ry-where!
Why not live it up a lit-tle bit and
Bg. Vox
why not live it up a
Lead Instr.
2 Fl.
1 A. Sax
2 Trpts
Brass
2 Bones
B.G.
3 Vlns
pizz.
arco
Harp
Guitar
Piano
Rhythm
Bass
Drums
Eb
Ab
Bbm7
Eb7

3
12
13
14
15
16
Lead Vox
bright-en your day? It's so eas - y you can do it, we're a 'phone call a - way. Fill your rooms with blooms from A - B - C Flowers!
Bg. Vox
lit - tle bit live it up A - B - C fill your rooms with blooms from A - B - C Flowers
Lead Instr.
2 Fl.
a2
1 A. Sax
2 Trpts
Brass
punch in
2 Bones
1
2
3 Vlns
3
Harp
Fm Eb Db Cm7 Bb; Bbm7 Bbm7 Eb7 Ab
Guitar
Db
Piano
Rhythm
Bass
Drums

4
17
18
19
20
21
Lead Vox
No mat - ter where you live__ get on the line; __ call five fif - ty five, nine - ty nine, nine - ty nine. __
Bg. Vox
o-o-o
o-o-o
Lead Instr.
2 Fl.
1 A. Sax
2 Trpts
Cup Mutes
to open
Brass
B.G.
2 Bones
Cup Mutes
to open
1
2
3 Vlns
3
a2 pizz.
arco
pizz.
arco
Harp
Guitar
Ab
Ab/G
Fm
Ab
Cm7
Fm
Ab
Db 7
C
Piano
Rhythm
Bass
Drums

5
Lead Vox
A - B - C Flowers makes it eas - y for you to get flow - ers to - day just a 'phone call a - way. Fill your rooms with blooms
just a 'phone call a - way. fill your rooms with blooms
Lead Instr.
2 Fl.
a2
1 A. Sax
2 Trpts
Brass
punch in
2 Bones
3 Vlns
Harp
Guitar
Fm
Ab Cm7 Ab
C+7 Fm7
Db maj7 Eb
Fm Eb Db Cm7 Bb m7
Piano
Rhythm
Bass
Drums

6
27
28
29
30
31
Lead Vox
from A - B - C Flowers. Why not live it up a lit - tle bit and bright -en your day? It's so
Bg. Vox
from A - B - C Flowers. Why not live it up a lit - tle bit
Lead Instr.
2 Fl.
a2
1 A. Sax
2 Trpts
punch in
Brass
2 Bones
1
2
3 Vlns
3
a2
Harp
Guitar
Bb m7 Eb 7 Ab Cm7 F7 Bb
Bb
Piano
Rhythm
Bass
Drums

7
Lead Vox
eas - y you can do it we're a 'phone call a - way. __ Fill your rooms with blooms __ from A - B - C Flowers! __
Bg. Vox
live it up A - B - C ___ Fill your rooms with blooms __ from A - B - C Flowers! __
Lead Instr.
2 Fl.
1 A. Sax
2 Trpts
Brass
punch in
2 Bones
a2
1
2
3 Vlns
3
Harp
Eb
Gm F Eb Dm7 Cm7 Cm7 F7 Bb+6
Guitar
Piano
Rhythm
Bass
Drums

APPENDIX C

JIM DANDY

Stone, arr. CES

IN BANK

Stone, arr. CES

© 1983 Al Stone

NIAGRA COUNTY
Fast Four
Stone/Lieber
Ni - a - gra Coun-ty is rain - bow coun - try!
Come to Ni - a - gra and see won-der - ous sights and fan - ta - sy,
not far a - way right out - side your door, wait - ing for you to come and ex - plore to -
geth - er. Ni - a - gra Coun-ty is rain - bow coun - try!
Ni - a - gra coun-ty with great things to do, a fami - ly ad - ven - ture is wait - ing for you; no
mat - ter which sea - son, a year 'round place. Now you can put some col - or in your
life! Ni - a - gra coun - ty is rain - bow coun - try!
Ni - a - gra coun - ty is rain - bow coun - try.

B & W PLUMBING

Stone, arr: CES/Lieber

RIVER BEND
:60 (:30 to #20)
Stone, arr. Lieber
♩ = 90-100
D11 Gmaj7 Bm7 Cmaj7 G Cmaj7 G
Riv-er Bend means liv-ing; Riv-er Bend means life; you're liv-ing life com-plete-ly;
5 Am7 D11 D7 Gmaj7 Bm7 C Bsus B7
you're liv-ing life in style. Riv-er Bend is mag-ic; Riv-er Bend is love!
8 Am7 D11 Bm7 Em7 Am7 D11 G Em D
So make the most of liv-ing; start liv-ing Riv-er Bend! Like South-ern Cal-i-forn-ia, like the
11 Gmaj7 Em Am7 Em C D D/C
South-ern coast of Spain. A place for spec-ial peo-ple, a place to live a-gain! Riv-er
14 Bm Em C G C Bm
Bend has eve-ry-thing to make your life com-plete, a-part-ment homes with style and grace where
17 Am7 D11 Gmaj7 Bm7 Cmaj7 G C Bm7 Em7
liv-ing is so sweet! Riv-er Bend means liv-ing; Riv-er Bend means life; the best part of liv-ing is
21 Am7 D11 G C D11 D7 E♭maj7 F G
just a-round the bend! Start liv-ing Riv-er Bend!
© 1982 Al Stone

LAFAYETTE BANK

Stone, arr: Lieber

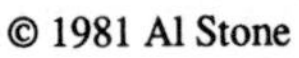

INDEX